Learning from the History of British Interventions in the Middle East

Learning from the History of British Interventions in the Middle East

Louise Kettle

EDINBURGH
University Press

Edinburgh University Press is one of the leading university presses in the UK. We publish academic books and journals in our selected subject areas across the humanities and social sciences, combining cutting-edge scholarship with high editorial and production values to produce academic works of lasting importance. For more information visit our website: edinburghuniversitypress.com

© Louise Kettle, 2018, 2020

Edinburgh University Press Ltd
The Tun – Holyrood Road,
12(2f) Jackson's Entry,
Edinburgh EH8 8PJ

First published in hardback by Edinburgh University Press 2020

Typeset in 11/13 Adobe Sabon by
IDSUK (DataConnection) Ltd

A CIP record for this book is available from the British Library

ISBN 978 1 4744 3795 0 (hardback)
ISBN 978 1 4744 3796 7 (paperback)
ISBN 978 1 4744 3797 4 (webready PDF)
ISBN 978 1 4744 3798 1 (epub)

The right of Louise Kettle to be identified as the author of this work has been asserted in accordance with the Copyright, Designs and Patents Act 1988, and the Copyright and Related Rights Regulations 2003 (SI No. 2498).

Contents

Acknowledgements	vii
1. Learning from History	1
Learning from History in Whitehall	3
Politicians Learning from History	8
Learning from the History of Military Interventions	9
How Do We Learn?	13
What is Learning from History?	15
Who Learns from History?	16
The Learning Process	18
Learning from the History of British Interventions in the Middle East	21
2. No End of a Lesson – Suez 1956	24
Planning the Intervention	26
During the Intervention	35
After the Intervention	43
Musketeer Learning	55
3. More like Korea – Jordan 1958	60
Planning the Intervention	63
During the Intervention	70
After the Intervention	80
Fortitude Learning	86

Learning from British Interventions in the Middle East

4.	Suez in Reverse – Kuwait 1961	90
	Planning the Intervention	92
	During the Intervention	103
	After the Intervention	113
	Vantage Learning	123
5.	A Re-Run of Port Stanley – The Gulf 1990–1	129
	Planning the Intervention	131
	During the Intervention	146
	After the Intervention	158
	Granby Learning	165
6.	Afghanistan Part Two – Iraq 2003–9	169
	Planning the Intervention	171
	During the Intervention	182
	After the Intervention	194
	Telic Learning	205
7.	Failing History or Lessons Learned?	209
	Learning from History since Iraq	218
	Conclusion	227
Notes		229
Index		279

Acknowledgements

There are too many people who have helped me with this project to thank each individually. However, I am particularly grateful to Dr Andrew Mumford who has provided enthusiasm, invaluable insight and support throughout the research and writing of this book. I would also like to thank Professor Alex Danchev who offered inspiration and sage advice from the outset; he is sorely missed.

I am also indebted to: Professor John Young, Professor Richard Aldrich, Professor Wyn Rees, Professor Michael Goodman, Dr Rory Cormac, Dr Geoffrey Sloan, Sir Alan Munro, Sir Jeremy Greenstock, Lord Williams of Baglan, Major General Tim Cross, Michael Herman, John Stubbington, Patrick Salmon, Richard Smith, Bob Evans, Lieutenant Colonel Judith Dando, lessons teams across the Ministry of Defence and all of the obliging archivists I have been fortunate to encounter. Each has taken the time and trouble to help in different ways and for this I am extremely grateful.

I am thankful to the Arts and Humanities Research Council, Economic and Social Research Council and Royal Historical Society, as well as the University of Nottingham's School of Politics and International Relations, Centre for British Politics and Centre for Conflict, Security and Terrorism, for funding my research.

In addition, I am grateful for permissions granted by the following: the RAF Historical Society; Air Power Review; The Naval Review; The Guardian; © Telegraph Media Group Limited 2012/2013; the Trustees of the Harold Macmillan Book Trust in relation to the diaries of Harold Macmillan – housed at Bodleian Libraries, University of Oxford; former diplomats (where individual copyright was retained) and the Master and Fellows of Churchill College, Cambridge for reproduction of transcripts from the British Diplomatic Oral History

Programme; and the Trustees of the Liddell Hart Centre for Military Archives with respect to extracts from the Liddell Hart archive and the Suez Oral History Project at King's College, London.

I would like to thank my wonderful family and friends who have been patient and understanding throughout this process. I am especially thankful to Suzanne and Christopher Sullivan, for keeping me smiling, checking in on me and always being supportive; I am extremely lucky to have them. I am also grateful to John Sullivan for providing my pedant tendencies and the education to get me here, as well as Robert and Margery Kettle who have shown me kindness and generosity in innumerable ways.

Finally, I owe more than I can possibly express to David Kettle – whose love, faith and encouragement have made all of this possible – and to William, whose impending arrival kept me focused and who has already brought so much joy to our lives. It is to David and William that this book is dedicated.

1 Learning from History

> If men could learn from history, what lessons it might teach us! But passion and party blind our eyes, and the light which experience gives is a lantern on the stern, which shines only on the waves behind us.
>
> *(Samuel Taylor Coleridge, 1831)*[1]

In 2003, shortly after the beginning of the Iraq War, British Prime Minister Tony Blair arrived at the United States Congress to rapturous applause. At the end of a standing ovation he began a speech in which he announced that the use of history in developing foreign policy was defunct. For him, at the beginning of what would become the most controversial and criticised war of a generation, there had never been a time when 'a study of history provides so little instruction for our present day'.[2]

It was not long after this speech that Iraq descended into post-war chaos and accusations of blame for the disastrous events emerged. Historians and commentators quickly asked how, given Britain had so much experience in Iraq, had policy-makers got post-war planning so wrong? Britain had been responsible for the founding of the state of Iraq in 1919 and established its Hashemite monarchy. It had governed the country under a League of Nations mandate until 1932 and maintained close links throughout the twentieth century: intervening against a coup in 1941, maintaining military occupation until 1947, keeping the country as a satellite state until 1958 and intervening again in 1991. How then, with all of the lessons of history at its disposal, had the government failed to understand the complexities of governing the Iraqi nation? The accusation was soon made that British policy-makers had failed to learn the lessons of history.

Despite Tony Blair's statement to Congress, the government quickly searched for ways to counteract the allegations that it had not learned from the past. A flurry of reports were produced to demonstrate to the public that lessons were at least being identified from the Iraq operation. As the 20th Armoured Brigade lowered the mission flag in Basra, Whitehall discussed culminating their efforts with a public inquiry. By the summer of 2009 the Iraq Inquiry had been announced under the Chairmanship of Sir John Chilcot. The inquiry was given the specific objective of determining lessons for the future:

> Our terms of reference are very broad ... to establish, as accurately as possible, what happened and to identify the lessons that can be learned. Those lessons will help ensure that, if we face similar situations in future, the government of the day is best equipped to respond to those situations in the most effective manner in the best interests of the country.[3]

Initially, the inquiry seemed promising, with the pledge of full government cooperation and the power to call the highest echelons of Whitehall to the witness stand. Even the former Prime Minister, Tony Blair, made an appearance for public questioning; attending the inquiry in January 2010 and again a year later. These appearances were highly anticipated with widespread media coverage and over-demand for seats in the hearing room leading to allocation via public ballot. They were also controversial: surrounded by large protests and punctuated by intermittent heckling and booing from the audience.

Over time, expectation dissipated. The inquiry progressed at a painfully slow pace, its duration being longer than that of the war it was investigating. It was also plagued with difficulties. In particular there was continual wrangling between the inquiry and the Cabinet Office over what information could be released to the public, with the inquiry succumbing to Cabinet Office demands to restrict the release of letters between Tony Blair and the American President George W. Bush. Furthermore, politicians were accused of delaying tactics through the 'Maxwellisation' process, allowing those facing criticism in its report the right of response before publication.[4]

Nonetheless, whilst the seven-year inquiry continued, politicians were increasingly keen to stress that lessons from Iraq had been learned. Such lessons were regular rationale for foreign policy decisions, including Britain's response to the Arab Spring and the 2011 crisis in Libya. The shadow of lessons from Iraq also lingered over two crucial parliamentary votes on action in Syria, in 2013 and 2015, and impacted the approach to tackling the threat of Daesh. In 2014, Prime Minister David Cameron addressed the United Nations (UN) Assembly on the plans to defeat the extremist group. Purporting the opposite view to Tony Blair a decade before, he stated that history, in particular the lessons from the Iraq War, was a vital consideration in the creation of current policy: 'it is absolutely right that we should learn the lessons of the past, especially of what happened in Iraq a decade ago'.[5] However, details surrounding the claims to have learned lessons remain distinctly hazy; who is learning what lessons, how and for how long, are unknown. This book examines these questions to uncover whether the British government learns from past interventions in the Middle East. In so doing it will explore both the criticism that Britain does not learn from its past, as well as scrutinising the contradicting claims made by politicians that lessons have been learned. It does so at a decisive moment, as the continued threat of Daesh, instability in Libya, regional boycotting of Qatar, concerns over the regime in Turkey and ongoing conflict in Syria, Yemen, Iraq, Israel and Palestine all ensure that the possibility of further British intervention in the region remains a contemporary and contentious reality, where lessons from the past could prove invaluable for shaping the future.

Learning from History in Whitehall

The debate about the role of history, evidenced by the opposing views of Blair and Cameron, is not new. Between the mid-1950s and the late 1970s a debate emerged amongst key historians as to whether history should be used within the development of policy. This debate came to fruition as the writing of the wartime official histories began to draw to a close and consideration was given to the future of the project. The discussions reignited a wider debate of whether history was a useful policy-making tool; did history provide lessons and could or should they be used in the creation of British policy?

Whilst the prominent historians Sir Geoffrey Elton and A. J. P. Taylor fiercely disagreed with the idea that history provided lessons, an alternative perspective was beginning to gather pace, pushed forward by historians including Allan Bullock, Margaret Gowing, William Keith Hancock and Michael Lee.[6] Instead, they urged for the increased use of history within Whitehall and accused policy-makers of 'a lack of historical depth'.[7] This view built upon a long-standing historical tradition; Thucydides wrote his *History of the Peloponnesian War*, recounting the war between Sparta and Athens in the fifth century BC, in order to inform policy-makers of the future. He stated the writing was for 'those who want to understand clearly the events which happened in the past, and which (human nature being what it is) will, at some time or other and in much the same way, be repeated in the future'.[8] This has become a fundamental assumption of social scientists who emphasise the importance of understanding past political and international relations phenomena in order to inform current decisions and, taking the argument even further, to form theoretical positions to provide a predictive function for the future through inductive reasoning.

In fact, a few Whitehall departments invested in the notion of learning from history throughout the twentieth century. Following the end of the First World War, a number of international history and international relations chairs were introduced to universities, often under the title of 'Peace Studies'. These were funded by the government to encourage the study of the First World War and to consider how lessons could be learned from the events to prevent war in the future.

Similarly, the civil service placed significant emphasis on the importance of historical knowledge in its entrance examination and the study of history was considered one of the recognised roads to the higher ranks within the service. In 1946 A. L. Rowse argued that the work of the civil service was 'for the most part concerned with nothing so pure and abstract as mathematics, but with the administration of human affairs . . . for which the appropriate background and training are provided by history'.[9]

Government also invested in the production of Whitehall official histories. These began under the Committee of the Imperial Defence (CID), the forerunner of the Cabinet Office. The CID's Historical Section was started in 1908 to compile the military history of Britain and to learn lessons from the Boer and Russo-Japanese Wars. In 1939, when the CID lapsed, the Historical Section became the responsibility of the Cabinet Office and in 1941 it was tasked with the preparation and publication of the Official History of the Second World War from a military, intelligence and civil perspective. The aim of this was to record 'experience for government use' in the event of another war.[10] The focus upon official histories has been supported by a series of Public Record Acts – beginning in 1958, amended in 1966, again in 2000 with the Freedom of Information Act and most recently in 2010 with the Constitutional Reform and Governance Act – to establish a public record closure period but also requiring departments to adopt more methodical procedures for processing and preserving records of historical value.

In 1957, the year after the Suez debacle, the Cabinet Secretary, Norman Brook, invested further funding to encourage all Whitehall departments to follow this lead and use history more systematically in their everyday work. When Brook's initiative was taken to the Foreign Office Steering Committee in April 1958 it produced a positive response. A background paper, written by the Head of the Permanent Under-Secretary's Department, revealed support for learning from history:

> Looking back can be a salutary exercise. If we could spare the time or the staff we should probably derive great benefit from examining in retrospect the accuracy of the information on which policy was based and the correctness of the conclusions drawn from it . . . past experience can be a useful guide to recurrent problems.[11]

In addition, in 1964 Lord Plowden's 'Report on Representational Services Overseas' emphasised the use of historians by stating 'Full use should be made of their services by executive departments so as to ensure that action on current problems is not taken in ignorance of the lessons of the past.'[12] Then, in 1966, Prime Minister Harold Wilson agreed to extend the official histories to the examination of events during peacetime; a programme which continues today.

However, despite these many endeavours to learn from history there have equally been many failures, omissions and difficulties. The investment in university chairs or recruitment of history graduates has not always equated to the consideration of lessons from history in the policy-making process. Instead, relationships between Whitehall and academia have always been encouraged but difficult, for a number of reasons.[13] For history graduates the pressures of the civil service can often overcome their historical dispositions and policy-making is a complex process where the lessons of history form only part of the consideration in any decision-making. Furthermore, there is now a much wider range of disciplines considered for entry and promotion within the civil service. In the Foreign and Commonwealth Office (FCO), for example, the subject of law has become increasingly of interest but applications are accepted from all disciplines.[14]

The official histories have also been limited and received criticism for being both time-consuming and expensive. When, in 1957, the Select Committee on Estimates examined the cost of producing the official histories it reported losses of £15,000 on the publication costs of the civil histories and £11,000 on military histories, in addition to the £79,517 paid in salaries to historians that year. This was not portrayed positively in the media and led to wider criticisms of the programme including in relation to the duplication of work and the occupation of valuable premises in Westminster.[15]

The selection process of official histories has also seemed limited; a shortlist of topics were to be prepared by an interdepartmental committee based on the criteria of presenting the British case of events, usefulness and, crucially, avoiding matters of controversy which may have party political or foreign policy implications. As a result, the official histories which were produced took the form of a narrative and, aware of their publication for a wider audience, offered little criticism or clear identification of lessons for the future. Each history was also agreed by a group of Privy Counsellors and the Prime Minister And all official histories, as with all documents released by the government for public consumption, were 'weeded' to ensure no harm could be done to British interests or offence given to other governments or political leaders. For this reason the five-volume diplomatic history of the Second World War, written by Llewellyn Woodward, was only published over a decade after completion.[16]

As a combination of the selection and weeding processes, there were accusations – including from A. J. P. Taylor – that the official histories merely served as a propaganda tool. Rather than providing a reliable account of history, from which useful lessons could be drawn, the series presented a one-sided view to vindicate the actions of the British government.[17] Even worse, some media reports suggested 'calculated inaccuracy' and pointed to the concealment of sources.[18]

Woodward's heavyweight history also illustrated another fundamental problem with the official histories; they were often too long and unwieldy to ever be read by even the most interested of parties. For busy Whitehall staff the opportunity to read such histories, and attempt to learn lessons from them, was minimal. As a result, the official histories were underutilised and became increasingly expensive. Even the 1957 history funding experience put forward by the Cabinet Secretary proved largely unsuccessful; few government departments took up the mantle, with many citing the lack of resource as a fundamental barrier.

By 1976 the Treasury's history department was closed. In response to the closure, in a 1978 lecture, the former Treasury historian Margaret Gowing explained the lack of history within Whitehall. She advised that even though central government employed nearly 18,000 scientists and engineers and 900 social scientists, it employed only a handful of historians and historical courses were not included in the syllabus of the Civil Service College: 'Historical knowledge, it seems, is not a necessity but a luxury.' She found this incredible:

> But why, if the status and usefulness of historical knowledge are so high, is there so little use of it in central and local government? Since the machinery of government is reorganised so often and ministers,

civil servants and policies are so ephemeral, surely a collective memory is required? Surely governments need to understand the complex roots of policies and problems? Surely analysis of past experience should be fed back into the system?[19]

Politicians Learning from History

As the ultimate policy decision-makers, with government departments acting as the advisor and implementer, the ability of politicians to learn from history can counteract any of Whitehall's historical failings and provide some credence to the contemporary claims of having learned lessons. Many key politicians throughout the twentieth century have been interested in history, following a long tradition of Greeks, Romans and men of the Renaissance who read history not for pleasure but for practical benefit. This is because history has always, as John Tusa argues, provided a useful tool for policy-makers confronted by the challenges of uncertainty by offering a pattern from which to draw answers: 'The truth is that outlines of an answer are far more likely to lie in historical examination of the past than wholly unfounded speculation of the future.'[20] For politicians, therefore, history provides a useful road map. In fact, history was the favourite reading of Napoleon, Lloyd George, Hitler and Sir Winston Churchill. Churchill, who declared 'Personally I'm always ready to learn, although I do not always like to be taught', believed in the benefits of the lessons of the past for informing policy and famously stated 'The farther backward you can look, the farther forward you are likely to see.'[21] More recently a number of politicians, including Paddy Ashdown, William Hague and Boris Johnson, have also published their own history books.[22]

One regular use of history by politicians is through analogy, which is widely used within both policy decision-making and policy rhetoric.[23] The most commonly used analogy throughout the twentieth and early twenty-first centuries was that of 'appeasement' or 'Munich', with many aggressive dictators compared to Hitler or Mussolini.[24] Both Anthony Eden and Harold Macmillan used this analogy in their analysis of Colonel Nasser's nationalisation of the Suez Canal. Margaret Thatcher compared General Leopoldo Galtieri's attack on the Falkland Islands and Saddam Hussein's 1990 invasion of Kuwait to the Anschluss.[25] The analogy was similarly echoed by Tony Blair in relation to Slobodan Milosevic over Kosovo and the dictatorial rule of Saddam Hussein in Iraq in 2003.[26] However, this use of history has two key failings. Firstly, analogies provide a shortcut to rationality, offering a simplified overview of a historical event. At times when politicians are working under extreme pressures the analogy handily reduces a complex and nuanced historical event to a mere sound bite or one sentence overview; hence the lesson of 'Munich' has become that all foreign acts of aggression must be met immediately with military might.[27] Again, this is often used in an attempt to provide a predictive function or even to offer a form of evidence to reinforce pre-existing ideas about how to manage a situation. Either way, this single-minded and simplified view would not be one accepted by many historians as a lesson from history.

Secondly, analogies are often retrospectively applied as rhetorical support for policy decisions and not used within the policy-making discussion itself. In this way analogies, and history, provide politicians with support for the presentation of policy to the public, rather than in its creation. Arthur Schlesinger, on reviewing Ernest May's book *'Lessons' of the Past*, claimed 'The past is an enormous grab bag with a prize for everybody. The issue of history as rationalization somewhat diminishes the force of the argument that history is per se a powerful formal determinant of policy.'[28] Following 9/11 a plethora of analogies were drawn by policy-makers as rationale for policy.[29] This has led Andrew Mumford to conclude that the use of analogy shifted away from a tool of using history to help decision-making to one of abusing history for ideologically informed policy justification.[30]

Learning from the History of Military Interventions

Learning from history can be utilised by policy-makers across government – both politicians and civil servants – but this book will specifically focus upon learning from history in military

Learning from British Interventions in the Middle East

interventions. Whilst many Whitehall departments are involved in these forms of intervention abroad they are primarily managed through the Prime Minister's Office (No10), FCO, Ministry of Defence (MoD) and the intelligence agencies and thus these departments will form the prime focus of this book.

Throughout the terms 'Britain' and 'British government' – as the decision-makers over British foreign and security policy – will be used interchangeably. In addition, for consistency, 'the FCO' will be referred to as such throughout with the term to encompass both the Foreign Office and Commonwealth Office (which only merged in 1968). Similarly, although the MoD only came into existence in its present form in 1971 it will also be referred to as such throughout with the term subsuming its five previously separate departments: the Admiralty, the War Office, the Air Ministry, the Ministry of Aviation and the Ministry of Defence itself. These merged in 1964 with the defence functions of the Ministry of Aviation Supply absorbed in 1971, when the MoD took over responsibility for supplying military aircraft and guided weapons. The MoD is also a duality as both a Department of State and a military headquarters for the three services (the British Army, Royal Navy and Royal Air Force) therefore the work of the services will also be included under this heading. Furthermore, the intelligence community (IC) will be considered as one body because of the many overlaps across the relevant intelligence agencies – including the Security Service (SS – more commonly known as MI5), the Secret Intelligence Service (SIS – more commonly known as MI6) and Government Communications Headquarters (GCHQ) – and because all of the intelligence agencies are subject to the setting of priorities by the Joint Intelligence Committee (JIC). As a result, the Defence Intelligence Service (DIS) – which although forming part of the MoD budget is also represented on the JIC – and the JIC's supporting staff (the Joint Intelligence Organisation) – will all be examined as part of the IC. This will not only prevent confusion but will additionally overcome some of the challenges of trying to attribute specific intelligence to one particular body when these lines of accountability remain blurred due to secrecy.

Each of these bodies has established unique ways and means to try to record, manage and draw lessons from history. At the same time as the Cabinet Office was commissioning official histories from external historians, the FCO and the MoD invested in permanent in-house historians, sometimes supported by the additional commissioning of works. The MoD even established independent historical branches for each of its three services, with only the Army Historical Branch being centrally managed in the MoD since 1970. The work of the in-house historians was also excluded from the centralised procedure of the Cabinet Office's Historical Section – which was established in 1966 – allowing them greater control over the subjects of their histories.

The FCO initially chose to use their in-house historians to focus upon the publication of Documents on British Foreign Policy (DBFP). This was a series of volumes featuring an edited, chronological selection of documents – considered by the historians to be the most important documents in the FCO archives – relating to British foreign policy between 1919 and 1939. This series was only completed in 1986. In 1973, the government announced its intention to publish a new collection with the aim of providing documents from the post-Second World War period; Documents on British Policy Overseas (DBPO) began with the Potsdam Conference in July 1945. DBPO continues to be published today along thematic lines.

The focus on DBFP and DBPO meant that little was produced that offered an analysis of history or identified lessons for the future. Rohan Butler, who became the senior editor of DBFP in 1955, argued that this provided 'a balanced view of British foreign policy' and this stance continued throughout the twentieth century.[31] Although the FCO in-house historians' role has now expanded and includes additional publications across a range of topics – which are written as narratives and often in the form of much shorter essays or occasional papers – their main activity remains the publication of DBPO.[32]

In the MoD, one maxim has always been that the military only study their last war and thus do poorly in the next. In fact, unlike in the FCO, there has been a long-standing tradition of both writing and teaching history across the services. The historian Margaret Macmillan claims 'Two groups in particular in our society have always taken history seriously as a guide. People in business and in the military.'³³ Unlike the FCO historians who were publishing for public consumption, the primary objectives of the historical branches within the MoD were to write classified histories, which provided narratives of campaigns and details on specific aspects such as command structures or bases.³⁴ However, these histories were often written in a functional way and were regularly concerned with the minutiae of a particular operation, not longer-term trends. In addition, subjectivity over the selection of topics remained. Sir Michael Howard noted, in a keynote address to the first 'Past Futures' conference on military history at the Royal Military Academy Sandhurst, that when he was a regimental historian the role was 'to chronicle triumphs, not disasters. The purpose is morale building, not dispassionate analysis, which rather limits its didactic value.'³⁵ Brigadier General Sir James Edmonds, the man in charge of the official military histories of the First World War, felt similarly. He often stated that he could not provide the entire truth in an official history because of loyalty to the service and former comrades.³⁶

Nonetheless, teaching of military history does form part of the curriculum within service Staff Colleges and historical vignettes are included within doctrine. There is a history department at the Royal Military Academy Sandhurst, there are opportunities to complete degrees in War Studies and there are many links with academic historians. Service specific publications (such as the *British Army Review*, *Air Power Review* and *The Naval Review*) also often include articles of historical interest whilst battlefield studies and staff rides to locations of past battles, to learn the history of an operation, have increased over the years.

In contrast, within the IC very little has been published in terms of histories. Some history of intelligence during the Second World War has been published but many documents have remained classified, exemplified by reports relating to the cracking of the enigma code only being released to the public in 2011.³⁷ Besides the official history volumes on British intelligence in the Second World War there have only been three official histories produced, all published within the last few years; Christopher Andrew's history of MI5, Keith Jeffrey's history of MI6 until 1949 and Michael S. Goodman's first volume of the history of the JIC.³⁸ This lack of published history is perhaps inevitable given that it was not until 1992 that the name of the Head of MI5 was first revealed: Stella Rimington. In addition, the SIS was only officially recognised as existing for the first time through the words 'There shall continue to be a Secret Intelligence Service' in the Intelligence Services Act 1994.

Instead, the IC relied upon a few, limited, internal histories but has not benefited from a British equivalent of the US Central Intelligence Agency (CIA) journal *Studies in Intelligence*.[39] A handful of specific reports have also been produced after intelligence failures, including the 1968 Russian invasion of Czechoslovakia and the 1973 Syrian and Egyptian attacks on Israel, in an endeavour to identify lessons for the future. However, unlike in the MoD, no history training programmes have existed for IC recruits. Often training has been focused upon more technical aspects, particularly for those starting employment at GCHQ, or the craft of intelligence collection, analysis and report reading. Nonetheless, as intelligence analysts examine current and past evidence in order to try to assess the present and anticipate the future course of events, there are a number of similarities between the approach to researching a problem and the approach of the historian. Consequently, the lessons of history should always be enshrined in their assessments.[40]

Overall, each department has approached history, and learning from it, very differently. The question is whether any of these approaches have made any difference to decisions affecting interventions.

How Do We Learn?

The study of learning is traced back to the epistemological – how knowledge can become known – debates of Plato and Aristotle. Whilst Plato had a rationalist epistemology, arguing that knowledge could be discovered through self-reflection, Aristotle had an empiricist approach, believing that knowledge was found externally through the senses. These conflicting philosophies have influenced the understanding of how we learn ever since.

Cognitivist psychologists follow a Platonic, rationalist epistemology and see learning as similar to an information processing model, whereby inputs are managed into short-term memory and coded for long-term recall.[41] For cognitivists, such as Jean Piaget, the study of how learning occurs is the study of the internal – of perceptions, beliefs, desires, motivations and thought processes.[42] L. S. Vygotsky extended Piaget's work to examine the impact of social interaction on learning and as a result he placed greater emphasis upon social factors, including the role of culture and language but continued to focus on internal processing.[43] For cognitivists, therefore, learning is defined as the appropriation of new knowledge and this knowledge does not necessarily need to be utilised, or observed externally, to have been learned.

On the other hand, behaviourist psychologists, such as I. P. Pavlov, follow the empiricist tradition and view learning as a reflex to outside stimuli which may or may not be conditioned.[44] For the behaviourist psychologists Edward Thorndike and B. F. Skinner learning is an active process whereby an action and its consequences reinforce each other; behaviour followed by reward is repeated (positive learning), whilst behaviour which is not rewarded is not repeated (negative learning).[45] This is known as operant, or instrumental, learning. Therefore, for behaviourists, the study of learning is about the examination of specific stimuli that change behaviour and learning itself is the gaining of knowledge which affects behaviour.

A third epistemological approach was put forward by Immanuel Kant who modernised the idea of rationalism and empiricism through the concept of 'a priori' knowledge.[46] For him the two could be brought together through the understanding that experience awakens awareness of pre-existing, innate knowledge. This philosophy is used by constructivist psychologists who emphasise that learning is about actively seeking meaning through real life experiences in order to construct knowledge.[47] This idea is used in theories of adult education whereby knowledge is constructed rather than transmitted in the manner of the education of children. Consequently, constructivists view learning not as defined by an effect on behaviour but by an effect on beliefs.

In education studies, George Siemens extended the work of constructivist psychologists to develop a further theoretical approach to learning: connectivism. He argued that the digital age changed the way in which learning takes place and drew upon chaos theory to explain that learning occurs by the connection of information. He argued

> Learning (defined as actionable knowledge) can reside outside of ourselves (within an organization or a database), is focused on connecting specialized information sets, and the connections that enable us to learn more are more important than our current state of knowing.[48]

This theoretical approach is particularly useful for providing a connection between the analysis of individuals and the organisational structures and systems within which knowledge can be found, such as digital archives.

What is Learning from History?

The different approaches to learning mean that there is no agreed definition of learning. This book will define 'learning from history' in the context of British interventions in the Middle East as 'a process which runs between the acquisition of knowledge of the past and its use to inform policy decisions'. In this definition learning is the action and the lesson is the object. The 'what' is learned is defined as 'knowledge of the past' and the condition of this knowledge being 'of the past' adds the specificity of learning from history, rather than learning by other means such as deductive or logical reasoning.

However, it would not be enough to define learning from history as only 'the acquisition of knowledge of the past'; this is history rather than learning from it. Although there is no requirement for this learning to have an immediate effect, what distinguishes learning from history is the use of this knowledge to inform policy-making; it is the utilisation of history, taking its understanding from the passive to the active, impacting beliefs, behaviour or both. Without this utilisation nothing is learned, it merely is and it is only once the knowledge has been used to inform policy decisions that a lesson can claim to have been learned. This does not presume that there needs to have been a 'change'[49] or 'adaption'[50] in policy. Whilst change or adaption may be one outcome of learning, existing beliefs and behaviours can also be confirmed, compounded or the conclusion drawn that a preferable alternative does not exist leading to repetition or maintaining of the status quo.

The definition also does not include an accuracy or efficiency requirement; the lesson does not have to be 'right', nor does it require that it leads to an improvement. Although a number of scholars provide these criteria as essential precursors to learning, this book assumes that learning which is considered to be 'wrong' or ineffective is still learning.[51] The inclusion of such precursors is fraught with normative difficulties, of judging 'right' and 'wrong' lessons and providing a standard measurement for assessing efficiency as well as methodological challenges of assessing an effect upon belief systems. The position of judging right and wrong is also subjective in time, consequently this book seeks only to examine whether learning occurs, not to judge whether lessons were right or wrong.

Who Learns from History?

The question of how learning from history occurs within military interventions is further complicated because of the number of actors involved in any learning process: individuals,[52] groups of individuals,[53] generations,[54] society,[55] states[56] and organisations.[57] This book will focus on the three most significant learners for military interventions: individuals, institutions and generations. The state will not be examined as a 'learner' itself but instead learning will be examined at the more devolved level of the individuals, generations and institutions which influence the making or enacting of the foreign and security policies of the state.

The individual has been selected due to the impact of certain key individuals on the policy-making process. It will be limited to those who work or worked within the FCO, MoD and IC. The one exception will be the additional consideration of the

Prime Minister due to the office's influence and control over policy direction.[58] The FCO, MoD and IC will also be considered learners within their own right as institutions. These institutions are important to examine because they define the organisational framework and culture within which learning occurs.[59] Institutions also offer the possibility for more formalised learning processes than those made by individuals; they can turn tacit lessons, or those held by individuals, into explicit lessons which can be shared.

Generations will also be examined as learners. As a result of societal learning, generations absorb many of the most significant values and beliefs that dominate the majority of opinion at a particular time.[60] They provide a collective memory of lessons of events which were considered to be important during specific times. In addition, the comparison of learning across different generations allows for the analysis of the development of learning over a longer period of time and a consideration of which lessons survive across generations and why. For the purposes of this book, generations are defined as groups of individuals who worked within the FCO, MoD or IC at a particular point in time. Three generations will be considered: those based within the FCO, MoD or IC at any time between 1956–61, 1990–1 and 2003–9. There may be some personnel who served as juniors in 1956 and had reached senior level positions by 1990, with even higher numbers of personnel who were serving in both 1991 and 2003. Consequently, it will be noted where any key individuals overlap across these generations.

Clearly, none of the three groups of learners exists in a vacuum or is mutually exclusive to the others; individuals form the workforce in institutions and the collective group of people that create a generation. Similarly, a generation of employees exist within an institution whilst an institution frames the experiences of individuals and generations. Consequently, this book will consider the three groups of learners as spheres which overlap and interact with each other (as illustrated in Figure 1.1). The very centre of the diagram – where all three spheres of learning overlap – is where learning is the most effective, in terms of impact and longevity.

Learning from British Interventions in the Middle East

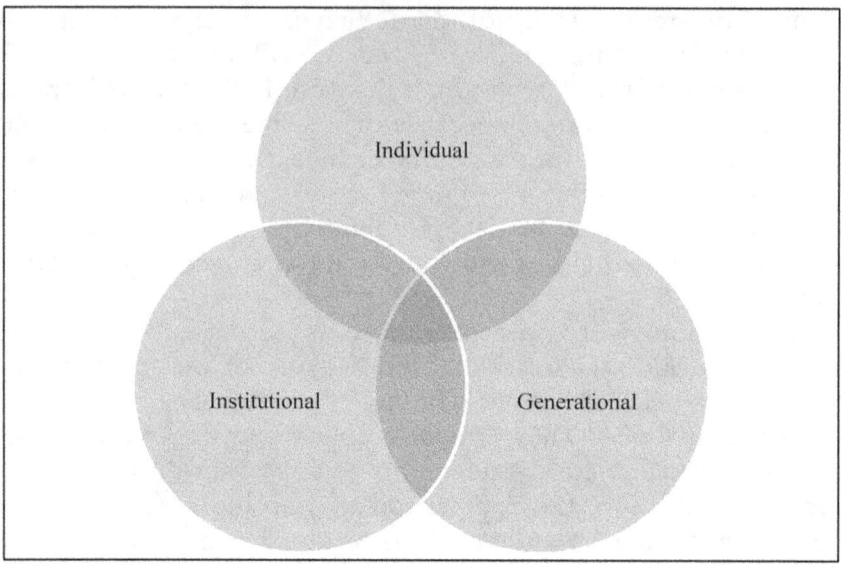

Figure 1.1 The spheres of learning

In many cases the spheres of learning are likely to be defined by the historical source which evidences learning. For example, personal papers reveal learning in the individual sphere, ministerial parliamentary speeches reveal learning in the institutional sphere and notes from retrospective conferences reveal learning in the generational sphere. However, identifying patterns of who is learning will provide further information to be able to identify which learners, if any, are driving the learning process within British military interventions.

The Learning Process

Drawing upon the work of psychology and organisational theorists, this book will assume that learning does not occur as a monolithic action but is a process which can be broken down into further stages across all three spheres of learning: lesson identification, lesson implementation, lesson distribution and lesson

Learning from History

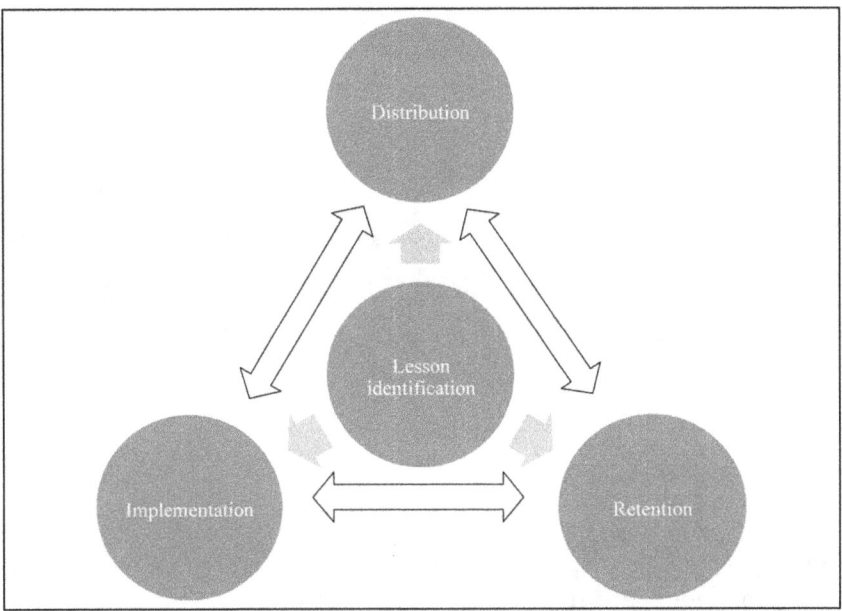

Figure 1.2 The learning process

retention (as illustrated in Figure 1.2).[61] Each of these stages will be examined in assessing whether the British government learns from its history of military interventions, and the relevant terms used accordingly throughout.

Lesson identification is always the first stage of the learning process. It is at this stage that, in line with the definition, the 'acquisition of knowledge' occurs. This idea draws upon the cognitivist theory of learning whereby such knowledge is considered relevant. Knowledge can be acquired through a number of different methods and from various sources although the ambition is to acquire knowledge from the action of others. As Otto von Bismarck famously stated 'Fools say they learn by experience, I prefer to profit by other people's experiences.'[62]

After knowledge is acquired it becomes understood and is given value and meaning – it is interpreted (as illustrated by Figure 1.3). This idea draws upon the constructivist approach to learning. How it is interpreted will depend on the learner but at this stage

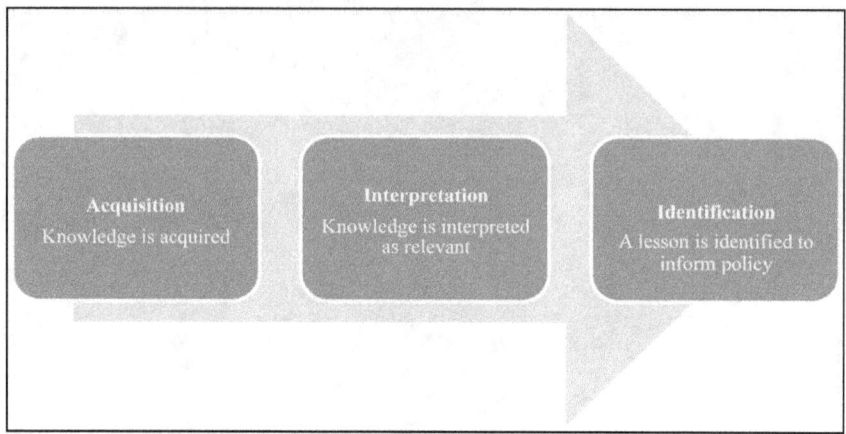

Figure 1.3 Lesson identification

biases, beliefs, goals, and current and future activities will impact the knowledge and the lesson which is ultimately identified.

Once a lesson is identified, there is no determined order for the other stages of the learning process. Implementation is the stage in the learning process when the knowledge of the past, the lesson identified, is used to inform policy. This is most closely aligned to the behaviourist approach to learning and it is only once a lesson has been implemented that it can be claimed to have been learned. If a lesson is not implemented it risks being forgotten.

In order to advance the learning process, distribution of lessons to other learners must also occur. Lesson distribution is important to ensure that all relevant learners learn from history and that lessons are not lost if individual learners are removed from office, personnel are changed within an institution or a generation dies out. The distribution of lessons by one learner can also become a source from which another learner may identify lessons. It is for this reason that the distribution of lessons across Whitehall is so important.

The fourth stage of the lessons process is retention. Retention is the recording of the lesson for the future and aligns with the connectivism theory of learning and ideas of memory. In some cases it is not necessary to implement or distribute the lesson immediately and therefore it must be retained to maintain the possibility of satisfying the second part of the definition of learning from history: 'to inform policy decisions'. Even if the lesson has been implemented and distributed, it should nevertheless be retained for the benefit of future learners. If lessons are not retained there is a risk that such lessons will become unlearned. Unlearned lessons are those which were 'learned' at some time but, having been implemented, the implementation process has now ceased or decisions have since been taken which contradict the original lesson thus the lesson has been unlearned. The key difference between whether a lesson is forgotten or unlearned is whether a lesson was ever implemented, or learned, in the first place.

Learning from the History of British Interventions in the Middle East

When British troops returned to Helmand Province in Afghanistan in 2001 many of the inhabitants thought that they had come to avenge the defeats of their predecessors in the nineteenth century. Similarly, Middle Easterners have long memories and – in a region where many policy-makers stay in power for decades, if not their whole lives, or form part of a political dynasty – scars of the past can run deep and supersede the career of a British politician, civil servant or serving personnel. In the Middle East the British also have a particularly long and unflattering historical legacy to understand and overcome, but it is one which provides a significant resource for lessons to inform foreign and security policy. In the twentieth century alone Britain has been involved in numerous interventions and was responsible for the defeat of the Ottoman Empire, the occupation of a significant amount of territory – following the Sykes–Picot Agreement of 1916 – and the establishment of the state of Israel and subsequent 1947 partition of Palestine. Iraq was under a British mandate until 1932, Jordan until 1946, Israel until 1948 and British troops were permanently stationed in Egypt until 1956. Britain maintained the Aden protectorate in Yemen until 1963 and only finally withdrew from Qatar, Bahrain and the United Arab Emirates (UAE) in 1971; as such there is much from which to learn.

This book examines learning from history before, during and after five key British interventions in the Middle East in the last seven decades. Chapter 2 opens on the most infamous intervention of the twentieth century – the disastrous 1956 Suez operation. This was a watershed moment for Britain in the Middle East and has since become one of the most frequently used analogies in British foreign policy, akin to Vietnam in the United States (US), and synonymous with failure. After Suez the government worked hard to avoid prolonging the embarrassment of the events – by avoiding any public identification of lessons – but behind the scenes much reflection was made. Two years later the implementation of these lessons were tested in the 1958 Jordan intervention. Chapter 3 examines this operation and considers the impact of 1956 on decision-making. In contrast to Suez, Jordan proved successful and provided a template for how best to intervene in the region without appearing imperial. By the time of the British intervention in Kuwait in 1961, the subject of Chapter 4, the government had a recent history of both success and failure to be used to inform decisions. A glance around the Cabinet table in 1961 provided a very similar view to 1956, with key members of the government having a personal history of events from which to draw lessons and to help inform policy.

Chapter 5 moves towards the end of the twentieth century to examine the 1990–1 Gulf War, by which time personnel had changed and individual experience of the region could no longer be relied upon to inform decision-making. Consequently, lessons from the previous decades were forgotten and mistakes repeated. However, the lessons from the war itself became politically divisive; as the first major conflict in the post-Cold War era, lessons were used to define the future of British foreign and security policy in a new international context. Twelve years later Britain faced the same enemy but, according to the Prime Minister, history was irrelevant. Chapter 6 examines the most notorious war of the twenty-first century thus far – the 2003–9 Iraq War – and uncovers the disparity of approach across Whitehall to history at this time. This was another defining moment for Britain as failings in Iraq led to a loss of public and parliamentary appetite for overseas military engagement and forced a new reflection upon the importance of learning from the events.

Finally, Chapter 7 explores how learning from history has changed since the Iraq War, reveals why lesson learning has stalled in the past, leading to disastrous consequences, and exposes the reality that Britain is still failing history. In order to combat this problem, suggestions for how learning from the past could be improved are presented. This learning is vital if there is to be any future profit from the difficult events of Britain's recent history of military interventions in the Middle East.

2 No End of a Lesson – Suez 1956

Let us admit it fairly, as a business people should,
We have had no end of a lesson: it will do us no end of good.
(Rudyard Kipling, The Lesson, 1901)

Rudyard Kipling wrote his famous poem *The Lesson* about the Boer War (1899–1902) but Anthony Nutting, the only Minister who was privy and opposed to all of the secrets of Suez from the outset, felt Kipling's poetic lines to be equally appropriate to Suez. As a result, he titled his published version of events *No End of a Lesson: The Story of Suez*.[1]

The story of Suez began in 1856 when Ferdinand De Lesseps obtained a concession from Egypt to construct the Suez Canal. When the canal opened in 1869 it had an immediate impact on world trade and soon after Britain bought Egypt's 44 per cent shareholding in the Suez Canal Company with France holding the remaining 56 per cent. British influence over the vital waterway increased in the 1880s when Britain gained control of Egypt before negotiating free navigation of the canal, as a neutral zone under the protection of the British military, at the 1888 Convention of Constantinople. In 1914 when Suez came under German–Ottoman attack, Britain established a protectorate over Egypt and sent forces to the canal. Even when, in 1922, Egypt was declared independent, Britain retained control of the Canal Zone. Subsequently, the 1936 Anglo-Egyptian Treaty agreed to the withdrawal of all British troops from Egyptian territory except for those deemed necessary to protect the canal and its surroundings.

The Suez crisis was sparked as a result of post-Second World War nationalism. The Anglo-Egyptian Treaty had never been welcomed by Egyptian nationalists and its signing had caused a wave of demonstrations. In 1951 it was universally abrogated by the nationalist Wafd government. A year later, a military coup by the Free Officers Movement – led by Muhammad Naguib and Gamal Abdel Nasser – overthrew King Farouk and established a new nationalist and anti-imperialist agenda. With a popular new leader in power, President Nasser, Britain agreed to withdraw all troops from Egypt through the Suez Base Canal Agreement of 1954. The agreement provided for the gradual evacuation of the Suez Canal base and subsequent passing of control to Egyptian military forces. The agreement was also dependent upon the freedom of navigation through the canal and the proviso that British troops were permitted to return to protect the Canal Zone should it be threatened by an outside power. Britain completed the Suez base evacuation on 13 June 1956, five days early.

In the meantime, in 1954, Nasser had begun plans to build a new dam at Aswan. Discussions between Egypt, the US and Britain on financing the dam took place in Washington in November 1955. A few months later, on 1 March 1956, news reached London from the British Ambassador in Jordan that King Hussein had dismissed the British General John Bagot Glubb from the post of Chief of the General Staff and Commander of the Arab Legion, Jordan's Royal Army.[2] General Glubb had commanded the Army since 1939 and the British Prime Minister, Anthony Eden, blamed the humiliation on the influence of Arab nationalism and the President of Egypt.[3] This event, compounded by the backdrop of the Cold War and the growing relationship between Egypt and the Soviet Union, eventually led Britain and the US to pull out of the Aswan Dam finance negotiations.[4] Seven days later, on 26 July 1956, Nasser declared the nationalisation of the Suez Canal Company and his plan to use the revenues from the canal to fund the Aswan Dam project. For the international community the nationalisation created a crisis for worldwide trade. For Britain it was a humiliation which impacted national and strategic interests; troops had only left the area the month before and each year 60 to 70 per cent of Britain's crude oil passed through the canal, as well as more than 50 million tons of British shipping.[5]

The FCO immediately became embroiled in diplomatic negotiations to find a solution to the crisis. They also sought to create a new Suez agreement and set up a London conference, followed by a Suez Canal Users' Association. However, Eden's patience with diplomacy rapidly declined and alternative options for removing Nasser and recapturing the canal were considered. At the end of October 1956, secret meetings to discuss a military intervention were held in Sèvres, France, between a small group of representatives from Britain, France and Israel. It was agreed that Israel – who had been in disputes with Egypt since the 1948 Arab-Israeli War – would attack Egypt thus providing a pre-text for Anglo-French action as 'peacekeepers' to separate the two warring factions. In so doing, Britain and France would invoke the 1954 Suez Base Canal Agreement to send troops to protect the Canal Zone and subsequently regain its control.

On 29 October 1956, Israeli forces crossed the border and attacked the Egyptian Army. The next day an ultimatum to stop the fighting was issued by Britain and France. When Egypt refused to relent, the Anglo-French forces began their attack – codenamed Operation Musketeer – with Valiant and Canberra bombers attacking Egyptian airfields. The conflict lasted from 31 October until 6 November 1956 when, under intense political and economic pressures, Britain and France were forced to agree a ceasefire.[6] By 21 November 1956, a UN force arrived in Port Said, allowing French and British troops to complete withdrawal before Christmas.

As well as the humiliation of withdrawal, accusations of collusion between the three nations soon became rife. When the government came under increasing pressure over these allegations Eden lied to Parliament by explicitly denying any pre-knowledge of the Israeli attack; 'We have been accused of being ... in collusion with the Israelis ... that Her Majesty's Government were engaged in some dishonourable conspiracy is completely untrue, and I most emphatically deny it.'[7] Under mounting pressure, on 9 January 1957, Eden resigned from the Premiership.

Planning the Intervention

History was important for the decisions made by the Prime Minister. There was concern that Britain was losing its position in the world and in the region; India was granted independence from the British Empire in 1947, Burma and Sri Lanka in 1948 and Sudan at the beginning of 1956. These events were compounded by the dismissal of Glubb Pasha from Jordan and ongoing troubles in Cyprus and Malaya, setting a tone of retreat which Eden was keen to rectify. As Shadow Foreign Secretary he had been highly critical of the Labour government's 'scuttle' from Palestine in 1948 and the 'appeasement' of the newly installed Prime Minister of Iran, Mohammad Mosaddeq, over the nationalisation of the Anglo-Iranian Oil Company in 1951.[8] In fact, lessons identified from the 1951 Abadan Crisis loomed large over decisions in 1956. At the time, the Minister of Defence, Emanuel Shinwell, had prophetically declared 'If Persia is allowed to get away with it, Egypt and other Middle Eastern countries will be encouraged to think they can try things on; the next thing may be an attempt to nationalise the Suez Canal.'[9] It also created a hard-line Conservative opposition front bench as they criticised the government's decisions, raising expectations for their own handling of crises after coming to power later that year. Eden himself confirmed the link between the events of 1951 and 1956 in his memoirs. He wrote 'the troubles fomented on the Shatt al Arab, festered on the Nile'.[10]

Events in the recent Buraimi dispute and in Nizwa, Oman, had also provided some lessons. Eden's Private Secretary, Guy Millard, mused 'The successful use of force on a small scale at Buraimi and Nizwa suggested that it could be employed to resolve larger issues; and that, provided force was swiftly and effectively applied, American and world opinion would acquiesce.'[11] In fact, Eden had taken the personal decision – as he would do in Suez – to send British troops to the region without informing the Americans in advance, and had done so without repercussion.

At the same time, Eden was influenced by lessons identified from his personal experience with Nasser. Despite repeated demonstrations of friendship, Nasser openly spoke against the British government on Cairo Radio,[12] payments due for the 1954 agreement – which Eden had steered as Foreign Secretary – remained unpaid, UK–US attempts at recruiting Nasser for peace talks with the Israelis – project Alpha – had failed and Egypt continued to flout the UN Security Council resolution calling for the end of interference with Israeli shipping passing through the canal.[13] Since 1955

Eden had also been receiving reports from the SIS that Nasser was tilting towards the Soviet Union, which appeared to be confirmed by the Czech arms deal – whereby the Union of Soviet Socialist Republics (USSR) agreed to supply Egypt with weaponry through Czechoslovakia.[14] Then, six weeks before nationalisation, on 10 June 1956, Nasser had signed an agreement with the Suez Canal Company on financial arrangements which encouraged the investment of large sums of money into Egypt, an agreement that directly impacted Britain and France as the company's major shareholders.[15] Nationalisation, therefore, was the final straw. For the Prime Minister, the grabbing of state assets was reminiscent of the pre-Second World War years and the events of the crises of Abyssinia, the Rhineland and the Anschluss when Eden had resigned as Foreign Secretary over appeasement and the Munich Agreement.[16] Consequently, Eden began to view Nasser as a ruthless dictator, akin to those of the 1930s, who was also not to be appeased. Eden's later autobiography, *Full Circle*, was so-called to emphasise the repetition of history and he stated in his foreword 'The lessons of the thirties and their application to the fifties ... are the theme of my memoirs.'[17] To him, Nasser looked like a new Hitler or Mussolini. He wrote to President Eisenhower 'the parallel with Mussolini is close. Neither of us can forget the lives and treasure he cost us before he was finally dealt with.'[18] These analogies were fuelled by their wide use within Whitehall. Even across the aisle the opposition leader, Hugh Gaitskell, declared that nationalisation 'is exactly the same that we encountered from Mussolini and Hitler in those years before the war'.[19]

The secrecy surrounding Musketeer meant that very few people were involved in its planning. Instead, Eden used an inner cabinet – the Egypt Committee – for all decision-making and, in line with wartime protocol, none of the committee papers were circulated, keeping all military plans closely guarded. When the argument for the use of force was finally presented to the wider Cabinet many members were reserved. They argued that the UN needed to be further consulted, that all diplomatic options had not been exhausted and therefore military action was not the last resort. There was also concern that public and international opinion would condemn any such actions.[20]

Although the Foreign Secretary, (John) Selwyn Lloyd, and his Private Secretary, Donald Logan, had both been present at Sèvres, officials in the FCO were intentionally kept in the dark about the conspiracy on the initiative of the Permanent Under-Secretary, Sir Ivone Kirkpatrick.[21] They were also excluded from most of the planning process and therefore unable to implement any lessons from past experience. In fact, for many diplomats it was a great shock when the news of the bombing of Port Said reached London. Donald Hawley, who worked in the Permanent Under-Secretary's Department, described how 'when the actual operation started, the first I knew of its launch was when I bought an *Evening Standard* when I went out for lunch that day'.[22] Many within the FCO were also horrified at British actions. Ivor Lucas who worked in the Economic Relations Department in 1956, but who would later go on to become Head of the Middle East Department, described how he 'wept for shame'.[23] Such was the strength of reaction that Kirkpatrick was forced to urge workers to remain in their posts and to offer reassurance that what had happened was an aberration which would never happen again.[24]

In contrast to the FCO, the MoD had more time for planning, although the government's true intentions remained concealed and there were still protests when they finally emerged.[25] Immediately after the news of nationalisation, the Chiefs of Staff were asked to consider plans to restore the canal to international control by armed force. The outline plan developed in July 1956 was visualised as Anglo-French action against Egypt and was to be launched in September. Integrated planning with the French began in mid-August 1956 and initially favoured landing forces at Alexandria. Some preparations for Musketeer began, under the telling codename Poker, but these had to be kept secret and balanced against causing provocation during a time when a peaceful resolution to the crisis was still being negotiated.[26] Due to security restrictions, Headquarters Middle East Land Forces was excluded from the planning process.[27]

In the meantime, lessons were identified from training and last minute exercises. 16 Parachute Brigade had conducted exercises in 1952 to ascertain how best to drop personnel, containers and heavy equipment into the same drop zone and lessons from these exercises were implemented in the planning and execution of Musketeer.[28] In addition, having been embroiled in fighting the Greek Cypriot guerrilla organisation, the EOKA, the brigade had not jumped for nine months and was immediately flown back to Britain from Cyprus for training. The aircrew of Transport Command also required updated training and it was soon identified that there was a lack of trained Forward Air Controllers who were also parachutists. Consequently, four Army officers from 16 Parachute Brigade underwent special training to fill the role, which was unusual as Forward Air Controllers were usually pilots.[29] However, there remained a lack of trained air crew throughout the operation. In the end, French paratroopers proved to be better trained and equipped, whilst the French also had to make up the numbers of Forward Air Controllers.[30] Lieutenant Colonel Bill Howard, of Air 2 Corps, later identified in his lessons report 'wherever the Regular Parachute Brigade is located – for whatever reason – the men and air crew should be able to keep in training all the time.'[31]

Early planning and training also allowed for the identification of the lack of vehicle waterproofing equipment which would be required for an amphibious assault. Consequently, a practise exercise in Malta (Septex I) with 1 Commando had to be limited to one squadron of tanks and a few vehicles from 6th Royal Tank Regiment.[32] However, by the time of intervention, 3 Commando Brigade had not done any amphibious training for eleven months with Musketeer being the first amphibious operation since the Second World War.[33] General Hugh Stockwell, the Commander of 2 (BR) Corps, identified these lessons and recommended a review of policy. He also proposed that a nucleus Force Headquarters be maintained during peacetime to take responsibility for supporting inter-service workings, including amphibious warfare and parachute operations.[34] A working party was subsequently established to investigate the lack of waterproofing equipment and implement lessons identified.[35]

Once a plan was in place, it was presented to Eden but there were political objections, particularly over the required fifteen days' notice to put it into action. To overcome the objections, a new plan was developed to allow a prolonged period of readiness: Musketeer Revise. For Revise, the assault would focus on Port

Said rather than Alexandria, an idea which had been rejected in August 1956 for tactical reasons.[36] Musketeer's Commander-in-Chief, Charles Keightley, later identified 'certain changes of orders required for political reasons but clearly unsound militarily inevitably cause a grave lack of confidence in Commanders'.[37]

Throughout planning, the main challenge for the MoD was syncing the political, diplomatic and military priorities and timetables. As time progressed, there was also a concern over the changing weather. On 1 October 1956, a directive was received to develop a new plan – Musketeer Winter Plan. This was to be based on receiving ten days' warning, but the Joint Task Force Commanders stated that the impact of weather conditions would mean a warning period of fourteen days was required. On 19 October orders were issued that Winter Plan was to be dropped and Musketeer Revise to return to force.[38] The ongoing changes in planning later led to the identification of lessons about the need for clear political direction from the outset. The 'Lessons from Musketeer' document, produced by the Deputy Chief of the Imperial Staff Sir Richard Hull in June 1957, identified 'The lack of a clear political aim and of consistent political direction bedevilled the mounting and execution of the operation.'[39] General Keightley had noted the same lesson and urged that a 'sound and comprehensive political appreciation must be made beforehand'. To implement the lesson, he recommended that Supreme Commanders be given a political adviser with the ear and confidence of the Cabinet.[40]

Ironically, all of the planning was conducted against the backdrop of possible operations against – rather than in cooperation with – Israel: Operation Cordage. Cordage was devised at the end of 1955 as part of the Anglo-Jordanian alliance, to protect Jordan in the event of Israeli aggression. Cordage rumbled on throughout the following year and in October 1956 a deteriorating situation on the West Bank led Sir Gerald Templer, the Chief of the Imperial General Staff, to advise ministers that Britain could conduct Cordage or Musketeer but not both.[41] The next day King Hussein of Jordan called for British assistance. Flights of Hunters were organised from Cyprus in a show of British support and a warning was issued that British bombing attacks on Israeli territory would be used if necessary.[42] For much of October 1956 it was clear that if

Cordage was put into action it was to take priority over Musketeer in terms of resources.

On 14 October 1956, French representatives visited Eden at Chequers and presented him with a solution for both his Nasser and Israel–Jordan problem. This proposal was formalised at Sèvres when the Israelis agreed that – as well as the attack on Egypt – they would not attack Jordan during operations against Nasser if the British agreed not to support any Jordanian attack on Israel.[43] Therefore, although Cordage was only officially abandoned in 1957, Commanders had to quickly learn that their planned enemy was to be their ally in Musketeer.

Throughout this time, the only reference made to past operations were concerns in the MoD that an isolated assault force – and anything other than a rapid advance – would lead to another Operation Market Garden, the unsuccessful Second World War operation that failed at Arnhem.[44] This memory was also the reason why the Chiefs of Staff tried to avoid Port Said as the initial landing target – beaches were shallow, muddy, close to housing, with limited room for unloading and a water supply that was easily cut.[45] Most significantly, the drop zone was close to the concentration of Egyptian tanks.[46] However, Templer complained to the Head of MI6 that his lessons had little influence claiming 'Eden's barely consulting us'.[47]

Also prominent in the minds of senior officers was 'the Nuremberg factor'. With the Nuremberg war crime trials held only a decade before there was nervousness about the level of aerial bombardment required for Musketeer Revise in respect of civilian casualties.[48] The Chiefs of Staff also drew upon the British experience of occupying Egypt in the past to provide an assessment of a post-war Egypt.[49] They identified lessons on the large number of resources that would be required to set up and support a friendly government whilst counteracting any guerrilla activity or ongoing hostility from Egyptian military units. It would, they warned, be 'prolonged' and mean that other commitments would have to be compromised, including the planned ending of national service.[50]

The IC suffered similarly from a lack of openness about the government's intentions, despite the Chairman of the JIC – Patrick Dean – providing the signatory on the Sèvres protocol. A number of officials were bypassed, including MI6's Head of Political Intelligence, who was removed from the Middle East telegrams circulation list, and senior officers who soon became aware that they were not receiving regular telegrams from Israel.[51] The newly appointed SIS Director, Richard White – the previous Head of MI5 who had been in his new role twelve days when Nasser nationalised the canal – was only later informed of the Anglo-French-Israeli collusion. Furthermore, he was only advised of events by Cabinet Secretary Norman Brook because Eden needed to use the SIS to communicate with the Israeli Prime Minister, David Ben-Gurion. White was sworn to secrecy and remained excluded from any decision-making.[52] In addition, special security measures were placed across all intelligence to protect the secrecy of planning for Musketeer, only including people on a need-to-know basis. This procedure was codenamed Terrapin.[53]

At the same time, the IC had failed to predict the nationalisation of the Suez Canal and had little understanding of the force of Arab nationalism. Whilst MI6 had always had intelligence assets within Egypt's monarchy and Wafd party, they had not penetrated the new leaders, the Free Officers, forcing reliance on the sharing of intelligence by the Americans and GCHQ intercepts. The result was that the IC had little understanding of Nasser or his intentions but this lesson was not promptly identified and the SIS was still debating how to infiltrate the Nasserite movement years later.[54]

After nationalisation, intelligence assets were reduced even further when a SIS network in Cairo was uncovered. The Arab News Agency had provided local cover for MI6 but in August 1956 its offices were raided and closed down by Nasser. Thirty people were arrested and accused of espionage. Some were expelled, others executed and the SIS was effectively neutered.

Nonetheless, a number of assessments were produced by the JIC during the crisis and before operations began. Immediately after Nasser nationalised the canal, a report was produced which assessed its impact and declared 'Nasser's triumph has been spectacular.' It also examined possible future developments and the impact on UK relations with other Arab states.[55] The JIC separately considered the situation that might arise in the Middle East once the Suez Canal Conference concluded, the risk of sabotage of the canal by the Egyptians, possible courses of action by Nasser as tensions continued and the ongoing influence of the Soviet Union.[56] From the outset assessments seemed to support the idea of an armed intervention.[57] One assessment proved to be particularly timely. 'The threat to United Kingdom interests overseas' was presented on 18 October 1956 and surmised:

> it should be emphasised that any concessions made by the United Kingdom under pressure are likely to have repercussions throughout the world, encouraging further claims and exacerbating points of friction. Conversely, a successful demonstration or resolution and firmness by the United Kingdom would have the effect of discouraging similar pressure throughout the world.[58]

It concluded that if Nasser succeeded in the Suez dispute the outlook for specific threats in Middle East and North African countries looked concerning. This assessment supported the anti-appeasement lessons identified by Eden and emerged just before the agreement at Sèvres. However, none of the assessments explicitly examined lessons from the past, nor was there any reflection on lessons from events as they progressed in terms of intelligence collection and analysis. Even the failure to predict the nationalisation of the canal was quickly forgotten and when Doug Nicoll – the former Deputy Director of GCHQ – was asked in the late 1970s to examine the JIC's warnings of aggression, and identify lessons to be learned, Suez was overlooked.[59]

The IC was also involved in three other ways during the planning of Musketeer. Firstly, there had been Anglo-American attempts to destabilise Nasser since March 1956 through economic, diplomatic and military means and offering reconciliation after each phase. This plan was called Omega and was to be supported by covert action including the increase of propaganda, the encouragement of Canada and France to provide jet fighters to Israel and intervention in Syria to change the government, codenamed Operation Straggle.[60]

Secondly, as the year progressed, the policy of Britain and the US diverged as MI6 began to consider a possible coup to overthrow Nasser. The MI6 Deputy Director, George Young, had been heavily involved in Operation Boot, the joint UK–US operation which orchestrated the 1953 overthrow of Mosaddeq in Iran, and lessons from these events informed his ideas on how to deal with Nasser.[61] On 27 August 1956, the Member of Parliament (MP) and son-in-law of Harold Macmillan, Julian Amery and two SIS officers met an Egyptian 'shadow' government in France. In the meantime, Squadron Leader Isameddine Mahmoud Khalil, Egypt's Deputy Chief of Air Force Intelligence, was recruited into the 'Restoration Plot' to establish an organisation of Army officers in Egypt who would help to orchestrate the coup.[62]

The final area of activity was the most extreme: planning the assassination of Nasser. In March 1956 Nutting had received a phone call at the Savoy Hotel from Eden, angry at the mild nature of the plans for Omega. On an open phone line the Prime Minister shouted 'What's all this nonsense about isolating Nasser or "neutralising" him? . . . I want him murdered, can't you understand?'[63] Young took Eden's request literally and drew up various plans for assassination including the use of dissident military officers, kitting out an electric razor with explosives, using poison gas and sending assassins.[64] Young later denied such conspiracies, although at this time there were no set guidelines or restrictions for covert action.[65] Despite none of these activities proving successful, there was no attempt by the IC to identify lessons for the future.

During the Intervention

Once the operation started, the FCO was forced into a state of damage control as the shockwaves from British actions extended beyond London to the Middle East and across the world. Support for Arab nationalism increased as a result of British failure and, for many, went on to influence events which led to the start of the Oman war in 1957, the 1958 Lebanese civil war, the 1958 Iraqi revolution and the 1967 Six Day War. There was wide dismay that Europeans had attacked a Muslim country; Saudi Arabia broke off relations, the situation with Palestine was set back and terrorists attacked the Middle East Centre for Arab Studies (MECAS) – the Arabic language school in Lebanon where Britain sent young diplomats for training.[66] Even in Kuwait, where Britain had enjoyed a long friendship, Sir Anthony Acland described how 'It was different' and that the Kuwaitis 'wanted to remain friends with Britain but they didn't want to be seen to be too friendly to the representatives of Britain after the Suez affair'.[67] Most of the Commonwealth countries were equally unimpressed, with widespread opposition to British actions. The Commander-in-Chief's post-operational report identified 'The one overriding lesson of the Suez operation is that world opinion is now an absolute principle of war and must be treated as such.'[68]

The affair also damaged relations with the US; the Americans were furious that they had not been consulted and they objected to the imperial nature of the actions. Eisenhower was particularly unhappy that he had explicitly warned against war and that Eden had chosen the inopportune moment of the run-up to his presidential election to launch such an operation. He wrote in his diaries 'October 20, 1956 was the start of the most crowded and demanding three weeks of my entire Presidency.'[69] Guy Millard, Eden's Private Secretary, later identified the lesson that Britain had not fully understood US preoccupation with domestic politics during the run-up to an American general election, nor their predisposition to leave foreign policy to the UN during this time.[70]

As a result, the FCO spent the time during the intervention trying to repair relationships. The new British Ambassador to the US, Harold Caccia, was spared the initial anger in Washington by being sent from London by boat, leaving him at sea throughout the intervention. However, Lord Wright, who would later become British Ambassador to the US, explained that Caccia still 'had a fearfully difficult time, picking up the pieces post-Suez, when large parts of the American administration were virtually not speaking to us'.[71] It was later identified in both the FCO and the MoD that Britain would need to liaise closely with the US throughout all future wars. Keightley identified 'it was the actions of the United States which really defeated us in attaining our object' and the Chiefs of Staff concluded that in the future 'the United Kingdom would only act in cooperation with the United States and/or the United Nations'.[72]

In the UN, the UK Representative, Pierson Dixon, was forced to defend the Anglo-French ultimatum despite his own moral objections and suspicions of collusion. He was instructed to play for time, in order to prevent UN intervention before the Canal was recaptured and Nasser sufficiently weakened. Dixon had already refused to support America's calling of the Security Council on 30 October 1956 and then used Britain's first ever veto against a resolution labelling Israelis aggressors and calling for a ceasefire.[73] In fact, Suez forced a number of historic firsts in the UN. In response to the deadlock, the Americans transferred the issue of a ceasefire to the General Assembly for its first ever Emergency Special Session, which Dixon again opposed.[74] Eventually the Canadian delegation proposed sending a UN Emergency Force to Egypt – again the first of its kind – to act as peacekeepers. This time Britain only abstained from the vote as political and financial pressure for a ceasefire was mounting.[75]

Despite these events, it took some time for the FCO to identify lessons about the importance of the UN in interventions. In the short term there was some resentment for the part it played in British humiliation by forcing a ceasefire. In February 1957 Ivor Pink, the Superintending Under-Secretary in the UN Department, produced a memorandum for the Anglo-American Bermuda Conference which called for a reduction in power of both the General Assembly and the Secretary General, Dag Hammarskjöld. The memo was approved by the FCO but not the Americans and instead both states agreed to coordinate better through the UN and not to grant it primacy in their foreign policy. By mid-1957 the mood in the FCO had changed and the ongoing role of the UN in international relations was finally identified. This eventually led to an acceptance of the institution, whilst work continued to restore the Security Council to its primacy for decision-making in matters of peace and security.[76]

In the MoD, once Musketeer began, damage limitation management took over as lessons needed to be quickly implemented due to planning inaccuracies and changes in circumstances. As soon as the first bomb landed in Port Said the Joint Task Force Commanders were asked if they could bring troop landing forward from the planned 6 November 1956.[77] This was something that the Commanders found 'impossible' as plans had already been delayed by an American display of disapproval; the US 6th Fleet flew aircraft and submerged submarines in the path of the Anglo-French invasion fleet.[78] However, the Egyptian Air Force was eliminated much quicker than anticipated, further hastening the need for an earlier landing of troops at a time when the leading force, 3rd Infantry Division, was sailing from the UK and was not due to reach Port Said until 9 November 1956.[79]

Challenges in adapting to changes in plans and the slow arrival of troops were partly due to the lack of force flexibility. Keightley identified this lesson and made a number of recommendations for implementation, including always having two parachute brigades fully staffed and equipped and sufficient transport carrying aircraft. The Chiefs of Staff agreed with Keightley's proposal but concluded 'For various reasons, including financial ones, there is little possibility of implementing most of General Keightley's proposals.'[80] They could not, for example, afford to increase the airborne element of the Army but did set a new focus for infantry brigade groups to be trained for rapid movement by air.

A further reason for last minute changes was the lack of intelligence on Egyptian capabilities during the military planning phase. Commodore Charles Moore had complained to the Chiefs of Staff and JIC that the Air Ministry were worried about the lack of up-to-date intelligence on the Egyptian Air Force and Air General Stockwell found the same was true for ground forces.[81] One report revealed that, due to the lack of intelligence, the Assistant Naval Attaché in Port Said had to plan an urgent afternoon picnic to the coast whereby he could report that vital landing beaches were inhabited by happy Egyptian families, not Egyptian land mines.[82]

The problem was exacerbated by the inability to run advance reconnaissance missions in order to avoid political difficulties. This was especially challenging as it soon became clear that many of the British maps of Egypt were out of date leaving parachutist dropping zones and bomb targeting to be based on air cover which was several years old. In fact, the key bombing target of Cairo Radio's transmitter was postponed because outdated maps suggested it was in the centre of the capital, when in fact its transmitters were in the desert.[83] Lieutenant Colonel Howard identified in his lessons report 'A dropping zone cannot be selected from air cover that is two or three years old . . . The lack of PR [photo reconnaissance] in August was a handicap.'[84] To implement the lesson Stockwell recommended an earlier inclusion of the War

Office's Survey Directorate in operational planning and to impress upon an initial assault force the urgent need to capture maps from the enemy.[85]

To make matters worse, poor communications and inaccuracy of bombing caused further difficulties once Musketeer began. The bombing of the first target, the airfield at Cairo West, was rapidly cancelled because news reached London that US citizens were being evacuated by a nearby road.[86] However, the signal only reached Malta after six Valiants and five Canberras had departed. These aircraft were successfully recalled but Canberras in 139 Squadron had already left from Cyprus and, in the ensuing confusion, incorrectly bombed Cairo International Airport instead.[87] In addition, this was the first active operation for Bomber Command since the Second World War and it was going through a re-equipping process; only 50 per cent of the 1,962 bombs dropped were within 650 yards of the aiming point and Egyptian propaganda soon claimed excessive use of force.[88] The international outcry led the MoD to fund its own propaganda in return. The film *Suez in Perspective* dismissed the Egyptian claims as 'absolute nonsense' and utilised video from the air to demonstrate the controlled nature of the bombing of Port Said.[89] The need to produce the film reiterated the lesson identified in planning: the requirement for future bombing campaigns to focus on precision targeting and the avoidance of civilians.

There were also other incidents to overcome. In one case air support was allocated at the request of a destroyer without reference to the troops on the ground. This led to a British strike on its own troops with the lesson immediately identified: 'the need to conform to established procedures when engaging targets within the bombline, and the importance of recognition methods between the ground and air'.[90] Another incident was the shooting down of a Canberra aircraft by a Syrian Meteor. The Syrian government had refused Britain permission to overfly its territory, leaving the Royal Air Force (RAF) to fly illegally and hazardously to provide essential supplies.[91] However, the lesson of securing overflying rights was not identified in any key learning documents and would become a repeatedly re-identified lesson in future operations.

In addition, equipment deficiencies remained, despite a programme of re-equipping having taken place before the operation. There continued to be a lack of waterproofing equipment for vehicles, no appropriate headquarters ship or parachutable anti-tank gun and no hospital ship was available. Similarly, the amphibious squadron could only transport part of the Commando Brigade and Transport Command could only lift a small number of the Parachute Brigade, whilst much ammunition proved unsuitable for the hot climate – a lesson that was later considered an 'urgent requirement' for implementation.[92] Most embarrassingly, when the paratroopers landed they were amazed to discover that the Egyptians were armed with more modern and effective weapons than themselves. This lesson was quickly identified and it was 'most earnestly recommended that Para Battalions should be re-equipped with the best and latest British weapons as soon as possible'.[93] In the short term, the lesson was implemented through the rapid repair of jeeps, trailers and parachute equipment as well as the purchase of recoilless rifles and ammunition from the US.[94] However, equipment difficulties persisted throughout Musketeer and were compounded by logistics failures. One post-operational report identified 'Many items were misdirected, all shipping schedules were late and some items were never found.'[95]

A separate area of concern throughout the campaign was the management of public relations (PR). PR had not been included in planning and was hampered by inexperienced officers, new correspondents and poor communications. General Keightley identified 'We had no time to organise our press representatives, to study the conflicting claims of would be accredited correspondents or to try out press communications.'[96] This meant that there was inadequate reporting of the assault phase which had the knock-on effect of causing political pressure. This lesson was quickly identified and – in the end – learned; forces received good press, partly due to the implementation of full and authoritative daily press briefings, and partly due to the morale of troops under difficult circumstances.[97] Following the operation further lessons were implemented on issues of press accreditation and liaising with the press over communications equipment, with a study commissioned into Service requirements.[98]

Successful liaison across the MoD – the Force Headquarters, Service Ministries, Allied Force Headquarters, General Headquarters Middle East Land Forces and with the Ministry of Transport – was identified as a positive lesson. This was achieved through regular conferences across departments and visits between London and theatre as well as daily meetings with a Liaison Officer who worked between Allied Force Headquarters and Rear Headquarters Middle East.[99] Positive working relations also continued further down the chain of command at the divisional and brigade level and below, including with the French Airborne Forces. Sir Frank Cooper, Head of the Air Staff Secretariat at the time of Suez, identified the importance of Anglo-French cooperation and to highlight the cordial relations between the two countries the front sheet of the British news was always printed in both English and French.[100] The lesson identified by Stockwell was 'As far as possible this liaison should be maintained by joint exercises, since the mutual confidence and respect that exist between the Services are battle winning factors' and, in addition, 'the exchange of officers between French and British Airborne Forces, especially on the technical side, should be maintained'.[101] The British also learned a number of lessons from the French, both by observing their equipment and organisation on operation but also from the sharing of their lessons reports.[102]

For the IC, once the operation began, the focus was on defence intelligence, much of which was delayed and therefore ineffective. The Deputy Chief of the Imperial Staff, Richard Hull, complained to the Executive Committee of the Army Council that Intelligence Branch 'was unable to acquire background quickly enough to become fully effective'.[103] This was, in part, due to coordination difficulties between the three intelligence branches of the Services, between these and the broader IC and across British and French intelligence. No existing structure was in place for the immediate coordination of operational and political intelligence and this identified lesson was quickly implemented by establishing an ad hoc emergency Joint Intelligence centre in an empty office. However, challenges of effective coordination continued in both the collection and dissemination of intelligence throughout Musketeer.[104]

There were also challenges with image intelligence (IMINT) as the necessary image developing and printing equipment did not arrive on time at Akrotiri meaning that film had to be sent by road or helicopter to Episkopi. This caused a seven hour delay for prints to be available to intelligence staff. The French, on the other hand, had arrived at Akrotiri with all their equipment and were able to provide results in less than three hours.[105] Air Vice Marshal John Stephenson later noted that 'The Air Ministry were well aware of the shortcomings revealed by Operation Musketeer and were doing their best to correct them.' To implement these lessons he advised that improvements were being made to the organisation for processing and interpreting of photos, but the details of these changes remain unknown.[106]

Even psychological operations (psyops) were limited. There was no existing policy for this type of warfare at the time, and very limited training.[107] The appointed Director of Psychological Warfare, Brigadier Bernard Fergusson, had no previous experience in this area and there were difficulties in securing the required voice aircraft from Kenya where they had been used against the Mau Mau.[108] In addition, planned leaflet drops had to be cancelled. Canberra bombers were technically incapable of carrying out the operation and the reservists responsible for the production of the leaflets were unfamiliar with the machinery for the scattering devices. As a result blocks of leaflets – which were due to explode at 1,000 feet in order to scatter – were actually exploding at head height or not at all, causing injury to civilians.[109] Nonetheless, the value of psyops was identified by Stockwell as having 'enormous potential value ... particularly in an area such as the Middle East'.[110] Keightley agreed and made a number of recommendations for implementation, including the creation of a 'really first class psychological warfare cadre' which would have regular exercises.[111] Whilst progress on implementing these lessons was slow, it did not forestall the use of psyops in Britain's next military intervention in the region – Oman in 1957.[112]

Other challenges included the shortage of linguists – interpreters, translators and interrogators – available to gather human intelligence (HUMINT). General Keightley identified to the Chiefs of Staff 'The inability to have enough officers or Ors [other ranks] who speak foreign languages is now a national failing, but it will affect our future operations unless improved.'[113] Following the operation the MoD applied to the Treasury for funding to support implementation in this area.[114]

One part of the IC which continued to work well, in contrast to all other parts of the government, was UK–US liaison. In fact, as operations began US U-2 reconnaissance planes were overflying Egypt, and the CIA passed the images to the British; the RAF telegrammed 'Warm thanks. It's the quickest bomb damage assessment we've ever had.'[115] The CIA also produced and shared an assessment – partly based on further reconnaissance – when the Soviets threatened to become militarily involved in Suez.[116] In fact, even as Eisenhower was condemning Britain in the UN, the CIA was still liaising with the SIS and much of Britain's post-Suez 'special relationship' was reignited due to the network of UK–US covert operations taking place in the Middle East; the political quarantine placed by Eisenhower on the Eden administration was lifted just over a week later in an effort to reignite the joint Operation Straggle in Syria and the importance of the Anglo-American intelligence liaison for broader relations would later become an identified lesson.

After the Intervention

After seven eventful days – from the start of the operation on 31 October to the ceasefire on 6 November – there was much from which to learn and, as time went on, there were increasing demands for a formal, external inquiry. Although the rationale for an inquiry was predominantly led by MP calls for scrutiny of the executive and the public right to 'truth' over rumours of collusion, such an inquiry would have provided the opportunity to ascertain policy and procedural lessons for the future. Initially, the grounds for denying such an inquiry were 'The Government do not believe an inquiry should take place into a matter which is primarily the responsibility of the Government.'[117] However, as time passed, a range of reasons were given for its dismissal. In 1960, the Prime Minister, Harold Macmillan, denying the benefit of learning from history, declared he could not conceive of 'any purpose, national or international, that can be served'.[118] In the run-up to the 1959 debate on the Anglo-Egyptian Financial Agreement, when the Suez question seemed likely to be revisited, Norman Brook produced a memorandum on the precedent of inquiries. He concluded that since criticism was towards the honour of ministers, rather than their professional wisdom, precedent suggested that any debate should be confined to the floor of the House of Commons rather than any form of inquiry.[119] Even in 1967, when debate was reignited over the publication of Anthony Nutting's memoir, the government was still discussing ways in which an inquiry could be avoided.[120]

The FCO also did not wish to support an external inquiry. Diplomats were concerned that it would reopen wounds which they were trying to repair, particularly with the US, and would only serve to benefit President Nasser.[121] Even years later the Foreign Secretary, George Brown, informed Richard Crossman, the Chair of the Cabinet's Legislation Committee, that he believed any inquiry would have harmful effects worldwide. He concluded that whilst the relationships that would be most greatly affected would be with the US, France, Israel and other Arab countries, in no country would such an inquiry bring Britain any benefit.[122] Consequently, the power of the present day politics and diplomacy overtook the necessity to learn from the past.

However, whilst the FCO refused to support any external lessons inquiry, there was also no desire for an official history to be produced. In fact, Suez was notably rejected for consideration on a number of occasions. In 1957 when Norman Brook was funding his history initiative across Whitehall, Suez did not even make the shortlist and the pilot history project was completed on the 1951 Abadan crisis instead. In 1963 – when the employment of official historians on the official histories of 1939–45 were coming to a close – Cabinet Secretary Burke Trend suggested moving to begin writing accounts of other major events. In so doing, he specifically asked 'How, for example, would the Foreign Office and the Commonwealth Office react to the suggestion that we should publish an official "history" of the Palestine mandate or the Suez episode?'[123] Having highlighted this particular quote Douglas-Home responded that he did not much like the idea but preferred to produce work which could be released once the required fifty year time rule had passed.[124] Trend pressed the Prime Minister after a Cabinet meeting and a compromise was struck, albeit one where Suez remained explicitly off limits:

> He agreed that discussions might now go forward with a view to producing a scheme or making contemporary accounts of certain episodes. These should be in the political field, e.g. Britain's history of decolonisation; or the independence of India; rather than in the military fields e.g. Suez.[125]

As the ten year anniversary of Suez approached the ranks closed further around any official history of Suez. Trend declared that 'nobody should write anything on Suez' whilst the Permanent Under-Secretary, Paul Gore-Booth, agreed that 'the less said about Suez the better'.[126]

There was the same nervousness over the publication of memoirs from officials involved in Suez – an unofficial way of recording individual lessons from the experience. In part, this raised debates over political party loyalty, ministerial collective responsibility, protection of serving members of the service and official secrecy but also the role of the FCO in vetting history. There was concern from the Foreign Secretary, for example, in 1959 when Eden wanted to publish his memoirs that he had quoted confidential discussions with people who remained influential, that there was a strong anti-American bias, a negative attitude towards the Arabs and a lack of any acceptance of fault. For Lloyd, such an account was too soon after events, when relations remained raw.[127] However, in the event, the FCO could only advise on the manuscript and publication proceeded for 1960.

Anthony Nutting's book ten years after events also caused much concern. Even as Nutting was considering publication Macmillan tried to dissuade him from providing specifics on Suez. Gore-Booth recorded how Macmillan 'using all his best political experience and persuasiveness' suggested to Nutting 'that it would be far more useful, dignified etc. if he published something rather broader in its consideration of the Middle East question, rather than more spicy revelations about Suez'.[128] In so doing, Macmillan again allowed the politics of the day to overtake the emphasis on history, both for the protection of international relationships and for the protection of his party in the forthcoming general election.

It was not until Nutting's print proof was made available that greater concerns were iterated by the FCO: the risk of relations with France, the US and the Arab world, the adverse way in which the methods of British diplomacy may be questioned, the negative effect of revealing – that in at least one case – telegrams from Ambassadors were doctored to conceal the degree to which they were being deceived, and concerns over security, with Nutting quoting from secret telegrams and highly classified documents.[129] It was at this point that the dangers of public revelations associated with learning from history were more vigorously articulated by the FCO and the difficult tensions between history, policy and politics became truly exposed.

Even so, the FCO did not completely rule out a confidential internal history. Upon completion of the Abadan history project by Rohan Butler, the question of completing such a review of Suez was reconsidered. Having been impressed by Butler's works the Foreign Secretary, Michael Stewart, inquired:

> I would be grateful if you would consider whether a similar confidential report could be prepared within the Foreign Office on the lessons of Suez ... This might be of use when the time comes for a fuller analysis to be done of Suez. I think also that just as we have learned some useful lessons from Abadan, so something worthwhile could emerge from a study of Suez.[130]

Clearly, Stewart appreciated the benefit of learning from history although he also stated 'this would have to be done most carefully because I am sure it would be most unfortunate if the fact that this study was being undertaken became public knowledge'.[131] However, Gore-Booth was quick to dissuade the Foreign Secretary from pursuing the matter further. In a stinging response he replied:

> The lesson to be learned from Suez was a simple one. It was this: if Ministers consulted their officials and then rejected their advice this was perfectly proper and might on many occasions give them the

right answer. If, however, a government undertook operations by a process of deliberately refraining from taking official advice, or keeping officials informed, then the result in due course would be disastrous.[132]

As a result, Gore-Booth firmly laid any required learning at the door of particular ministers, rather than the acceptance of lesson learning for the FCO. Stewart relented and conceded that 'while in due course the true story ought to be told' in the circumstances such an inquiry 'would look like a vindictive diversion of time and effort'.[133] Consequently, the matter was promptly dropped, without further recorded discussion.

However, what Stewart did not know was that Guy Millard had already written a history of Suez which had remained secret. The document – 'Memorandum on relations between the United Kingdom, the United States and France in the months following Egyptian nationalisation of the Suez Canal Company in 1956' – identified two key lessons. Firstly, Britain had endeavoured to solve both the issue of passage through the Suez Canal and declining British prestige through a single operation. For Millard 'It was perhaps a British mistake to try to solve two problems simultaneously; and this was a criticism of British policy made during the crisis by the Americans.'[134] In reality Musketeer had sought to achieve even more objectives than this, simultaneously aiming to protect Jordan, weaken Syria and topple Nasser.

Secondly, Suez revealed that British policy-makers had not understood Britain's international or economic limitations. The day after Eden and Lloyd had been in Paris to discuss a possible joint intervention, the French had made the move to protect their currency reserves. However, no such protection was given to sterling and when Musketeer began, a run on the pound lead to an $85 million loss of reserves by 6 November, just as the amphibious assault arrived in Port Said in support of the paratroopers.[135] Washington then blocked any International Monetary Fund (IMF) financial assistance to the UK until a ceasefire was agreed.[136] As a result of both of these lessons, a complete re-evaluation was required:

we could never again resort to military action, outside British territories, without at least American acquiescence. Our capacity to act independently had been seen to be closely circumscribed by economic weakness. The experience of Suez may have led to a reassessment of British interests and of our relative position in the world.[137]

Nine months earlier, Eden had identified the same lessons. Five pages of general thoughts on the crisis were sent by the Prime Minister to the Foreign Secretary, Minister of Defence and Lord President and the concluding paragraph reassessed Britain's place in the world and its international relationships. Eden wrote 'The conclusion of all this is surely that we must review our world position and our domestic capacity more searchingly in the light of the Suez experience, which has not so much changed our fortunes but revealed our realities.'[138]

It was not long before the same lesson was identified within the FCO itself. In April 1958, the FCO produced a planning paper for its Foreign Affairs Steering Committee which stated:

> The last fifty years have seen a drastic diminution in our world status . . . our policies have outstripped our capacity or willingness to provide the means to meet them . . . This looks like the classic picture of an Empire in decline.[139]

Looking specifically at the Middle East, the paper revealed that Britain had been unable to resist recent attacks on colonial, strategic and commercial interests due to post-Suez domestic and world opinion about actions in the region and because of the prohibitive costs. The stark lesson was identified; 'we are no longer in a position to "go it alone"'.[140] Instead, to achieve British objectives in the region it was identified that it was necessary to 'Promot[e] United States involvement and the harmonisation of Anglo-American policy.'[141]

A further opportunity for the FCO to identify lessons arose in 1963 when the Permanent Under-Secretary asked diplomats to respond to a call by Lord Strang to critically review British diplomacy. Thirty-four replies were received from Ambassadors around the world and their ideas were compiled into a paper by Rohan Butler: 'A New Perspective for British Diplomacy'.[142] The third section of the paper focused on obstacles for a stronger British foreign policy of which three main problems were specified: the propensity to always seek good relations rather than pursuing tough policy lines, British economic weakness and failure at Suez. Suez was described as 'a traumatic humiliation' comparable only to Munich. The difference, it was claimed, was that the defeat in Munich was wiped out within a year by war whereas the 'long shadow from Suez . . . still lies heavy across our thinking' and the concern that 'the error of Suez should become a defeatist bogey to be regularly trundled out, without fresh or keen appraisal'.[143] This concern would prove prophetic. The paper was twice discussed by the Foreign Affairs Steering Committee and the lessons were widely distributed, with a copy sent to the heads of all FCO departments and a truncated version distributed to all Foreign Service posts.[144]

The implementation of these lessons is less tangible to discern. The attempts to work more closely with the Americans were certainly observable over the next few years and Britain would go out of its way to incorporate Washington in an intervention two years later in Jordan. There were also some structural changes which slowly emerged in the aftermath of Suez including the establishment of a new FCO section to deal with the repercussions.[145] In addition, the FCO, in line with Eden's conclusions, did appear to learn and re-evaluate Britain's position in the world and in 1964 the recommendation was made to merge the Foreign Office and Commonwealth Office as part of an endeavour to reinforce Britain's international influence.[146]

In contrast, the MoD had a more proactive and positive approach to historical learning from Suez than the FCO. As the Commander of 16 Independent Parachute Brigade stated in the opening lines of his lessons report 'sufficient lessons of lasting importance have emerged from the planning and execution of this operation to warrant a detailed and extensive review'.[147] As early as 26 November 1956 the School of Land and Air Warfare requested a team from Suez to be flown home to discuss lessons from the emergency, which Brigadier Weston and Air Commodore Radford considered would be 'of great benefit'.[148] Although this request was refused, it was on the basis that General Stockwell, the ground Commander of the Allied Task Force, wished to submit his own report to Allied Force Headquarters before any 'piecemeal discussion of lessons'.[149] However, learning was not rejected, merely delayed, with two officers flown back to discuss the Suez operation with the School before Christmas.[150]

By 14 November 1956 a report on the air aspects of the operation at Gamil Airfield had been produced and included lessons from air transport, technical, signals and the Army. This report was shared by the Air Ministry with the War Office in January 1957 and declared 'The Air Ministry considers that the Report discloses a number of points . . . which merit closer examination and follow up action in order that the lessons learned from the operation are not lost.'[151] In order to ensure that these lessons were disseminated and implemented, a conference was held and relevant actions were appropriately attributed.[152]

On 4 February 1957 separate loose minutes were sent to all of the large departments involved in Musketeer to announce a cross-departmental lesson initiative and the collection of 'major lessons . . . which you consider could be drawn from the operation, other than purely departmental matters with which you are dealing yourself'.[153] The request revealed the expectation that learning would occur within all departments and a volume of evidence suggests that this was the case; working committees were established, conferences held and actions attributed. In addition, the response to the request ensured the collection and retention of lessons across defence departments.[154] These were then collated into a paper entitled 'Lessons from Operation Musketeer' by the Deputy Chief of the Imperial General Staff, General Sir Richard Hull.[155]

'Lessons from Operation Musketeer' demonstrated the MoD's commitment to historical learning by aiming to identify important lessons, irrespective of the practicalities of implementation. The paper examined lessons in planning, mobilisation, operational efficiency and administration and recognised that many of the difficulties experienced were the result of factors outside the MoD's control, including policy decisions and financial limitations. However, although the paper was circulated, it was given very limited distribution and whilst some actions were taken to implement lessons it was suggested that the list of lessons were not tabled at the meeting of the Executive Committee of the Army Council.[156]

Concurrently, the Commander-in-Chief of Allied Forces, General Sir Charles Keightley prepared his own despatch on the Suez campaign, with the second half offering a critical analysis of the lessons of Suez.[157] Initially this report had a very tight distribution list – to the MoD's Deputy Secretary Sir Richard Powell, the Permanent Under-Secretary, the three Chiefs of Staff and Patrick Dean at the FCO – with requests that the report be returned to the Chiefs of Staff Committee once read.[158] It was later examined by the Chiefs of Staff and studies were commissioned to implement a number of identified lessons, including issues surrounding command and control which were implemented by the 1961 intervention in Kuwait.[159] Requests for immediate implementation of lessons on intelligence were also sent to the JIC, on psyops and PR to the MoD and on inter-service subjects to the Joint Planning Staff.[160] Furthermore, lessons reports were regularly followed-up to ensure implementation, including updates to the Chiefs of Staff as late as 1958.[161]

However, in May 1957, to Macmillan's horror, the MoD proposed publishing Keightley's report and the Chief of the Imperial General Staff quickly ordered a withdrawal of all circulated copies.[162] After some persuasion by Richard Powell, Macmillan agreed to the report's publication on the understanding that it was to provide a purely factual and military focused account.[163] More specifically, the version was to be 'harmless', not give rise to 'public difficulties', 'political controversy' or 'friction in foreign relations'.[164] In order to enforce such requests it had to be approved for publication by Macmillan, Lloyd, the Minister of Defence Duncan Sandys, and Eden himself. Unsurprisingly, as a result, the second part of the report, where lessons were the most prominent, was not published externally. Consequently, despite the MoD's best attempts to widely circulate lessons, politics had again won over history.

Later, in 1963, the question of lessons from Suez again arose when the Chiefs of Staff approved a study by the Combined Staff College. This was the perfect opportunity for the MoD to implement lessons in the training of their personnel and would provide an ongoing method to ensure the lessons of Suez were not forgotten. However, even six years later Macmillan's view had not changed. He instructed the study to be immediately abandoned and his decision came to be considered as a comprehensive ban across Whitehall for any such study of the Suez crisis, including any form of history.[165]

Even before this, the Working Party on Joint Service In-House Histories had shied away from tackling the thorny topic of Musketeer and as late as 1973 the Party concluded 'Suez would have to be excluded because of political sensitivity.'[166] It also reported that even a purely military history of Suez would 'meet difficulties'.[167] Little had changed five years later, in 1978, when the concerns over the ramifications from producing a history of Suez remained prevalent. In writing to the Head of the Air Historical Branch, one section head emphasised the legal issues surrounding the internal history programmes, with a specific reference to Suez:

> ... even 'in house' documents which impugn someone's character or reputation are open to damages. We have to think about reflections upon both individuals and organisations ... it would be amazing if the top people in the MoD did not make mistakes in the difficult time from 1956.[168]

Therefore, even though the Air Historical Branch Steering Committee demonstrated a recognition that the history programme was beneficial to 'meet a genuine professional need of the RAF and of the Air Force Department', and Suez offered some important and relevant lessons, it was rejected as a subject for a standalone history.[169] Even with the protection of classification, and a distribution list as small as 200, learning from Suez through internal histories was abandoned.

In 1957 a formal defence review was carried out allowing for more reflection and formalisation of lessons.[170] The Defence White Paper re-evaluated British defence needs based upon economic constraints, decolonisation, nuclearisation and lessons from Suez. An early draft of the paper explicitly stated 'The operations undertaken in Egypt at the beginning of November 1956 have been studied.'[171] Furthermore, just as Eden had identified lessons for the FCO, he had also written notes on the strategic lessons for the MoD and sent a copy to the Minister of Defence, Antony Head, who was soon replaced by Duncan Sandys.[172] There had been severe difficulty and delay in putting together an expeditionary force for Suez and, embarrassingly, the French had been able to send almost double the numbers of paratroopers; by the end of Musketeer 668 British and 1,014 French paratroopers had been dropped. Eden therefore identified that the MoD required a more mobile force supported by modern equipment: 'This probably means that we have in proportion to our total Army too much armour and too much infantry but too small a paratroop force.'[173] The lesson was echoed by Keightley and the White Paper.[174] Consequently, the lesson was implemented through force restructuring and by the time of the 1958 intervention in Jordan a new, more mobile force was ready to be sent to Amman.

However, few other lessons identified from Musketeer were included within the review. The reality was that Suez had only re-emphasised that defence policy had to be compromised due to the economic situation and consequently it was not possible to implement all lessons as requested. The Chiefs of Staff wrote to the Secretary of State for Defence on the topic of Keightley's identified lessons, 'their value will depend on our ultimate resources and commitments arising from our new defence policy'.[175] In addition, time and resource would continue to remain a barrier to learning. One handwritten note on a report by 2 Corps on Musketeer stated that they agreed with the lessons identified but asked 'What is happening about M [Musketeer] lessons in general? We are supposed to be processing but have almost too much on our plates.'[176]

In the IC, despite prediction and covert operation failures, the disbanding of intelligence links and ongoing operational challenges, there was little reflection on lessons from the events of Suez. Instead, a remarkable continuity remained. Soon after the ceasefire all intelligence departments were asked to find fresh evidence that they could give to the Americans to persuade them that Nasser was a tool of the Soviets.[177] However, there was no improvement in British intelligence assets in Egypt, leaving the JIC unable to provide any intelligence on the post-Musketeer internal situation and forcing the FCO to beg other nations to share their assessments.[178]

A number of the pre-Suez crisis operations also quickly resumed with the search for an alternative government continuing into the Premiership of Macmillan. The Restoration Plot to overthrow Nasser only ended on 23 December 1957 when the President himself revealed the conspiracy during a speech at Port Said. At this speech he triumphantly handed over £166,500 to the port's reconstruction fund; money that had been paid by MI6 to Squadron Leader Khalil, who had been recruited into the plot but who turned out to be a double agent.[179]

In addition, the IC did not have the same mechanisms and processes in place for learning as the FCO or MoD and, as the existence of the SIS was not formally recognised by the government until 1995, there were no calls for any form of external inquiry, oversight, scrutiny or review. Internally, Dick White decided against commissioning a post-Suez report where lessons could be identified. He considered that such an investigation would be unsettling when he was already managing a number of other changes across the department.[180] The JIC only commissioned one specific report on Musketeer: to examine security measures around the secrecy of Musketeer.[181] Any other reflections were made through much broader assessments of Egyptian and Soviet behaviour rather than reflections upon British conduct.[182]

However, the regional Chair of the JIC Middle East (JIC(ME)), Henry Hainworth, was much more reflective and produced a report which identified a number of lessons 'which may be of use in any future limited war' and was sent to London.[183] These lessons included increasing communications with Whitehall during planning and coordination as well as lessons on command and liaison of intelligence throughout the operation. In particular, the JIC(ME) stressed the importance of collection and assessment of intelligence locally, where there was expertise. It emphasised that local assessment of Middle East intelligence was important because of understanding the specific tendency of sources in the region to 'exaggerate and dramatise the most ordinary events'. It was also identified that 'the intelligence plan produced in London failed to take important local problems into account'.[184]

In Whitehall, the report was quickly dismissed. The British Defence Coordination Committee considered it without offering any comment and it was agreed that the report was to be shelved until General Keightley's report was produced.[185] Once Keightley's report was complete, Patrick Dean asked his Secretary to take a view on referring the JIC(ME) report to the JIC in London. By then it was August 1957 and the Secretary sceptically concluded 'that an inquest on intelligence in "Musketeer" per se would be profitless, the more so since the episode is now nearly a year old and the official reports to be suppressed'.[186] Dean noted on the minute that he agreed leaving the identified lessons not to be implemented or further distributed.

The one significant lesson which was implemented was the lack of oversight of the IC within government, which had allowed Eden to bypass the FCO and Cabinet to the SIS in pursuit of his own agenda. This loophole was compounded by the lack of guidelines for the covert operations Eden pursued and that the new SIS director, Richard White, had little understanding of the SIS machinery and ways of working. Consequently, this lesson was implemented by moving the JIC into the Cabinet Office and giving the JIC Chair a clearer structure of management. It also restricted MI6's pursuit of extreme operations, which may have led to Young's eventual disillusionment and resignation in 1961. Additionally, Dean took advantage of the opportunity to reorganise the SIS Information Research Department used for covert propaganda. He split the section into two, with one solely focused upon the Middle East.[187]

Musketeer Learning

In planning the intervention it was clear that Eden was influenced by the recent past. His lessons were in the individual sphere, from personal experience of appeasement, observing imperial decline, managing smaller scale interventions and his relationship with Nasser. These lessons overrode any considerations of learning from elsewhere and the secrecy surrounding Musketeer meant that there was little opportunity to gain opposing views. He did, however, try to identify further lessons after the intervention and distributed these to key ministers for implementation.

In the FCO there was no opportunity to learn during planning but little was learned from Suez either. For many, the learning that needed to occur was within No10 and the Cabinet, not within the FCO itself. For other officials, the concern was to look forward rather than back and to avoid the connotations surrounding what was often negatively referred to as a 'post mortem'. For many, they wished the episode to be forgotten; for others there was nothing left to learn. Kirkpatrick, who played a key role during this time, refused to discuss Suez any further after the operation, even in writing his memoirs.[188]

The one exception for the FCO was learning in the institutional sphere through the paper 'British Obligations Overseas' which internally identified lessons echoing many of those identified by Eden in the individual sphere months before. Nevertheless, there is no evidence that these institutional lessons were formally implemented. Although they were distributed, this was limited and the failure to provide clear, institutional lessons allowed subjective and individual lessons to have primacy.[189]

In the MoD, learning occurred during planning through exercises, training and some reflection upon past operations. In addition, in contrast to the FCO, many lessons were formally identified and implemented within the institutional sphere after Suez. A plethora of methods were used, with many lessons reports produced quickly after the operation. In particular, the learning process surrounding the airborne operation worked well; a report was produced, circulated, a conference held and actions attributed to ensure identified lessons were implemented, whilst the Chiefs of Staff also monitored progress on implementing General Keightley's identified lessons. In addition, reports and working groups were set up to examine specific difficulties. As a result of the efficiency of learning, there was less need for outspoken individual learning and lessons were retained for future use. Although the learning was restricted to internal learning and the lessons were identified as part of a routine process of post-operational reflection, the scale of this process was extraordinary.

A number of strategic lessons which were identified were further formalised in the institutional sphere and distributed publicly, through the 1957 Defence White Paper. This paper echoed some of the lessons identified by individuals, including Eden and Keightley, but it is unclear whether it was individual learning which influenced the institutional sphere or simply that the same lessons were identified independently in the different spheres.

There was, however, still scepticism about learning lessons. General Keightley's dispatches warned of drawing broad military conclusions as much of the operation could have turned out very differently had there been either any opposition from the Egyptian Air Force or poor weather. In addition, a number of senior members of the MoD felt that the unique circumstances surrounding Suez meant that the operation was not worth studying for lessons. In response to the School of Land and Air Warfare request for an account of the operation it was stated 'I don't see that the peculiar circumstances of the Musketeer operation afford good cause for altering general doctrine and policy.'[190]

As time passed the pressure to restrict even internal historical learning documentation was increased. Although cross-defence departmental learning was encouraged through 'Lessons from Operation Musketeer' it received a limited circulation and was not tabled at the Executive Committee of the Army Council. Keightley's report was published but only under much duress, editorial persuasion from ministers and the deletion of the second half of the report. Even an internal study by the Combined Staff College caught ministerial attention and resorted in a political battle between the Chiefs of Staff and the Prime Minister. While the internal reports and inquiries became slowly muzzled, the internal and external histories were also silenced; Macmillan's strong reaction against historical learning from Suez was felt across Whitehall and as a result the MoD historians were reluctant to pursue a political hot potato. Further barriers to learning were also revealed, including the lack of time and resources to implement identified lessons.

In contrast, learning within the IC was limited. Although much could have been learned, the mechanisms for learning were not in place and Suez had little impact upon the institution; many of the operations continued, Arab nationalism remained, the relationship with the CIA continued throughout and policy was still focused upon the Cold War divide. This continuity meant that there was little incentive for self-reflection. Moreover, the SIS had a reputation of being stuck in the past and failing to change – something Dick White was keen to alter. The CIA representative Chester Cooper was shocked by the British IC's archaic tendencies. He described his first meeting with the JIC as a room full of tall men wearing identical Savile Row suits and Etonian blue striped ties. Greek verse was handed around along with the latest intelligence documents and the meeting was briefly interrupted for an update of the cricket scores.[191]

For the IC, the main learning from Suez occurred in the institutional sphere, through restructuring, and in the individual sphere by the Chair of JIC(ME). However, this learning was on a much smaller scale than the MoD and the response to the lesson document produced by JIC(ME) in London revealed this method of lesson identification was not part of a routine process. Instead, many of its lessons were ignored. Unlike the MoD, no lesson documentation was formally produced.

The approach to learning from Suez demonstrated some key themes across all three departments of government. In particular, Suez revealed the impact of politics upon learning. Many histories and reports were suppressed due to political difficulties, allowing politics to overtake the importance of drawing lessons for the future. Suez also revealed how history is shaped: officials with their memoirs, nations through propaganda and institutions through the destruction of documentation. During Suez some documents were destroyed at Eden's explicit request but there is plenty of other evidence of destruction throughout the government archive, including Cabinet documents discussing the publication of Anthony Nutting's book and routine destruction of FCO documents.[192] Gore-Booth acknowledged this fact when trying to dissuade the Foreign Secretary from producing an internal history on Suez. He noted that any investigation would prove difficult as little evidence had been retained and that it would quickly be discovered that 'sometime after the nationalisation the records would, so to speak, thin out and that on the crucial events leading up to the hostilities there would be no confidential evidence in the

Foreign Office official archives at all'.[193] Even Lord Mountbatten, who objected so strongly to Musketeer, removed all Royal Navy records containing any evidence of conspiracy.[194] No copy of the Sèvres protocol exists in British archives and Eden specifically ordered members of the Egypt Committee to stop recording in personal diaries. In addition, no minutes from Egypt Committee meetings exist between 17 October and 1 November 1956.

The examination of learning from Suez demonstrates the fine line between the positives to be gained from history and the negatives of looking back. Learning from history can have an impact for a country in terms of precedent, domestic politics and international relations. At some moments after Suez politicians banished historical learning for selfish reasons, at other times there was a feeling that there was an importance for the country to look forward to the future rather than reflect on the past. Consequently, it would soon be demonstrated that the events of Suez offered a number of relevant lessons for other British interventions in the Middle East which needed to be learned.

3   More like Korea – Jordan 1958

> With the loss of our positions on the Canal and the outcome of military intervention at the end of 1956, we were far worse placed from a military point of view. On the other hand the Western world had learnt much in the last two years and we no longer stood alone.
> *(Harold Macmillan, reflecting upon the events of 1958)[1]*

On the morning of 14 July 1958, news arrived in London that the Iraqi monarchy, which had been installed by Britain upon the foundation of Iraq in 1922, had been unexpectedly overthrown in a bloody coup d'état. Members of an Arab nationalist group named the Free Officers – after the Egyptian nationalist officers led by President Nasser – had rounded up and brutally murdered the Royal Family. The insurgents quickly took over Baghdad Radio. Using this platform they announced to the nation that the Iraqi people had been liberated from the corrupt regime which had been installed by powers of 'imperialism'. They also advised that the body of the Crown Prince, Abd al-Ilah, was hanging outside the Defence Ministry for all to see. His mother Queen Nafisa, his sister Princess Abdiya and King Faisal II had also been killed. The new Prime Minister, Defence Minister and Commander-in-Chief was to be Brigadier Abd al-Karim Qasim.

Initially, the events caused chaos in Iraq. The frontiers and airports were immediately closed and rioting and looting broke out. British buildings and expatriates were targeted by mobs as symbols of imperial domination. At a Cabinet Defence Committee meeting at 16:30 it was confirmed that there had been no contact from the British Ambassador in Baghdad, Sir Michael Wright, since 9:00 and reports had advised that the British

Embassy had been overrun and set on fire.[2] The Embassy had been the secretariat of the British High Commissioner, Sir Percy Cox, during the British mandate over Iraq (1920–32) and was fronted by a statue of General Frederick Maude, who had led the British Mesopotamia campaign during the Second World War and captured Baghdad. It therefore provided an icon of humiliation to be attacked; the statue was toppled and the mob ransacked the buildings whilst the staff took refuge in the registry. After some hours all members of staff were released, including the Ambassador. They moved to a Baghdad hotel where they set up a temporary Embassy on the third floor. It is speculated that the staff only survived because Qasim had learned his own lessons from history. In remembering the failed 1941 Iraqi coup, when British forces sent from Jordan crushed Rashid Ali al-Gaylani's rebel government, he quickly restored order, apologised for property destruction, promised to honour all Anglo-Iraqi oil agreements and guaranteed the safety of foreigners.[3]

Since Suez, the dynamics of the Middle East had changed significantly with increased feelings of Arab nationalism and anti-imperialism. In February 1958, Syria and Egypt had merged to become the United Arab Republic (UAR), under the leadership of President Nasser, and received funding and arms from the Soviet Union. To counteract the power merger, less than two weeks later, the British allies of Jordan and Iraq had formed the Arab Union and a propaganda battle between the two unions began.[4] The coup, therefore, had a substantial ripple effect in the region: suspicions were rife that Nasser – as the embodiment of Arab nationalism – and the UAR were behind the actions; a Western ally, the Arab Union, had effectively dissolved; the 1955 Baghdad Pact – the British-led regional defence agreement aimed at preventing Soviet Russian influence in the region – was threatened; and the visible rising tide of Arab nationalism left many Middle Eastern leaders nervous over their own positions.

On the same day as the coup the President of Lebanon, Camille Chamoun, called the UK and US Ambassadors to request the sending of Anglo-American forces to protect his presidency from a similar fate. The Americans agreed to oblige and when it became clear to Prime Minister Harold Macmillan that the US had taken a unilateral decision to land in Lebanon and the American Fleet were approaching Beirut, he joked to President Eisenhower 'You are doing a Suez on me.'[5] Two days later King Hussein of Jordan also formally requested a British and American military intervention for protection against a coup.

Britain's long established relationship with Jordan had recently gone into decline. Britain had been awarded a mandate over Jordan after the First World War. While the country had officially become independent in 1946 Britain had retained influence and connections through advisers, experts and military Commanders. However, in 1955 anti-Baghdad Pact riots began the shift in Anglo-Jordanian relations and pro-Nasser opposition called for the expulsion of the British from the country. In March 1956, under severe pressure, King Hussein dismissed General John Glubb, the British Commander of the Jordanian military and replaced all British officers with Jordanians, causing much resentment in London.[6] When Nasser nationalised the Suez Canal, King Hussein was the first Arab leader to send congratulations on removing the 'shadow of exploitation' from the region.[7] In March 1957, the newly elected Nationalist Socialist Party leader, Sulaiman al-Nabulsi, abrogated the Anglo-Jordanian treaty of 1948. The treaty agreed the presence of British military bases in Jordan with the promise of mutual assistance in war and an annual subsidy to be paid to King Hussein. It was supposed to last twenty years but its abrogation led to the withdrawal of British troops and the removal or disposal of all British stores, equipment, installations and other property in Jordan.[8]

By 1958 the Jordan relationship had declined to a level of resentment towards the British. Anthony Parsons, First Secretary in the Embassy in Amman, explained 'We were not popular ... Some of the more old-fashioned East Bank grandees clung to their British friends, but the younger, educated generation could not forgive us for having created the Palestine problem, [and] for Suez.'[9] Furthermore, the US had replaced the UK as Jordan's most prominent and popular Western ally, asking the Americans for help first before turning to the British.[10] Consequently, when King Hussein did request assistance it offered the opportunity for the British to improve Jordanian relations, reposition Britain's role in the Middle

East, re-establish a good working relationship with the US, demonstrate that Britain had learned lessons from Suez and overcome what the Lebanese Foreign Minister, Charles Habib Malik, described as a 'guilt complex' from the Suez intervention.[11] As a result, Britain agreed to intervene. On 17 July 1958, 16 Independent Parachute Brigade arrived in Jordan to secure the Amman airfield, protect King Hussein and the Jordanian government as well as the lives and property of British and friendly nationals. This military intervention was codenamed Operation Fortitude.[12] Forces remained in the country until 2 November 1958 as a deterrent and a coup did not transpire.

Planning the Intervention

Following Suez there was cross-Whitehall identification of the lesson to work closer with the Americans. The new Prime Minister, Harold Macmillan, and his Foreign Secretary, John Selwyn Lloyd, spent a considerable amount of time implementing this lesson by mending the UK–US relationship.[13] During the Second World War Macmillan had served with Eisenhower in North Africa as his British political advisor and, in January 1957, Macmillan drew on his personal connection with US President Dwight D. Eisenhower in inviting him to work on improving the Anglo-American alliance and publicly demonstrate the UK–US friendship.[14] The result was the Bermuda Conference of March 1957 where mutual plans for the future of the Middle East began to be discussed. By the end of the year a second conference was hosted in Washington and Anglo-American cooperation became institutionalised through several joint working groups to coordinate planning and policy for the region. These included one such group on Lebanon.[15]

In the meantime rumblings within the region throughout 1957 made diplomats nervous about the position of the rulers in Lebanon and Jordan. In October 1957 the FCO asked the Chiefs of Staff to examine the possibility of British military assistance to those countries in the event of outside aggression, insurrection or subversion.[16] Macmillan saw this as the perfect opportunity to further formalise the new US–UK relationship and by November 1957 Macmillan began to focus on securing joint contingency planning for an intervention in Lebanon or Jordan in the event of a coup.[17]

The FCO was significant in these working committees and also endeavoured to implement the lesson of promoting the UK–US relationship, even with animosity towards the Americans from Suez remaining amongst some diplomats.[18] As Macmillan stated on the eve of the Lebanon and Jordan landings, 'We would rather be wrong together than right separately' and the attempts at reconciling the relationship were largely successful.[19] Indeed, by June 1958, when Macmillan visited the US, *The Washington Post* reported 'Mr Macmillan will find the scars of Suez all but healed here.'[20]

At the same time the IC encouraged closer Anglo-American workings too, through the establishment of a Joint Intelligence Liaison Committee based in Washington. This body endeavoured to provide the structure 'to act as a link between the Intelligence authorities in this country and in the USA'[21] and at the time of the coup proved to be invaluable as the US shared news and intelligence on Iraq, including the information on the state of the British Embassy in Baghdad.[22]

However, the MoD found implementing the lesson of working with the Americans the most challenging as UK and US political and military objectives often did not align. During joint contingency planning neither the British military, nor their US counterparts, were prepared to sacrifice national autonomy or command structure to create a truly joint enterprise. On 19 November 1957, the Chiefs of Staff admitted that whilst ministers assumed effective military plans existed, hesitancy on both sides had meant that 'nothing of the sort was taking place'.[23] Instead, Britain developed clear contingency plans for independent interventions. For Jordan this was codenamed Operation Broil and would be executed almost exactly as planned nine months later under the codename Operation Fortitude.[24]

In the end, the failure to plan jointly did not cause any difficulties. When Lebanon requested assistance there was concern amongst the Cabinet that a similar request from Jordan may not be far behind and that they did not have the resources available to act in both states. There were also concerns over the security of Kuwait and a question over whether intervention in Iraq was a possibility. Jordan, Kuwait and Iraq were areas where British interests were described as 'paramount' in comparison to Lebanon and therefore had to take priority. The Cabinet concluded that the Americans should be allowed to take the lead in Lebanon with only 'a small token British contribution'.[25] However, Eisenhower was keen to work independently.[26] Macmillan noted the irony in his memoirs: 'This was indeed a strange reversal of the situation only eighteen months before.' In fact, he declared that American actions were 'a recantation – an act of penitence – unparalleled in history'.[27] A division of labour was subsequently agreed, with the US intervening in Lebanon and British forces sent to Jordan.

The arrival of British troops in the Middle East so soon after Suez was risky and controversial, with UK–Arab relations still damaged and accusations of imperialism echoing around the corridors of Whitehall. Even within the Conservative government there were serious concerns about another embarrassing diplomatic and military situation. Macmillan described the proposed intervention to the Cabinet as a 'quixotic undertaking' and noted in his memoirs 'It was impossible to foresee the end of the operation. It might have grave consequences for the nation and for the Government.'[28]

The FCO was also extremely nervous and had separately identified the lesson that any British intervention in the region would be unpopular and lead to accusations of imperialism, even with US support. As a result, it had already been stated that any assistance would have to be requested by King Hussein and involve a limited operation for troops.[29] Consequently, when news of the Iraqi coup arrived in London, the FCO quickly began implementing this lesson by working with the US State Department to recommend wording for the King of Jordan, should a formal appeal for help become necessary.[30] The appeal had to be written satisfactorily for both public and international opinion. The FCO wrote to the Embassy in Jordan:

> We have also considered the precise form of wording which the King should use if he decides to make a formal appeal for help from the two governments. This question, which is important in terms of public opinion and the United Nations, will be discussed in Washington.[31]

In the meantime, continuing to implement the lesson of working with the Americans, the Prime Minister contacted Eisenhower to urge for a UK–US 'joint intention' for an intervention and dispatched Lloyd to Washington to secure as much support as possible.[32] Whilst Lloyd was en route, on the evening of 16 July 1958, the formal request for a military intervention in Jordan arrived but Macmillan refused to provide any commitment until he had received confirmation of support from the US President. As a result, the first consideration listed on notes taken from a meeting with the Minister of Defence and the Chiefs of Staff, as to whether military assistance should be provided to Jordan, was 'the reply from President Eisenhower'.[33]

Macmillan also called an emergency Cabinet meeting. During the course of the three hour meeting, he twice phoned the US Secretary of State, John Foster Dulles, to gain assurance of US support and to confirm the American position.[34] In the early hours of 17 July, once Macmillan had received assurances from Dulles and had Cabinet agreement, the FCO was advised to inform the King that his request for military assistance had been granted.[35] The telegram sent to the British Embassy in Amman emphasised that this decision had been made in consultation with the Americans.

In addition, Macmillan had identified his own lessons from Suez about managing support for the operation within Parliament. From the outset of the crisis he had decided to keep the opposition informed, taking Labour leader Hugh Gaitskell into his confidence and agreeing with him how to handle the House of Commons. This implementation had worked well and he noted 'The whole atmosphere, tho [sic] charged, was different to Suez' and 'There is none of the rancour of Suez.'[36] The learning implemented in this careful planning appeared to pay off. Once Britain agreed to send troops even Anthony Nutting, one of the most vocal critics of Suez, was quick to support the Prime Minister's decision and declared that Jordan was not another Suez because Britain was acting at the 'specific request [of the] victims of aggression'.[37]

Macmillan had also identified the necessity of keeping the Cabinet informed and committed to the operation. He wrote in his diary 'I was determined not to repeat Anthony's [Eden] mistake and let them say – if this venture were attempted and proved a disaster – that they had not been properly informed.'[38] Consequently, he implemented the lesson by insisting that the Attorney General sat in on all relevant Cabinet meetings and providing the opportunity for each member to ask questions, and express doubts and views, before taking a final vote for intervention.

The MoD had also identified from Suez the importance of politics in any operation, particularly understanding the political context and agreeing the political aims in advance. For the Chiefs of Staff this lesson was easier to implement than working with the Americans and, by example, a combined contingency plan produced by the Washington Working Group in November 1957 was firmly rejected because of the lack of political information and direction included. Writing to the Minister of Defence, Duncan Sandys, the Chiefs of Staff advised:

> The Chiefs of Staff have examined this plan and find it quite unsuitable as a basis for detailed planning since it disregards all political factors ... The Chiefs of Staff have instructed the British team in the working party in Washington not to resume military planning until the political background has been agreed.[39]

Digging their heels in worked and by the start of Fortitude the operational plans had been amended to include limited political objectives: 'secure the airfield, and support the King and Government of Jordan ... confine operations to the Amman area'.[40] Throughout the campaign the Chiefs of Staff also continued to ensure the regular updating of contingency plans with similarly focused objectives and the FCO provided clear directives on actions to be taken should certain events arise.[41]

The MoD was also conscious of avoiding appearing imperial. Aware of local political sensitivities to the arrival of foreign forces Brigadier Tom Pearson – the Commander of British forces in Jordan – sought to secure a plan which minimised British presence. His outline plan specifically stated 'Politically the deployment of British forces to assist the Amman Garrison in performing their task in maintaining law and order in the capital is highly undesirable' instead 'action must be limited to that required to maintain the morale and confidence of the Garrison Commander and his units'.[42] Consequently, should the events get out of hand, assistance was to be strictly limited to the Royal Palace, British Embassy, two surrounding hills and the road communications to these areas and Amman airfield. It was also to involve the minimum use of force to extricate the King, the government, and British and friendly nationals if required.[43] There were even very strict limitations on the use of British force expressed by Pearson as he handed over to his successor, Colonel Chaplain, at the end of the operation. In particular, Britain was not to get involved in any dispute which may emerge between Jordan and Israel or any civil disturbances which did not directly impact British lives or property. It was also emphasised that all ranks pay proper compliments to officers of the Jordanian Arab Army and conform to their wishes.[44]

At the same time as the concern for Jordanian and local politics, no serious discussion was ever held over whether British troops should be sent into Iraq to counteract the coup. The Chiefs of Staff did initiate some precautionary moves for such an operation but further action never materialised.[45] British diplomat and Soviet spy Donald Maclean believed this decision was 'strongly influenced by the disastrous experience of the attack on Egypt eighteen months before' but it was also likely to be because of Qasim's immediate reassurances over oil agreements and Britain's continuing military commitments, and threats, elsewhere.[46] In fact the FCO soon considered Qasim to be more Iraqi nationalist than Nasserite and initially thought that he may even wish to remain in the Baghdad Pact after all.[47] In addition, the IC was caught unawares by the coup and was too rattled to identify means of resistance against the new regime. They also warned against any interference in the country.[48]

For the IC a lot had changed since 1956. On 14 October 1957 the JIC was moved from the MoD into the Cabinet Committee structure and the JIC Secretariat became part of the Cabinet Office – allowing closer government supervision of activities and a shift away from purely military intelligence to also include intelligence in the political, economic and scientific fields.[49] The JIC(ME) was also made obsolete. At the beginning of 1958, local British intelligence organisations were re-evaluated and the British Defence Coordination Committee (Middle East) suggested that the JIC(ME) – whose responsibility included Jordan, Lebanon and Egypt – be replaced by a smaller organisation at a lower level that would receive evaluated evidence, thus providing more of a liaison role.[50] The proposal removed the benefits of a local intelligence headquarters in favour of a more centralised intelligence structure, going against the lessons identified from Suez. Nonetheless, the proposal was agreed.[51]

Consequently, by the time of Fortitude the IC had very few Arabists in the region. Responsibility for the Middle East had been assigned to a European expert, Bruce Lockhart, whilst the new station chief sent to Beirut was Paul Paulson, a former solicitor who only spoke French.[52] In light of these limitations, on 7 July 1958, seven days before the Iraqi coup, a meeting was held with the Prime Minister and it was identified that in the Middle East 'further expenditure would be necessary on political intelligence and counter subversion'.[53] However, this lesson was identified too late to be implemented and the IC – just as they had in Egypt – failed to offer any warning of the Iraqi coup. In fact, in a repeat of the events bringing Nasser to power in Egypt, MI6 had committed the same intelligence error of recruiting agents amongst allies rather than within anti-British and pro-nationalist groups. As a result, the SIS station chief in Baghdad, Alexis Fforter, had no idea of the political views of those who had led the violent attack against the Iraqi monarchy.[54]

Intelligence from within Jordan had also reduced. In the 1950s Britain had developed the Jordanian security forces, including the training of Jordanian military intelligence personnel, and the Arab Legion had a British Director General of Intelligence, Colonel Sir Patrick Coghill. Although Coghill had been dismissed by King Hussein, with General John Glubb, the British initially retained close personal contacts within Jordanian intelligence circles, leading to some informal sharing of information.[55] However, the events of Suez disrupted many of the intimate relationships upon which the SIS had come to rely for information. Although Paulson had tried to improve the collection of intelligence on Jordan through the recruitment of informants, including one operation under the codename Operation Jester, these attempts largely failed.[56]

Nonetheless, the IC had kept an eye on Arab nationalism and provided an assessment on its impact at the beginning of 1958. The problem was that this assessment focused strictly on the threat to the Gulf Peninsular of nationalist and radical movements, therefore neglecting to examine either Iraq or Jordan.[57] This issue had also been raised as an important agenda item for the Heads of Middle Eastern Mission Conference which was due to be held in London in early August 1958.[58] In addition, in support of the ongoing military contingency planning, the IC had considered the likely Soviet reactions to any UK military action in Lebanon, but not in Jordan.[59]

When the coup emerged, the IC made a short intelligence assessment on the situation in Iraq and Jordan by 15:00. The lack of British sources meant that it relied on American sources, press reports, Cairo and Baghdad radios and reports from RAF Habbaniya – over sixty miles away from Baghdad.[60] The IC also could not confirm or deny whether the coup had spread to Jordan and advised that it was awaiting information from the British Embassy in Amman. Nonetheless, on 16 July 1958, British intelligence were able to provide King Hussein with an assessment that a coup would take place against him the following day, orchestrated by President Nasser.[61] This assessment was based upon the monitoring of UAR subversive activities and it was this intelligence briefing which convinced the King to make a formal request for military assistance.[62] Suspicion over IC asset availability and capability at this time has since led to some suggestions that the IC manufactured the assessment as part of a conspiracy to allow British troops to return to the region.[63] However, US Secretary of State, John Foster Dulles, had also seen intelligence reports of an impending coup and took the threat equally seriously. He spoke to the Director of Central Intelligence, Allen Dulles, about the situation who advised that the US had also sent a warning to the King.[64]

During the Intervention

Despite the FCO and Prime Minister learning from history in the planning of the operation, Fortitude was almost immediately placed in jeopardy because of an identified but forgotten lesson. In April 1958, the FCO had identified that the UAR and Israel presented an air barrier for the military to move between Europe and the Arab states, especially from the bases in Nicosia in Cyprus. It concluded 'The value of these overflying rights, the measures necessary to secure them and the prospects of their being denied to us ... are at present worth active study.'[65] In the confusion of the Foreign Secretary being sent to Washington, the lesson was implemented by requesting authorisation to overfly Israel but not until the last minute and the Israeli Prime Minister, David Ben-Gurion, initially refused the request. This was especially concerning given that illegal overflying of Syria during Musketeer had led to the shooting down of a RAF plane. It soon became clear that the Israelis had also identified the lesson from Suez of securing US support and Ben-Gurion would not give his consent until he received assurances from Washington that aid would be provided to him in the event of any retaliatory action from Arab countries. Similar to Macmillan, Ben-Gurion only conceded approval after having awoken Dulles at 2:30 in the morning to receive personal assurances.[66]

Consequently, whilst some aircraft, under the orders of Brigadier Pearson, continued to Amman with a parachute brigade to secure the airfield, others were forced to turn around. In fact, by the time the recall was received one Beverley had already landed. Four Hastings were successfully recalled but one Hastings and four further Beverleys continued on to reach their destination without overflying permission.[67] Once landed, Pearson and his men were required to wait for the rest of 16 Independent Parachute Brigade at the airfield – exposed and without any support – until the situation was rectified. The British Ambassador to Jordan, Charles Johnston, recorded in his memoirs that he was in a meeting with the Commander-in-Chief of the RAF at the time of the sending of the first wave of British paratroopers to Amman. During the meeting the Commander-in-Chief was called away and returned white faced to announce that the operation had been cancelled by London. Johnston recalled 'We looked at each other and I sensed that everyone in the room had the same thought: was this another Suez; had the British government taken fright in the middle of the operation?'[68] Similarly in Whitehall Macmillan had to announce to the Cabinet that the entire operation was in danger as only 400 men had landed.[69]

Even once initial permission was granted, the use of the Israeli route proved problematic throughout Fortitude. The British were reliant upon the provision of supplies by air but Ben Gurion quickly came under heavy domestic and Soviet pressure to renege on any overflying agreements.[70] The British, therefore, came to rely upon the Americans to manage the situation with Israel throughout the campaign and eventually Eisenhower agreed to US Globemasters taking over all of Britain's airlift requirements. Lessons from these events were quickly identified and implemented when the contingency plan was made by the FCO to request overflying Israel in the event of emergency caused by a coup in Jordan.[71] In addition, Israel and Lebanon were approached over two weeks ahead of planned withdrawal to secure overflying rights.[72] Ironically, in the end, the UAR allowed the evacuation to take place over Syrian airspace.[73]

The FCO also continued to implement the lesson of working with the Americans throughout the campaign, despite some strong disagreements. From the outset Washington was sceptical about the benefits of an intervention in Jordan and believed that the monarchy would collapse upon withdrawal of troops.[74] On the ground in Amman, Ambassador Johnston strongly disagreed with a number of American assessments, including that King Hussein was only supported by 10 per cent of the population. Johnston wrote to the FCO 'I distrust these facile statistics which rest on no scientific evidence whatever.'[75] When the Americans began evacuating women and children he accused them of being 'well-known panickers' and in his annual dispatch he also concluded 'The line taken by the United States Embassy here during the crisis was often fainthearted, or wrong-headed, or both.'[76] Nonetheless, it also revealed that he had managed to work with the Americans in Amman, whilst in Washington an informal working committee was soon established within the British Embassy to coordinate issues specifically related to Jordan. This committee met once a day and was described by Dulles as performing 'an excellent job'.[77]

Meanwhile, Macmillan worked hard throughout Fortitude to liaise with Washington and to secure support, for practical and political reasons. As well as persuading Eisenhower to take over the airlift of supplies and funding for the initial supplies of oil to reach Aqaba, there was close cooperation throughout the campaign with UK–US local operational liaison for forces and planning liaison in London.[78] Although Macmillan never succeeded in his ultimate ambition of a truly joint operation he was determined not to repeat the secrecy and lack of understanding between the two nations that had occurred during Suez.[79] He was also keen to continually reiterate to the President that they were 'in it together'. On 18 July 1958, the Prime Minister wrote to Eisenhower 'My great consolation is that we are together in these two operations in Lebanon and Jordan. We must at all costs not be divided now when we have been forced to play for such high stakes.' He ended by stressing 'our close and intimate cooperation together'.[80] Eisenhower would later describe his relationship with Macmillan at this time as being in 'finger-tip communication' and at the end of the campaign the President wrote to the Prime Minister 'We can take special satisfaction in the complete understanding and special cooperation which was evident between our two governments.'[81] In fact the events were so successful for reinstating the relationship that by December 1958 the Foreign Secretary began working towards achieving a joint Anglo-American policy on Iraq and its new regime.[82]

Throughout this time the FCO also recognised that securing UN support for the operation was required to implement a number of other lessons identified from the past: evade accusations of imperialism, save British resources, keep the public happy through a quick withdrawal, and avoid the abrupt and embarrassing withdrawal scenes reminiscent of the Suez crisis.[83] Therefore, from the outset of contingency planning for Jordan, the FCO had considered ways to make British actions 'look more like another Korea and less like another Suez'.[84] There was also concern throughout the operation that, unlike during Suez, the UN was to be 'handled'.[85] The FCO began to implement this lesson by negotiating with the UN Secretary General, Dag Hammarskjöld, for the replacement of British troops with a UN force shortly after the operation commenced and eventually a resolution was passed which paved the way for British withdrawal.[86]

Macmillan also leveraged his relationship with Washington for diplomatic support in handling the UN and Russian responses to the intervention, and all policy decisions came after full consultation with Washington.[87] In a revealing telegram from London to the UN delegation in New York, the FCO advised:

> In continuing your discussions with the Secretary General I hope you will take care to emphasise their informal, exploratory basis. Our present views are still tentative and until we have discussed them with the Americans we do not want to give Mr Hammarskjold [sic] the impression that they represent firm policy decisions.[88]

In fact the one nation who was angered during this time was France. General de Gaulle complained that he had not been consulted and pointed out the impact that the actions would have on French interests in the region if the operations in Lebanon and Jordan went wrong.[89] Perhaps influenced by the tri-nation Suez plot, de Gaulle quickly became deeply suspicious of the Anglo-American action and it was reported by the French Foreign Minister that he was convinced that he had been deceived by the Prime Minister and Mr Dulles when they had previously visited Paris. It was advised 'the General now has no doubt that there had been, what he called, an Anglo-American Turkish plot of long standing' for the occupation of Lebanon and Jordan.[90] The FCO, therefore, had to work hard to repair the damage.[91]

The FCO had also identified the dangers of declining press and public opinion at home and abroad and was conscious to try to avoid any direct comparisons between Fortitude and Musketeer where possible. Immediately after the coup *The Herald* had declared that it did not want Britain intervening in the region through the bold headline 'Keep Out!' and asking 'Has nothing been learned from Suez?'[92] The *Daily Mirror* reported 'The Mindless Muscle Men, who learned nothing from Suez, are all for trying it once more' and the next day, under the headline 'Blind Blind Blind' declared 'Suez will go down in history as a blunder. The British landings in Jordan are charged with even greater perils.'[93] Nonetheless, overall the British public were inclined to support the government, with a Gallup poll in the *News Chronicle* revealing two to one in favour of intervention.[94] Macmillan and the FCO wanted to keep it that way and the Prime Minister immediately sanctioned the creation of an FCO news executive which paid close attention to monitoring public opinion domestically and internationally, particularly in the US, and worked to maintain support by managing the reporting of actions in Jordan.[95] This included avoiding the publication of undesirable news stories which could influence public perception. In one case Johnston had to persuade King Hussein against the public execution of opposition collaborators, advising that such actions would be received badly in Britain and diminish confidence towards the operation. In understanding the need to cultivate public support Hussein agreed to commute the death sentences.[96]

The MoD had also identified the importance of media management and maintaining public support from the 1956 intervention. Lessons reports from Suez featured PR and world opinion as high amongst the lessons identified across the three services and, as a result, the MoD ensured that an Embassy Press Officer and PR Officer were assigned to the British Forces on the ground – although the Air Ministry could not detach a PR Officer for several days forcing them to rely on Army PR to look after its publicity 'which somewhat naturally suffered'.[97] The MoD also took the decision not to impose a 'D-Notice' – an official request to the media not to publish or broadcast specific stories for reasons of national security – upon journalists in the field.[98] In addition, the MoD worked with the Central Office of Information to put together a documentary on the operation and provided illustrated profiles of service personnel to the press to secure more personal stories. There was even some competition amongst the services to secure the most positive publicity, with reporters and cameramen being treated to ground and flying sequences to provide interesting footage.[99] However, some members of the press were still unhappy and complaints were made that much information remained withheld. Even worse, information was often only censored locally, with Whitehall providing more details of the operation to journalists in London than those in theatre, leading correspondents to send a telegram in protest to the War Office.[100]

Another lesson which the FCO identified and implemented during the operation was the need to protect the British economy. The FCO had already recognised Britain's diminishing means to achieve its ambitions but just before the intervention, on 7 July 1958, a Cabinet meeting – which included Selwyn Lloyd and his Permanent Under-Secretary, Sir Frederick Hoyer Millar – considered a report entitled 'The Position of the United Kingdom in World Affairs'.[101] As part of this meeting the Chancellor of the Exchequer emphasised the steady increase in the size of financial commitments to aid allied and dependent states – of which Jordan was one – and the requirement to reduce government expenditure overall. A British subsidy of approximately £1 million a month was being used to fund the Jordanian Army and the intervention, therefore, provided the opportunity to redress this balance.[102]

At the outset of the operation the minister in the Washington Embassy, Lord Hood, was asked to stress the British economic position to President Eisenhower, including that there was already great pressure on the pound which meant a lot of money being spent to maintain its value.[103] By 25 August 1958 Macmillan and Lloyd had decided to persuade the Americans to pay for Jordan on an ongoing basis, to be negotiated by the FCO.[104] This was successfully implemented and by the time of withdrawal the Americans had taken over the funding of the Jordanian Royal Family and Army – totalling around $40.5 million per year – and earmarking $10 million for Jordanian development.[105] Despite the British inability to pay this large sum, Macmillan noted 'It will be cheap if it helps get our troops out' whilst Johnston remarked 'it is only a fraction of what the United States spends each year on Korea'.[106]

Furthermore, in an awareness of the financial pressures that were placed on the government to withdraw from Suez, Macmillan was keen to ensure that economic issues, as a result of Jordan, were minimalised. In a personal minute to the MoD Macmillan suggested cost savings to offset the expenditure of Fortitude: 'Inevitably the military operations that we have had to undertake in the Middle East must have led to increased expenditure . . . Perhaps we should temporarily restrict training especially in flying, and other manoeuvres which cost money.'[107] These concerns were set against the backdrop of trying to manage the defence budget more broadly, and debates about investment into Britain's nuclear weapons programme.[108]

In the MoD, the Jordan campaign was very different to Suez. As soon as the coup occurred immediate moves were made by the Chiefs of Staff to prepare for an operation but in the end only two parachute battalions, a parachute brigade headquarters and an RAF signals detachment, totalling around 1,500 men, were sent from Cyprus.[109] Decisions on force size had to be made in the context of ongoing attacks in the region which required British troops, including in Oman and Yemen as well as a possible attack on Kuwait by Iraq and the defence of other UK interests in the Persian Gulf.[110] The operation was later supported by reinforcements, one battalion of Cameronians, which landed on 6 August 1958.[111] It did, however, immediately test lessons from Suez. During Musketeer there had been severe difficulty and delay in putting together an expeditionary force, which was only mobilised as a result of retaining National Servicemen beyond their usual time period. Although this was successful the cancellation of leave caused much resentment and a degeneration of discipline amongst the servicemen.[112] As a consequence, plans were developed for an expeditionary force which would mount 'limited operations in overseas emergencies' and avoid such situations.[113] This was formalised in the 1957 Defence White Paper and soon after its publication contingency planning for Jordan began in earnest. Consequently Jordan became a testing ground for the long-term changes that were being commissioned.

In some senses the lessons were implemented. The restructuring of forces proved beneficial but revealed that further lessons needed to be learned. Whilst Duncan Sandys had envisaged that the Strategic Reserve would ensure British troops arrived quickly into trouble-spots, Jordan demonstrated the restricted capabilities that remained in air power, specifically limited flying routes and take-off bases. No British transport aircraft could fly direct from Britain to the Middle East without passing through the air space of other countries or refuelling, and Israel's difficulties in this area revealed the precariousness of the situation. At one point the Chiefs of Staff were even forced to consider attacking Israeli airfields or jamming their radar in order to provide safe passage for the airlift.[114] In fact airlift difficulties remained throughout Fortitude and a proposal was put forward by the Joint Planning Staff to the Chiefs of Staff for a new system of Joint Planning Instructions and Joint Operations Instructions with the specific aim of improving the system of planning the air movement of troops, following the difficulties of entering and withdrawing from Jordan.[115] Suggestions included the re-examination of air routes as well as, crucially, that responsibility for ensuring clearance for overflying other countries would be given to the Air Ministry for future operations.

Despite the difficulties during planning, the MoD did continue to try to implement the lesson of working with the Americans throughout the operation. Prior to sending troops, Britain and the US had set up operational liaison of forces locally and planning liaison in London, with this relationship continuing throughout the Jordan campaign.[116] As the operation progressed UK–US military liaison became increasingly important as the Americans took over the airlift responsibilities and the Chiefs of Staff continued to consider ways to engage the Americans further. Ideas included the provision of civilian technicians to maintain US aircraft flying into Amman and ancillary forces to open up communications.[117] Two weeks later, further suggestions were made at the Cabinet Defence Committee meeting including, perhaps controversially, asking the US to charter merchant vessels to fly the American flag and bring supplies to the British down the Suez Canal. Requests were made for everything from the transport of drummed aviation fuel to maintenance of an airstrip and refrigerated containers.[118] As the operation came to an end there was a need to coordinate simultaneous withdrawal of US troops in Lebanon and British troops in Jordan, to ensure that Britain was not left exposed in the region.[119] This was successfully achieved and it was hoped that the relationship which developed between the two militaries during the operation would aid more successful UK–US joint military planning for the region in the future.[120] In fact the Anglo-American joint Planning Group soon produced a paper for the Chiefs of Staff on the coordination of plans for the Persian Gulf.[121]

Overall, the operation went very smoothly for the MoD. The only disturbances occurred on 29 July 1958 when a bomb exploded in the British Council library in Amman, without any injuries, and on 2 August when another bomb exploded at the Jordanian Development Board in Amman.[122] There was one accidental fatal shooting of a Jordanian civilian by a British soldier but both sides agreed to maintain silence over the incident.[123] However, much of Fortitude's success was due to good fortune. From the outset the Minister of Defence and Chiefs of Staff had warned that 'The force would be very vulnerable if the Jordanian Army became hostile – particularly in the face of an attack by Jordanian Armoured units' and 'there is little direct military advantage and a certain amount of risk'.[124] As the days went by, the MoD remained aware of the vulnerability of British forces and stressed 'should any portion of the Army in or near to Amman, however, actually march on Amman and attack the Government or the British forces in the area, the latter would be placed in a very perilous military position'.[125] In fact British troops had only been sent to support the regime and it had never been the intention to send land forces on the scale required to fight the Jordanian Army if an internal coup occurred.[126] Consequently, contingency plans were made in case the position of British forces was threatened but in the end troops were not engaged by opposition.[127] Nor was there any real threat to counter, including skirmishes between the Jordanians and Israelis, or the need to evacuate the King. In addition, the constant threat of supplies being halted by the closure of the Suez Canal did not become a reality. As a result, the dangers of intervening without a full strength force was not identified as a lesson and single brigade groups would go on to be sent to Kuwait and Rhodesia.[128]

Even withdrawal was relatively straightforward, despite concerns. Plans began in mid-September 1958 but the Chiefs of Staff were worried that forces may be required to return at short notice and so contingency plans were made for various eventualities.[129] In the end withdrawal began on 20 October and was completed by 2 November 1958 without event. The troops returned to Britain alongside two horses as gifts for Queen Elizabeth from King Hussein.[130] The King wrote 'The British force was small, but its very presence had given us a chance to breathe. The famous red berets in the streets made people realise we were not alone, that this was no time to despair.'[131] Ambassador Johnston stated '[the intervention] was extremely well conducted both by London and by the Commanders-in-Chief in Cyprus. It was a model politico-military operation and achieved everything that it set out to do.'[132]

For the IC no further lessons were identified or implemented. With the main objective focused upon looking to the future and providing predictive assessments, there was little reflection on the past. Instead, assessments were made on the outlook for Jordan, Soviet reaction to British actions in the Middle East and how Jordan would affect President Nasser's ambitions and objectives for the Middle Eastern region. Reports also examined the ongoing subversive activity of the UAR in Jordan but none of the reports assessed the past actions of the IC itself.[133]

The lack of attempt to identify lessons was surprising considering the number of intelligence limitations and failures that occurred during the intervention. In particular, intelligence sources predicted a Jordanian coup on 12–13 August 1958 – causing all of the flying squadrons in Cyprus to be brought to a state of readiness – but, similar to the predicted coup of 17 July, it did not materialise.[134] However, there is no record within the JIC files of attempts to learn from either the inaccurate predictions or the conduct of intelligence gathering and assessment.

After the Intervention

Despite the success of the intervention, the FCO made little reflection upon lessons from Fortitude. No internal inquiries took place, nor were there parliamentary calls for an external inquiry or any official or internal histories written. Instead, the only identified lessons came from Ambassador Charles Johnston in his annual review despatch. Primarily, Johnston identified that the decision to support allies in their time of need was correct and beneficial. He claimed:

> We have showed both types of Arab extremists that we (the West in general and the British in particular) are people to be reckoned with . . . We have not only gained time for the Nasser-Qassim split to develop, but have made sure that we are still in the game, with a political foothold.[135]

For him, the intervention revealed two key lessons: firstly, 'it proved that Anglo-American cooperation in the Arab world is possible, not only on the inter-governmental level, but in the field', and secondly, 'Britain still can and should play in the Arab world.' Johnston mused that the British were still the best placed Westerners to act in the Middle East and concluded that '[we] should not be inhibited by unnecessary feelings of guilt or mistaken complexes of inferiority'. Thinking about relying on the Americans in the future he advised 'we shall, I fear, find the Americans alone unequal to the task. (Their performance in Jordan this year shows how badly they need interjections of good sense and resolution from us in times of crisis).'[136]

The despatch – and consequently its identified lessons – was distributed to only four officials before submission to the Foreign Secretary. Whilst one official simply signed in acknowledgment, a further commented 'a beautiful despatch'. The other two were quick to dismiss the identified lessons because they felt much of the content was self-congratulatory and overestimated the importance of the operation and Jordan's continued survival.[137] There is no record of the Foreign Secretary's response.

Nevertheless, changes in the region, coupled with a major review in the US of its Middle East policy, led the Cabinet's Official Committee on the Middle East to reconsider Britain's policy towards the region and the FCO began to produce the paper 'Points for a Middle East Policy' in October 1958, whilst British troops were still stationed in Amman, but concluded after withdrawal.[138] The paper was written in two parts: part one dealt with UK aims in the region in a stable setting and in the long-term; part two examined UK aims in the region in the face of unrest and in the short term. Each identified a number of lessons for the future which mirrored the recent Jordan experience and some of the lessons identified by Ambassador Johnston. In particular, both parts acknowledged the stabilising factor and deterrent to President Nasser of the presence of British troops.[139] The paper also suggested that although the operation could not be repeated in Jordan again with the same level of success, British troops could be used to advantage, with the consent of the government concerned, to prevent or forestall crises or coups elsewhere in the region in the future.[140] The paper also reiterated the lesson that any future interventions would have to occur with American support: 'It seems clear that the UK cannot now successfully use force in the Middle East without at least moral support from the US.'[141] The Prime Minister's Private Secretary for Foreign Affairs, Philip de Zulueta, had reached the same conclusion two months before. He wrote to Macmillan identifying 'I doubt whether action without the United States now has a chance of success.'[142]

The paper went on to emphasise the importance of working with the UN, especially to aid in British disengagement from the region.[143] The management of public opinion for any future interventions was also stressed and the paper prophetically considered that whilst the public may rally behind interventions, providing it was in defence of a British interest, 'it is not certain that it would remain steadfast over a long period of occupation'.[144]

Some individuals did question the role and ability of the FCO during the operation but failed to interpret these into lessons which could be implemented. Ivor Lucas, who worked in the Eastern Department of the FCO, thought that during 1958:

> expertise was on occasions rather sadly lacking ... The Iraq Hashemite monarch was overthrown and assassinated; there was trouble with Jordan and the Lebanon ... and all these crises seemed to have occurred without the Foreign Office or the embassies on the ground foreseeing them at all.[145]

There were similar concerns externally. Three years later Lord Plowden's report on the use of manpower in the Foreign Service noted that the FCO suffered recruitment difficulties between 1956 and 1958 because there was a view that the FCO had not improved since Suez. It reported that there was 'dissatisfaction in some quarters with British Foreign Policy' and a feeling that there was 'diminished importance of work within the Foreign Service'.[146]

The MoD also failed to thoroughly consider lessons from the events and the records are not filled with the same plethora of internal inquiries and identified lessons which were present after Suez. Instead, the majority of post-operational reports were presented on specific issues, such as from the technical officer on pilot training requirements, some of which led to further investigation.[147] In fact, there is only evidence of one significant attempt to learn lessons from Fortitude: the Commander of 16 Independent Parachute Brigade Group held a debriefing conference at General Headquarters Middle East Land Forces (GHQ MELF) 'to hear from Brigadier Pearson the outstanding lessons of Op "Fortitude" from his point of view'. The conference was attended by members of the brigade and GHQ MELF, and it was intended to examine and record 'the major lessons of this op, against the time when we have to undertake a similar one in the future'. The lessons identified included the requirement of a Staff Officer from the Transport Task Force to be made available during planning phases. It also re-identified a lesson from Suez: the need for interpreters, stating 'the need for interpreters for the initial contacts between troops and civilians. Shooting could result from a failure to understand each other.'[148] However, the conference record is very short and does not state that actions for implementation were attributed. In addition, identified lessons were not widely distributed. Beyond the attendees of the conference, who were involved in the operation, the record was only distributed to four others, including the assistant to the Commander-in-Chief and Staff Officer for the Chief of Staff.

Nonetheless, it is difficult to know for certain whether all documentation on the operation is available for analysis. Despite the 1958 Public Records Act gaining royal assent during the Jordan intervention, a 1977 study of the MoD Departmental Record System revealed a high level of destruction of documents at an early stage.[149] Even Service Historians 'concerned in trying to discover the reasons for past policy or organizational decisions' had difficulties in tracing archival material.[150] In part this was due to the decentralised nature of the MoD, with many documents destroyed locally. The report also suggested that narrative accounts of operations were not regularly produced, nor were new recruits trained in lessons learned despite recognition that this would be 'useful'. In addition, the few studies which were produced were not widely circulated or well publicised.[151]

An official history of Jordan was not considered until 1973. At that time the Working Party on Joint Service In-House Histories described the Jordan intervention as a 'minor operation', arguing that a history of Fortitude did not warrant a monograph, only a narrative, and so did not merit a full Joint Service History. However, it was concluded that the history of the Jordan intervention was to be researched and written as part of a wider study, examining the history of post-war deployment and intervention operations, written as an account without any analysis of lessons.[152] Therefore, whilst other commissioned histories addressed difficulties and developments of operations within their terms of reference, the Jordan in-house history was written primarily utilising chronological, factual information from the war diary without any analysis.[153] It was not until 1989, when the Air Historical Branch published *Wings in the Sun*, featuring a small section on Jordan, that a few additional lessons were identified and retained by this method, including the identification of poor accommodation and the subsequent attempts at implementation: converting marquees into covered messes, taking rooms at Amman's Philadelphia Hotel and persuading the Jordanian government to allow the British to use some of the old RAF Amman buildings.[154]

Learning from the intervention in the IC was also limited. There is no record that internal reflections upon the improvement of intelligence for the future were made either institutionally or individually and, with the removal of JIC(ME), no lessons reports were produced. Externally, some lessons were identified in the individual sphere. Philip De Zulueta wrote to the Prime Minister to complain that 'the MI6 activities in the area ought to be looked at very carefully in any case. We have lamentably failed to get information of any of the recent major events.'[155] Nonetheless, very little was done to counteract this problem. Instead, the broader focus remained on Arab nationalism, Nasser and the influence of the Soviet Union in the region. A review of intelligence targets in November 1958 focused almost entirely on the Soviet Union and Sino-Soviet bloc, with countries in the Middle East barely receiving a mention.[156]

Instead, the only attempt to identify lessons was focused not upon the conducting of intelligence gathering and assessment but the impact that the operation had in securing Jordan and on tensions elsewhere in the region. These suggested that Fortitude had very little long-term benefit: 'the situation remains fundamentally unstable, with only a fine balance between loyalist elements and those with pro-UAR leanings'.[157] However, the assessments also identified that as a by-product the operation had created unrest elsewhere in the region. The JIC noted the impact of British actions upon a possible coup in Lebanon and the threat to Aden and the Aden Protectorate if the operation failed.[158] In addition, in Kuwait, Bahrain and Qatar a relationship with the British was beginning to be viewed as a liability.[159] The Ruler of Kuwait had become particularly nervous, believing a connection with the British to be 'outmoded' and that any further success by Nasser, or an additional Western intervention, would spark riotous demonstrations within his own country. A JIC assessment stated 'The Anglo-American interventions in Jordan and Lebanon have not reassured him – rather the contrary – since he does not believe his regime can in the long run be bolstered.' In addition, the Ruler considered that 'the introduction of British troops, even with the Ruler's consent, would stimulate unrest and might provoke strikes and sabotage in the oil fields'.[160] This would be proven to be an incorrect conclusion by the end of 1961.

Macmillan's son-in-law, the MP and SIS agent Julian Amery, did write one paper which identified the need to strengthen Britain's subversive and propaganda activities in the Middle East in order to help counteract the rising tide of Arab nationalism.[161] Anthony Parsons, in the Amman Embassy, agreed:

> During my short stay in Jordan I had experienced the palpable influence which Nasser's activities exercised over the political climate . . . Everyone read the Cairo newspaper (except when they were banned) as their main source of information and political guidance, just as they listened to Cairo Radio . . . Cairo was the centre of the Jordanian universe and, love him or hate him, Nasser was the man who made Cairo's heartbeat audible.[162]

By December 1958 the JIC had written a full report on 'The activities and influence of Cairo Radio', as they had in 1956, but again the nature of the document was to report, not to identify any lessons for the future.[163] Even with the 1958 Iraqi coup and Lebanese crisis changing the dynamics of intelligence sharing within the region, continuity of security communications continued through the Liaison Committee of the Baghdad Pact, which was later renamed the Central Treaty Organisation (CENTO). Biannual meetings between Britain, America, Turkey, Pakistan and Iran continued to offer a forum to share intelligence, particularly on communist activities, until CENTO's dissolution in 1979.

Outside the formal methods of learning, the success of the intervention did allow the British to reinstate some intelligence networks within the country. In particular, in October 1958, Duncan MacIntosh, the former British security advisor to Baghdad who had escaped the recent coup, was appointed advisor to Jordan. He identified the need to reorganise the Jordanian police and laid the foundations for the General Intelligence Department which remains today, with the responsibility to 'safeguard the security of the Hashemite Kingdom of Jordan domestically and abroad by means of carrying out necessary intelligence operations'.[164]

Fortitude Learning

The UK intervention in Jordan in 1958 was an intervention that occurred in the shadow of Suez and presented the opportunity to demonstrate that lessons had been learned from that experience. Although little was formally learned from Suez in the institutional sphere of the FCO it is clear that thoughts of Musketeer influenced its, and the Prime Minister's, actions during the Jordan operation. In fact, the learning which had the greatest impact in the planning of Fortitude came from the driving forces of learning in the individual sphere from Harold Macmillan and, to some extent, Selwyn Lloyd. Although similarly identifying the lessons of working with the Americans and managing British decline and economics, the Prime Minister and the Foreign Secretary moved the learning process forward to the implementation of these lessons at a strategic and operational level, through the establishment of working committees and joint contingency planning. Following their lead the FCO also implemented these lessons which were, therefore, learned.

Whilst most of the lessons from Suez were negative in nature – what not to do – there were many positive lessons to be learned from Jordan. However, equally to Suez, very little lesson identification took place in the FCO, revealing that learning from history was not dependent upon the outcome of an intervention. There was no attempt to identify lessons through specific inquiries or full histories and, unlike Suez, the idea was not even debated. Instead, there is only evidence of two attempts to learn from the operation itself: one in the individual and one in the institutional sphere.

In the individual sphere, Ambassador Johnston identified positive, strategic lessons through the formal and routine method of the annual review despatch. However, the despatch was only distributed to five officials, two of whom dismissed its content. Consequently, despite some lesson identification, there is no evidence that the identified lessons were implemented or retained for learning purposes. In the institutional sphere, 'Points for a Middle East policy' identified lessons through an extraordinary method, formalising and retaining them for the future. This included the identified lesson that British troops could be successfully used again in a similar situation; a lesson which would become significant three years later.

Overall, learning in the FCO was primarily within the individual sphere. Little consideration was recorded of tactical or operational lessons and more lessons were drawn from the negative experience of Suez than identified from the positive experience of the Jordan operation. The incident with Israel also revealed a barrier for learning: whilst Britain had identified the need to secure overflying rights, Israel had learned to secure US support before granting such permission. This demonstrated the potential of other learners to inhibit implementing the lessons of history.

In the MoD, during the planning phase of the operation, a number of lessons from Suez were implemented but were successful to different extents. In particular, the Chiefs of Staff insisted upon establishing the political aims and direction of an operation before they would consider contingency planning and the newly restructured force was tested for the first time. Other identified lessons were not successfully implemented during the operation. These included the management of the media and ongoing working relations with the US military. The experience reiterated the new barrier to learning: opposing external actors. For the media specifically, the methods of personnel provision, access to increased information and the lack of imposed restrictions did not go far enough, especially as the MoD did not manage a consistent policy in both London and Jordan. For the US, working together was successful in terms of coordinated, if not integrated, action but it did not last long term, with the working group collapsing shortly after Fortitude. However, although the MoD struggled to connect with their US counterparts in a meaningful way, the experience of working with American support in Jordan would set a precedent for all future British interventions in the region.

In addition, although the MoD had the methods available for retention, through in-house histories, these were not maximised. The Jordan operation was dismissed as 'minor' despite its strategic and political importance.[165] Lesson identification after the intervention was also limited, perhaps reflecting – in comparison to Suez – the size of the operation. This lesson identification remained internal and any strategic and operational lessons were not widely distributed.

During planning the only evident implementation of lessons for the IC was working with the Americans but, unlike in the FCO and MoD, this cannot be formally traced to an identified lesson. During the operation itself lesson identification was restricted to the institutional assessment of other actors, not an internal reflection upon the conducting of the intelligence operation or learning in the individual sphere. Once the operation was complete, some learning occurred externally in the individual sphere by Philip de Zulueta, Ivor Lucas and Julian Amery. However, although the identification of lessons by Amery led to a further JIC report, it was written in the same way as previous reports and assessments, without any reflection upon lessons. Overall, whilst the IC learned little from Suez, even less was learned from Jordan. The lessons which were identified were negative and strategic. Consequently, the biggest barrier to learning was revealed: the lack of a learning culture.

Consequently, learning was primarily in the individual sphere in the FCO, the institutional sphere in the MoD and significantly limited in the IC. This is likely to have been heavily influenced by the structure of these organisations as well as their general culture and specific approach to learning. For the FCO there was a clear driver of learning, the Prime Minister and Foreign Secretary, in the MoD the driver was the institutional post-operational process of reporting, whilst in the IC a driver was lacking post-Suez.

Learning across all three government bodies was primarily at the identification and implementation stages, from internal sources and methods. There was little evidence of wide distribution or retention. In fact, no external inquiries took place and no histories were written with any form of analysis. Those lessons from Suez which were both identified and implemented – such as the FCO working with the Americans, the MoD creating a new force and the IC restructuring – can be claimed to have been learned. However, despite Fortitude lasting twelve times as long as Musketeer, more appeared to be learned from the latter than the former.

One element that was noticeably absent throughout Jordan was the use of historical analogy. Macmillan did continue to use analogies in regards to Nasser during this time, with frequent references to his actions 'as a sort of Mussolini'.[166] However, in comparison to the debates over Suez, this form of the use of history was almost non-existent. The only prominent analogy was the result of the lesson of working with the Americans and the UN to make Jordan look 'more like Korea'.

4   Suez in Reverse – Kuwait 1961

> History this weekend is staging a brief flashback of the far-off days of Pax Britannia. It is nothing to be ashamed of. It is not, of course, another Suez . . . Rather it is Jordan and the Lebanon again, without the Americans.
> *(Author unknown, Sunday Telegraph, 2 July 1961)*[1]

Three years after the intervention in Jordan, events in the Middle East led the British to return to the region to defend Kuwait against the threat of annexation by Qasim's Iraq. This intervention was codenamed Operation Vantage. It provided the opportunity to utilise and implement lessons from Suez and Jordan, and to demonstrate to the British public and the international community that lessons from these previous crises had been learned for the long term. Furthermore, policy-makers at the time could not have predicted that the lessons from Vantage might prove invaluable for informing the planning of an operation almost thirty years later, when the need to defend Kuwait against Iraqi attack reoccurred.

Following the 1958 Iraqi coup, attempts were made to establish diplomatic relations between Britain and the Iraqi revolutionaries. Humphrey Trevelyan, who had been the British Ambassador to Egypt during the Suez crisis, was sent to represent the government on the ground but relations between the two nations did not improve. A few months later Iraq withdrew from the Baghdad Pact. At the same time, the dynamics between Britain and Kuwait – a British protectorate – were also changing. Kuwait had been significant to Britain for decades as part of a major trading route between India and the Mediterranean. It offered one of the few harbours in the Northern Gulf with waters deep enough to dock British ships and in 1775, when the Persians invaded Basra, many trading routes had been diverted to Kuwait where the British East India Company established new offices.

Kuwait was run by a line of hereditary Sheikhs owing allegiance to Turkey, but had operated semi-autonomously since 1756. In 1896 the hereditary line was broken following the assassination of Sheikh Muhammad Al-Sabah by his half-brother, Mubarak. This change in leadership, combined with resurgent Ottoman aggression, made Mubarak concerned over annexation by Turkey. In 1899, fearing invasion or political interference, he requested British military protection. At this time the Ottomans were receiving economic and diplomatic support from Germany. Plans had been made for a railway from Berlin to Baghdad to allow Germany access to Iraqi oil fields and a quicker trading route to the eastern parts of its colonial empire.[2] The railway plans included an extension as far as Kuwait and the British, fearing displacement in the region, were quick to agree to Mubarak's request for support. On 23 January 1899 Kuwait was made a British protectorate; Britain provided naval protection and an annual subsidy to the ruling family. In return the Kuwaiti authorities allowed Britain influence over foreign policy decisions.

During the next decade Britain sought to define the limits of Ottoman jurisdiction in the Gulf, including the boundaries of Kuwait. This was eventually formalised in the 1913 Anglo-Ottoman Convention which agreed that Kuwait was 'an autonomous kaza of the Ottoman Empire', and that the Baghdad railway would not extend into Kuwaiti borders. The Convention was never ratified and, after the defeat of the Ottoman Empire in the First World War, the British invalidated the agreement, declaring Kuwait an independent Sheikdom under British protection.[3]

In 1936 the Anglo-Persian Oil Company and the American Gulf Oil Group drilled the first well in Kuwait. Commercial activity continued after the Second World War and Kuwait's prosperity flourished. During the 1951 Persian Oil Crisis, when the Iranian government voted to nationalise the assets of the Anglo-Iranian Oil Company, Britain pressured foreign countries not to purchase Iranian oil. The revision of oil company negotiations led to a review of Kuwait's Concessionary Agreement and Kuwait's annual oil income rose from £5 million in 1950 to £90 million in 1954; Britain had become increasingly reliant upon Kuwaiti oil whilst the protectorate was rising in wealth and becoming less reliant upon British patronage.[4] Consequently, there were increasing calls from Kuwaitis for formal independence from Britain and in June 1961 a compromise was reached; independence would be granted but, in order to protect British assets and interests, Kuwait could call upon British military protection if required. This agreement was formalised through an Exchange of Letters on 19 June 1961.[5]

Days after the declaration of Kuwaiti independence, President Qasim of Iraq caused alarm by verbally annexing Kuwait, asserting it as part of Iraqi territory based on historic claims. By 28 June 1961, Trevelyan was reporting from Baghdad that a military attack on Kuwait, to annex the country forcefully, was imminent.[6] On 30 June, the Ruler of Kuwait – Emir Abdullah III Al-Salim Al-Sabah – made a formal, urgent, request for British military assistance – under the terms of the Exchange of Letters – for protection against such annexation. The first forces landed the next day.

The military operation in Kuwait was the largest mobilisation of British forces in the region post-Suez and the scale of operation would not be exceeded until the British troop contribution to the Gulf War in 1991. On 1 July 1961, Royal Marine Commandos landed by helicopter from HMS *Bulwark*, paratroopers arrived by air, Centurion tanks landed from HMS *Striker*, the Coldstream Guards were flown in from Bahrain and 24 Brigade from Kenya. Transport aircraft from the Royal Rhodesian Air Force helped in the build-up of forces and units of the Kuwaiti Army were also deployed. By 7 July, the force had been substantially reinforced. All three services had major units involved with a total of 7,000 servicemen taking part and an additional 3,000 on standby and auxiliary duties.[7] Despite this demonstration of force, and in similarity with Jordan, not a single shot was fired. Redeployment began on 20 July but British troops remained in the country until 19 October 1961, when Kuwait's security was handed over to an Arab League Security Force (ALSF).

Planning the Intervention

For the FCO very little had changed since Jordan. Attempts to develop a meaningful relationship with the US over long-term planning for the Middle East region had faltered and, with the

Berlin crisis starting in November 1958, almost all of Washington's focus had quickly turned away from the region. When the crisis in Kuwait began to unfold, the US, by now under the administration of President John F. Kennedy, took very little interest, providing a new, high risk backdrop to British military action in the region.

The FCO was, however, deeply involved in the run-up to the Kuwaiti crisis and therefore had the opportunity to incorporate identified lessons into the planning of the intervention. It was Ambassador Trevelyan who provided a stream of reports from Baghdad and advised on troop movements and the Iraqi threat. Initially, Trevelyan dismissed Qasim's speech as sabre-rattling but his tone soon changed and he advised 'We shall watch Iraqi actions closely here and in Basra. Rumours of troop manoeuvres in Baghdad.'[8] By 27 June, Trevelyan appeared more alarmed, 'On further consideration I am inclined to think that . . . Qasim's original plans may have been further developed than we guessed and may have included an early internal coup supported by military action.'[9] The next day two further telegrams were sent: the first emphasised that an early warning of an Iraqi attack could not be given,[10] the second recommended a pre-emptive, deterrent British force be sent to Kuwait. He advised:

> My most recent information reveals Qasim's intention to build up in Basra a striking force suitable for an attack on Kuwait. It would help to deter him from using it if he could see that we had collected forces in the vicinity which he would have to meet.[11]

In some quarters of the FCO post-Suez nervousness towards intervention still remained and the Eastern and Arabian Department were split over Trevelyan's recommendation.[12] Earlier in the year, in a letter to Sir Roger Stevens, the Governor of Aden, Charles Johnston – who had been Ambassador to Jordan during Fortitude – had written:

> As I see it, one of the worst things that have happened to us since the war, and more particularly since Suez, is that in the Middle East we have lost our confidence in our own ability to deal with situations . . . Our Suez fiasco seems, in effect, to have left a far deeper mark on ourselves than on the Arabs.[13]

In addition, in the run-up to the crisis, Prime Minister Harold Macmillan had written of his own concerns regarding 'a show of animosity against Britain for interfering in Arab affairs'.[14] To make matters worse, Qasim's press statement had already set the media tone by accusing Britain of behaving imperially in the Middle East since the eighteenth century and providing a history of 'British imperialism for military and economic purposes'.[15] Sir William Luce, the Political Resident in the Persian Gulf, advised 'I cannot believe that even Kuwaiti oil could make it worth our while to take part in such a putting back of the clock, with all its dire political and military consequences.'[16] Consequently, once the decision had been made to intervene, the FCO worked hard to avoid accusations of imperialism. Lessons identified from Jordan – which had shown that British troops could be used to benefit in such a situation with the consent of the government concerned – were drawn upon. The FCO advised, 'What we wish to achieve, if we have to move, is something like the Jordan situation.'[17]

In the first instance, lesson implementation meant insisting that the Emir of Kuwait formally request British military assistance under the terms of the Exchange of Letters. Although the Ruler had been reluctant in asking for British military measures, for fear of jeopardising his support from Arab countries, it was important to the FCO to present the intervention as a Kuwaiti initiative. This would ensure that the FCO could circumnavigate any accusations of imperialism and that Britain would not be viewed as undermining Kuwaiti independence or delegitimising its position in the region.[18]

The FCO also endeavoured to maximise Arab support, which was not straightforward. Although initially supportive of Kuwaiti independence, the Arab response to Qasim's statement had been indecisive and hesitant. Jordan was particularly reluctant to offer support, having developed friendly relations with Iraq founded on a common aversion towards Nasser. In addition, King Hussein was frustrated that, despite his best efforts, Kuwait had not established diplomatic relations with his country and was concerned that suspicion would surround any British intervention in the Middle East; he advised the British Ambassador that he had to be careful not to meet with him in order to avoid any possible accusations of collusion.[19] King Hussein only changed his mind when the Iraqis rejected his proposal of a Jordan–Kuwait–Iraq federation.[20] On the other hand, King Saud quickly declared his solidarity with Kuwait and a small detachment of thirty-one Saudi paratroopers landed with the first British troops. However, as Saudi Arabia had also broken off traditional diplomatic relations with Britain in 1956 – leaving the FCO to rely upon the US government as a diplomatic intermediary – the paratroopers refused to liaise with British forces.[21]

The return of British troops to Arab soil did lead some commentators to revisit the events of 1956 and draw unflattering comparisons. Many Cairo newspapers declared disgruntlement, with headlines including 'A bad day for all Arabs' and 'Forces of British imperialism find the opportunity and land in Kuwait'. However, in an ironic turn of events, President Nasser of Egypt allowed British warships to pass through the Suez Canal to reach the Gulf state and he used the intervention to scold Iraq for attacking fellow Arab nations rather than criticising Britain for its response.[22] These sentiments were echoed by Mohamed Heikal, the editor of the popular Egyptian newspaper *Al-Ahram*, who declared Vantage to be 'Suez in reverse'.[23] For him, Suez had been hailed as a triumph of Arab rights over British imperialism but, by threatening Kuwait, Qasim had directly caused the return of British troops to the region. Paradoxically, therefore, five years after Suez, the 'imperialists' had returned by invitation to protect the rights of an Arab nation.

Outside the region the FCO worked to gain and maintain the support of the wider international community. After the scuffle during Fortitude the FCO had learned the lesson of informing France of the situation, although this may also have been due to the ongoing European Economic Community (EEC) negotiations.[24] Britain was also quick to explain its position to Commonwealth countries and kept them informed of its intentions throughout.[25] The response from most countries was overwhelmingly supportive, with the exception of Pakistan.[26] Pakistan advised that they could not publicly be seen to take sides over the Iraq–Kuwait dispute however sympathetic they felt because of the prestige they lost in the Arab world after supporting the British over Suez.[27]

From the outset the FCO also paid special attention to the UN. The FCO wrote to the British Ambassador in Washington, Harold Caccia, 'We are very conscious of the United Nations angle on this.'[28] Learning from the successful action in Jordan, the FCO was keen to replicate the experience in Kuwait and the UK representative in New York, the former Chairman of the JIC, Patrick Dean, agreed 'we should aim to follow the Jordan precedent as closely as possible'.[29] The US also agreed to support Britain in the UN and follow the 'Jordan precedent' to gain a good position in the Council. This precedent required the Ruler of Kuwait to send a letter to the President of the Council as a deterrent for Iraqi aggression. Once British action had been taken Britain and the US would take the initiative to call the Council to meet and would report on the situation. No resolution would be tabled, for fear of Russian veto, but the British case would be stated and supporting speeches welcomed from other delegates so as to provide a form of international political endorsement.[30] In addition, British forces were instructed not to enter Kuwait before 7:00 on 1 July 1961 in order to comply with UN formalities.[31]

Given the importance of history in Iraq's claim over Kuwait, in preparation for the Security Council meeting, the FCO's Arabian Department prepared three historical works for reference.[32] The UK's UN Mission advised that the information was useful but that the information would have been even more worthwhile if it had been available more promptly.[33] This demonstrated the benefit of producing ongoing and timely histories.

The FCO further implemented the lesson of keeping the Americans informed throughout the planning stage of the intervention. Anglo-American discussions about the possibility of an Iraqi threat, and consequences of military action in Kuwait, had taken place for some time and by the summer of 1961 a specific study had been produced. Immediately after Jordan, in September 1958, a UK–US Planning Group was set up for this purpose. Macmillan expressly wrote to Washington in 1959 requesting that the Group be used to develop 'joint planning on the lines we prepared for Lebanon' for the protection of Kuwait.[34] In the early stages of planning Britain experienced the same challenges of working with their American allies as they had in planning Fortitude, with the

US continually reluctant to share any military plans.³⁵ In 1960, an agreed paper concluded that ground operations would be undertaken by either UK or US troops but in each case logistical support would be provided by the other due to the shared American and Western interests in Kuwait's independence. By June 1961, however, the Arabian Department at the FCO identified the American's lack of commitment: 'The net result therefore is that we have no details of American plans, the Americans have always refused to discuss joint planning and seem now, on the military level, likely to close the door.'³⁶ In the end, coordination was never achieved; US forces did not take part in the operation and Washington was keen to leave the British to manage what they deemed an essentially Arab affair.³⁷

Nonetheless, as a result of the attempts at joint planning Prime Minster Macmillan was confident of gaining US support for the operation and declared 'I think the Americans will be alright on this occasion', although reassurance from Washington was still sought.³⁸ On 28 June 1961, the FCO instructed Caccia to advise the US Secretary of State, Dean Rusk, of London's intentions to intervene. Macmillan explicitly referenced the close working relationship between John Foster Dulles and the former Foreign Secretary, Selwyn Lloyd, during the Jordan intervention and advised of his hope that 'we could act in the closest cooperation' again.³⁹ He was quickly reassured 'Your thinking coincides with ours . . . and we are prepared to render the full political support you request.'⁴⁰ Rusk offered the assistance of a small naval force, if required, and vital diplomatic, moral and political support. This support was quick and forthcoming.

The IC also continued to work on the UK–US relationship, which the FCO considered to be invaluable. In fact, diplomats were convinced that it was ongoing intelligence sharing that persuaded the US to support British actions in Kuwait. In the FCO's Arabian Department, Edwin Maynard wrote 'The way we took the Americans and Canadians fully into our confidence on Iraq/Kuwait intelligence matters is believed to have influenced their policy.'⁴¹

In the meantime, Macmillan also remained aware of the lessons which he had identified from Suez and Jordan on the importance of maintaining Cabinet and parliamentary support. In the first instance, to implement the lesson and try to avoid the 'dithering' that had occurred over launching Musketeer and Fortitude, Macmillan convinced the Cabinet to leave the management of the crisis to him. However, he was also cautious with this approach and wrote in his diaries: 'Remembering Suez, I was careful throughout to have meetings of ministers (including Chancellor of the Exchequer, Lord Chancellor and Home Secretary) and also – before the final decision to launch the forces – of the whole Cabinet.'[42] In fact, Macmillan went around the Cabinet table and asked ministers individually if they had all the information that they wanted to make a decision, and whether they agreed to send troops.

For the MoD, much had changed since Jordan but not because of it. Jordan had occurred during a period of transition in the military – after Suez and the reforms of the 1957 Defence White Paper – and had provided an initial, small scale, test of these changes. The Defence White Paper was subject to a five year development plan that was coming towards its conclusion and Kuwait offered the first large scale test of the amendments under emergency conditions. As a result, the success of the operation was politically important. Similarly, lessons identified from the operation would be significant for feeding into the 1962 Defence White Paper, shaping Britain's future defence policy as it withdrew east of Suez.

Despite MoD difficulties of working with the Americans, contingency planning had continued and military plans for Vantage had been drawn up since November 1959, even further in advance than the contingency plans for Jordan or Suez. Movement appendices for Vantage had been revised in December 1960 and equipment had been stockpiled to improve readiness. At the beginning of 1961 a rehearsal exercise had also been conducted in the Trucial States allowing further lessons to be identified. A revised concept was in preparation to implement these lessons – codenamed Bellringer – and was due to become effective in September 1961. When the Iraqi threat emerged sooner than expected a number of elements of Bellringer were quickly incorporated into Vantage.[43]

In July 1960, the state of readiness was relaxed to no less than four days due to intelligence on Iraqi intentions. However, the events of June 1961 progressed rather more rapidly than expected and the FCO quickly recommended a military, rather than diplomatic, route be pursued. In the event, Commander-in-Chief Middle East, Air Marshal Charles Elworthy, criticised the assumption of a four day warning as 'ill found' and 'might have led to the most dangerous situation', openly accusing the JIC of providing assessments too late.[44] The last assessment had been provided on 12 June 1961 and stated that it was unlikely that Iraq would risk attack on Kuwait, that for political reasons such an attack would probably be preceded by an attempted insurrection and that a warning period could be expected. However, for Elworthy, much of the revised assessment provided on 18 August would have been equally valid in June and the lack of the planned warning period caused problems in the build-up phase; the imperative of getting troops quickly into Kuwait delayed the arrival of headquarters and administrative personnel. In addition, pre-planned reinforcements – to be dropped off in Cyprus and Aden – had to make way for the parachute battalion, 45 Commando and 11th Hussars.[45]

For the IC concerns over the spread of communism had continued to dominate its agenda since 1958. Nonetheless, the IC had been warning of the threat of Iraqi aggression and, in contrast to Suez and Jordan, the IC had been predicting Iraqi actions towards Kuwait for years. As early as January 1957, the JIC had described the Iraqi government, suffering from financial difficulties, as 'having for some time been casting covetous eyes on Kuwait' and between 1958 and 1961, the IC demonstrated some lesson identification and implementation through the continual re-evaluation of assessments on the Iraqi threat to Kuwait, often at the request of the MoD.[46]

Immediately after the 1958 Iraqi coup, the Joint Planning Staff produced a paper for the Chiefs of Staff which considered means of rapid intervention in Kuwait to protect British oil interests.[47] The ability to intervene was also reconsidered on 17 September 1958, whilst the political and economic implications for military intervention were considered in December 1958.[48] At the same time, assessments from the IC predicted that the new Qasim regime would maintain claims to Kuwait but aim to achieve its objectives of annexation through internal subversion rather than outright aggression.[49] In fact, the early capability assessments of the JIC suggested that Iraq was incapable of going to war abroad, being both disorganised and lacking training and experience, largely due to the anti-nationalist purge of officers in 1959. In March 1959, military planners asked the JIC to disregard assessing the likelihood of an invasion and focus upon how an Iraqi invasion into Kuwait might take place. The JIC assessed Iraqi attack scenarios and provided predicted warning times for Iraqi aggression which fed into the MoD plans. It was this assessment which concluded that Britain could expect 'to receive not less than four days' warning of the assembly of an invasion force in the Basrah [sic] area, but, once this is assembled [Britain] could expect little or no warning of an actual invasion'.[50]

At the beginning of 1961, the JIC provided another long-term assessment which concluded that Qasim was focused upon improving relations with Arab countries and was therefore unlikely to act aggressively towards Kuwait, another Arab country.[51] The report also concluded that the Iraqi Army was incapable of conducting an operation outside Iraq, reinforcing its disorganisation. The JIC concluded 'The Iraqi Armed Forces, at present capable of little more than an internal security role, are unlikely to show any marked improvement in their capability', a conclusion which had also been reached by the Military Attaché in Iraq, Colonel J. W. Bowden, in January; 'Due to lack of experienced commanders, the state of training and lack of the normal supply organisation, it is not considered probable that the General Staff would consider, let alone launch, an offensive operation.'[52] This assessment led to a lack of urgency in updating the contingency planning of Vantage with Bellringer.[53]

The IC also had more intelligence assets available in 1961 than they had in the areas of crisis in 1956 or 1958. A new SIS station had opened in Kuwait, in 1958, after pressure from British Petroleum executives. It was opened by one of the few Arabists in the service at the time, John Christie, who was dispatched from Bahrain to persuade the Al-Sabah ruling family that Kuwait's security depended upon an SIS created counter-intelligence service to infiltrate Kuwaiti society. He was also to escort British Army officers to the Mutla Ridge on the Iraqi border to prepare maps in case Iraq invaded.[54] Across the border in Iraq there was also a SIS station in Baghdad, under Henry Coombe-Tenant, which exploited long-term relations with officers in the military and security services to get intelligence.[55]

Once Qasim issued his threat of annexation on 25 June the intelligence reporting from on the ground came thick and fast. With assessments required from both the Embassy in Baghdad and the Consulate in Basra information was gleaned through a variety of informants, sources and means. These included confronting senior officers, speaking to rail officials and interviewing friends and families of regiment members.[56] One telegram even suggested monitoring the demands for large quantities of diesel fuel as a possible indicator of the mobilisation of armoured regiments.[57] In addition, propaganda monitoring of the Iraqi press and radio continued, as did liaison with the Kuwaiti military intelligence. However, the SIS station in Baghdad assessed the announcement as propaganda whilst intelligence reaching the FCO soon contradicted this conclusion, with reports from the Ambassador and Colonel Bowden showing increasing concern over the movement of troops.[58] Bowden also liaised with the other Military Attachés in Iraq in order to pool resources, despite some of their dubious competences; the Turkish officer was described by one diplomat as really 'off the wall'.[59] Britain's alert status was heightened on 28 June 1961 and it was also on this day that Trevelyan advised that he could no longer guarantee the anticipated warning time that had been determined by the IC for the military contingency planning. In fact, it was Bowden's assessment of Iraqi preparation for invasion which led to the MoD's preparatory moves on 29 June and over time the IC leaned increasingly on the members of the British Embassy in Baghdad and Consulate in Basra for intelligence.[60] In his memoirs Ambassador Trevelyan described the different methods through which information was sought and summarised some of the evidence that was collected by himself and his team. These included large orders for aviation spirit, requisitioning of railway wagons and the widening of the road from Basra to Kuwait at night for heavy traffic.[61] Asking FCO staff to gain intelligence on the ground put personnel under pressure and in danger but on 5 July 1961 the FCO wrote to Baghdad 'War Office greatly appreciate information Her Majesty's Consul

General Basra has been able to supply under difficult conditions and much regret lack of other sources compels them to ask for more.'[62] This left one government representative in Kuwait to conclude 'One lesson of the recent events appears to be that we cannot rely solely on accurate intelligence of Iraqi troop concentrations.'[63] In fact, it had been assumed that intelligence of any force concentration in Basra would solve this problem but it was confused by preparations for a military parade to celebrate the 1958 coup on 14 July.[64]

Where Trevelyan and his team were unable to provide further intelligence was on Qasim's intentions.[65] There were some suspicious signs: rumours were circulating that the Minister of Housing had been ordered to visit Kuwait to draw up plans for housing projects, there was a report that a senior official in the Ministry of Finance had his leave cancelled to draw up a new budget to incorporate Kuwait and it was announced that Kuwaitis no longer had to conform to foreigner regulation in Iraq.[66] However, this was speculation and the information passed to the Cabinet failed to emphasise that intentions remained unknown. The IC seemed to be able to offer little more on Iraqi intentions. Certainly none of the JIC assessments released in the public archives made clear the distinction between capabilities and intentions. Trevelyan did, however, portray Qasim as obsessed with history and the historical justification for the annexation of Kuwait. He was described as displaying Ottoman documents, letters and old maps 'like a child displaying its toys' and went to great effort to produce materials about Iraq's historical claim.[67]

The IC had already identified its collection weaknesses during planning. In an attempt to corroborate HUMINT the IC relied on signals intelligence (SIGINT) from Baghdad and Cyprus, the continued monitoring of Iraqi media and increasing the observation of trains on the Baghdad to Basra line.[68] The IC also placed much emphasis on the use of IMINT to substantiate HUMINT reports. The benefit of reconnaissance for substantiating HUMINT had been identified as a lesson by the Commander-in-Chief in Musketeer and the IC had agreed.[69] Upon reading the Commander-in-Chief's report the JIC stated 'this report only serves to re-emphasise the pressing need for the maintenance of an adequate and up-to-date reconnaissance force ... in any theatre of operations'.[70] Furthermore, in January 1960 the Air Ministry had suggested that Canberras could deliver blanket coverage of photo reconnaissance of Southern Iraq to implement this lesson.[71]

However, there soon proved to be a number of difficulties at the operational level with lesson implementation of IMINT. In particular, entering another state's territory during peacetime required approval from the Cabinet and this caused significant delays in the process. Once approval was given, reconnaissance did not solve the problem as missions were unable to locate an armoured regiment which was reportedly on the move. Canberras were routinely flown but severe haze often degraded their images and by mid-August the JIC was still unable to confirm any reports of movement.[72] This was significant as George Hiller, the Head of the FCO Western Department, admitted '[the] decision to send troops was based on military appreciation [of the] situation following realization Intelligence had lost track [of a] squadron'.[73] Furthermore, one report from the bridge of HMS *Bulwark* revealed that the ship's crew were aware of being badly in need of up-to-date intelligence, images and maps, none of which could agree on the nearest position to the new civil airport.[74]

During the Intervention

Once the operation began, the implementation of many lessons identified from Musketeer and Fortitude was immediately tested, beginning with the movement of troops by air. In fact, the air movement of around 700 tons of stores in the first six days of the operation revealed a significant increase in speed and efficiency due to intensive and combined training of the Army and the RAF.[75] However, the issue of overflying rights immediately re-emerged, despite it previously being identified as a lesson. There was already a ban on the British overflying certain Middle East countries, forcing long routes from Cyprus via Turkey and Iran into Kuwait. Although Iran granted permission, Turkey and Sudan initially refused to permit flying in their air space.[76] As a result, within hours of taking the decision to implement Vantage, the Defence

Committee was recalled and the parachute battalion was forced to stand down, just as it had in Fortitude. Emergency alternative flying routes were considered, all of which were longer (at least 7,000 miles more) and had additional complications.[77]

The failure to successfully implement the lesson forced the FCO to request that the US Ambassador in Ankara, Raymond Hare, persuade the Turkish Foreign Minister to grant overflying rights. Washington agreed and Hare drew upon the analogy of the US approval of overflying rights from Israel in the 1958 intervention in Jordan to provide reassurance.[78] He also provided an official reply advising of US government approval of UK actions and reassuring that any attack from Russia would be treated under Article V of the North Atlantic Treaty Organization (NATO) treaty; that an attack on one NATO country would be viewed as an attack on them all.[79] The next day Turkey agreed to overflying, but only by night and with specific conditions which were to be 'scrupulously observed'.[80] This meant that aircraft could not fly and return in one day, leading to congestion and aircraft grounded and exposed to attack in Kuwait during the day.[81]

In the case of Sudan, the government refused overflying and refuelling. However, not wishing to irritate the British, the Sudanese Minister for Foreign Affairs hinted that flying should continue without a request. If all went well no one would ever know and he advised 'even if by ill fortune an aeroplane landed in Sudan it could easily be hushed up'.[82]

Despite these difficulties, the identified lesson of securing overflying rights was still not fully implemented. There was soon an additional requirement to overfly Saudi Arabia with troop supplies, but gaining these rights proved equally difficult. As the Saudis had broken off diplomatic relations, the FCO initially requested the US to gain overflying rights on its behalf.[83] A positive reply was promptly returned.[84] However, King Saud insisted the request for overflying came from the Emir, not from the British or via the Americans, and when permission was granted it also was given with strict limitations.[85] Even worse, the Air Ministry had been overflying Italy for four days before it was realised that permission had been overlooked. The unfortunate British Ambassador was dispatched to apologise and handle the situation in Rome 'in whatever manner you think appropriate' only to report back to London that the Italian Air Ministry were 'maddened'.[86] Commander-in-Chief Elworthy would again identify the overflying difficulties as a lesson for the future, acknowledging that the delay in obtaining permission to overfly Turkey and the Sudan could have been critical and reconfirmed the existence of an air barrier. For him this meant either that deliberate overflights without permission would have to occur or the lesson could be implemented through 'the stationing of sufficient air transport on the right side of any potential air barrier'.[87] Sir William Luce agreed and to implement this lesson in the short term it was fixed that a parachute battalion would be permanently stationed in Bahrain, despite the vast expense of building and maintaining new air conditioned barracks.[88]

The operation was also a test for the new Middle East Command based in Aden. One of the lessons identified from Suez had been that the existing command structure was unreliable and 'not a set-up recommended in any future operations'.[89] The lesson was subsequently implemented through the division of the existing Middle East Command into two in 1959: one based in Aden and one in Cyprus (which was renamed Near East Command). The new Middle East Command allowed for a Commander-in-Chief to have regional command of decision-making and report directly to the Chiefs of Staff in London. Once the Iraqi threat was perceived to be imminent initial operational management was slow, with piecemeal alerting of different parts of the force, delays in getting the Canberra photo reconnaissance detachment to the Persian Gulf, further clarification required on actions to be taken in the event of an attack and misunderstandings over codewords. The lesson was identified: 'There seems a clear need for an organisation in the Ministry of Defence to be nominated to perform this function in the UK and for parallel action in overseas command.'[90]

Once troops had landed, Air Marshal Charles Elworthy moved 1,200 miles closer to theatre – joining Sir William Luce in Bahrain, which allowed daily visits to Kuwait and twice daily meetings with all Commanders.[91] Being situated in the Residency also enabled the Commander-in-Chief to be provided with copies of all FCO telegrams and intelligence. In his post-operational report Elworthy identified 'The Command structure established at Bahrein [sic] worked very well and I am convinced of the need for the source of military command and political direction to be situated together in an operation of this type.'[92]

However, the command structure was still not successful for managing a tri-service operation. Whilst the Army and RAF were happy to work within a joint service headquarters, the Royal Navy resisted and Admiral Talbot insisted on operating off-shore.[93] To add further complication, lower down the Vantage command structure, infantry came from three brigades, each organised differently. There were also equipment and communication incompatibilities and, as a result, organisation and standardisation issues became overwhelming for the Joint Administrative Headquarters in Bahrain. This lesson was quickly identified and a team from the School of Land and Air Warfare was despatched to study the difficulties, implementing their lessons through an update to operating procedures and techniques.[94] Commander-in-Chief Elworthy concluded 'The lack of an established joint organisation and procedure was seriously felt . . . More practise is required to improve inter-service working.'[95] This lesson was soon implemented and the 1962 Defence White Paper announced the set-up of a permanent Joint Service Staff within the MoD to improve the framework of joint working in the future and to run joint service exercises worldwide.[96] In 1963, an additional White Paper, 'Central Organisation for Defence', increased defence coordination further with four new organisations created to work with the Joint Planning and Joint Warfare Staff: the Defence Operations Executive, the Defence Operational Requirements Staff, the Defence Signals Staff and the Defence Intelligence Staff.[97]

Once forces had landed, the FCO was aware that the longer British boots remained on Arab soil, the more political criticism would emerge. A few days into the operation Macmillan recorded in his diaries 'It is going to be difficult, and expensive to stay; hard to get out. The Opposition in Parliament have behaved pretty well – so far. But this will not last.'[98] In fact, by 17 July 1961, Emanuel Shinwell had submitted a parliamentary question leading to comparisons with the failed operation in Suez.[99] Luce also advised 'it seems inevitable that the longer we keep any troops in Kuwait the greater will become the pressure to force us out of the

Gulf altogether'.[100] Consequently, in order to avoid a prolonged operation and declining opposition, public, Arab and wider international support, plans for a prompt withdrawal of British troops were immediately considered.

As before, the lessons of history were examined to consider how the UN could assist. The FCO UN Department identified a number of lessons from the past including the emergency UN force sent to Suez in 1956 and the observation group which lead to a resolution allowing the withdrawal of UK and US forces from Jordan and Lebanon in 1958.[101] However, in a final ironic turn it was the Arab countries, through the provision of the ALSF, who came to British aid by relieving its troops. The FCO had encouraged the Kuwaiti Ruler to send a diplomat to each of the regional capitals to seek support for an Arab League application which was eventually granted.[102] In addition, it was Patrick Dean, the former Chair of the JIC and one of the few people who had been aware of the Suez conspiracy and who was now stationed at the UN, who advised the US State Department that to secure such a force and allow British withdrawal 'Cairo may be the key'.[103] He was right. It was with UAR agreement that the ALSF allowed the withdrawal of British troops from Kuwait.

Once the ALSF arrived and the British had withdrawn, there was some pressure on the MoD to bolster the ALSF force by providing tanks and aeroplanes. However, learning from past experience, Macmillan refused and declared that such action would lead to the threat of the weapons being used against the British or the Ruler in the future. Not only had there been a close call in selling two new Z class destroyers to Egypt just before the Suez crisis, but tanks that the British had sold to Iraq had been used to overthrow the Hashemites in 1958.[104]

The alleviation of responsibility by the ALSF did, however, help with the previously identified lesson of cost management, which was implemented throughout. The economic situation at home remained difficult and Harold Macmillan wrote in his diary, just before writing about the Kuwaiti intervention, 'Economic situation at home has not improved . . . The real question is how to cut down military expenditure . . . something must go.'[105] As early as 2 July 1961 it was agreed in a Defence Committee meeting that the FCO should begin to recover as many costs as possible from Vantage.[106] A month later Macmillan wrote to the Foreign Secretary 'I know it is bad manners to talk about money with Sheiks but at some point we must raise the question of a contribution by the Sheik to our very heavy expenses.'[107] The FCO also drew on the identified lessons of recovering costs from Jordan in order to negotiate its position with Kuwait. The Embassy specifically wrote to London 'It would be most useful for me to know, in context of forthcoming negotiations with Kuwaiti authorities, what settlement of both local and general costs was reached with the Jordan Government, after the 1958 operations.'[108]

Another previously identified lesson – managing the media – was also implemented in Kuwait, but with only partial success. Securing priority for the movement of PR officers and staff to Kuwait was challenging. The first officer arrived just after the troops, albeit that he quickly contracted chicken pox resulting in initially incomplete and imbalanced reporting.[109] The remaining PR team was not effective until forty-eight hours after the troops' arrival, leaving the press without access to official sources. Once in place, the team in Kuwait worked hard to keep the media informed and onside but were hindered by a number of challenges. Initially, no provision was made for RAF representation at Kuwait airfield – the request got lost in London leading to a ten day delay – and only one Army PR officer was stationed in Bahrain throughout the majority of the operation. There were also restrictions placed upon correspondents by the Kuwaiti authorities and poor communications remained, with MoD announcements being released in London before in theatre. There was also a lack of direction from the MoD on what could be released to the press. Commander-in-Chief Elworthy later identified 'a lack of clear positive guidance from London made it more difficult to present the situation to the Press in the best possible light'.[110]

Nonetheless Elworthy and Brigadier Horsford held many press conferences accompanied by the FCO Regional Information Officer in Beirut, who was temporarily despatched to Kuwait, and Sir William Luce or one of his staff. The Commander-in-Chief also tried to avoid any negative publicity, or political embarrassment, through accidental crossing of the Iraqi border; land patrols, Twin

Pioneers, Austers, Canberras on photo reconnaissance and helicopters were restricted to five miles behind the border and other air sorties to ten miles. The 11th Hussars roadblock was seven miles within Kuwaiti territory and the use of land mines was forbidden to avoid Kuwaiti casualties.[111]

Despite PR efforts and the success of the operation, the media did provide some negative reporting, particularly over the difficulties associated with working within extreme weather conditions; the surface sand was regularly over 140°F. Extreme temperatures caused grenades to smoke, batteries to lose charge, radios to fail, boots to degenerate, explosives to give off headache inducing fumes and water jerrican linings to disintegrate causing nausea and vomiting. In addition, Centurion tanks were too hot to carry infantry and it was suspected that, due to disintegration, much of the ammunition would have been useless had it been used.[112] The high temperatures were also unfavourable for flying helicopters, whilst the maintenance and serviceability of the aircraft and pilots meant that helicopters were often kept onboard ships rather than in the required vicinity.[113] Furthermore, with troops flown in from all over the world, no time for acclimatisation, poor discipline in heat protection and a lack of suitable equipment and food, there were many heat casualties. A report by the Army's Operational Research Group (AORG) identified that 10 per cent of troops arriving from the UK were out of action due to heat disorders within the first five days.[114] As it happened, HMS *Bulwark* was on its way to undertake hot weather trials in the Persian Gulf when Vantage commenced. It was carrying additional Royal Navy medical personnel and subsequently diverted to Kuwait allowing 200 men to board the ship each day for a sleep in air conditioning. The Kuwaiti Health Service also assisted, allowing men to be nursed in air conditioned wards rather than under canvas.[115]

However, much to the dismay of the MoD, by 6 July 1961 the *Daily Mirror* claimed that a Royal Marine Commando had been withdrawn because one third of the men were suffering heat exhaustion.[116] Another story stated that a Commanding Officer was forced to pay for ice for his troops out of his own pocket, causing one sympathetic member of the public to guarantee the supply of £10,500 worth of ice to the troops.[117] To 'damp down any political criticism in this country [Britain] about the living conditions of our troops in Kuwait' the Under-Secretary of State for War, James Ramsden, was quickly dispatched to theatre.[118] The trip achieved its objective and was triumphantly described in a letter from John Profumo, the Minister of War, as 'a great success and the publicity here has been splendid'. Upon Ramsden's return Profumo also wrote 'Well done indeed . . . the more colourful, personal and tough stories you can tell about how good the soldiers are . . . the better.'[119] However, the visit was not appreciated by all; one War Office bureaucrat noted 'P.S. Have just seen signal from C-in-C [Commander-in-Chief] asking to be protected from such visits.'[120] Ramsden wrote a report on his observations which identified lessons surrounding the conditions of the troops and was distributed to relevant departments for the implementation of these lessons.[121]

In addition, as early as 13 July 1961 the War Office commissioned AORG to conduct two pieces of operational research. The first sent a scientist to collect data across seven specific areas of concern, including equipment and weapons. The second saw a specialist in physiology survey all factors related to the health and efficiency of serving personnel, particularly heat and acclimatisation difficulties.[122] Both research groups produced reports which identified lessons for the future. The reports led to further heat exercises, conducted in Aden in 1962, to identify lessons through the study of the acclimatisation of troops, appropriate rations for hotter climates and new equipment. Consideration for implementation included acclimatising soldiers through heat chambers or carrying them to theatre in heated aircraft. The lessons identified from the reports and exercises were widely distributed through lectures to the War Office, Strategic Reserve and Southern Command.

As well as the heat and forty cases of heat exhaustion a day, the political agent in Kuwait also mentioned problems caused by severe dust storms.[123] The first Commandos landed in difficult weather with poor visibility and aircraft in the initial anti-tank role were also severely limited by poor visibility at the beginning of July, whilst flights into Kuwait New Airfield were hampered throughout Vantage. In some cases transport aircraft were unable to land and had to return to Bahrain. Lighting and other aids were installed at airfields for a short time to assist but facilities on the ground were limited. Incomplete buildings had to be used as accommodation and Elworthy noted 'such refinements as ablutions and latrines were non-existent'. On the other hand, the Kuwaiti Oil Company opened its doors to British troops offering a large swimming pool for recreation and exercise and private homes for washing, sleeping and eating.[124]

As well as the heat challenges, many of the communications difficulties of past operations remained. The Commander-in-Chief advised 'the difficulties which were experienced with communications had been foreseen and various projects were in hand to improve them'. Nonetheless the previously identified lessons of inflated precedents, over-classification and the ongoing need to integrate the communications systems of the three services 'was again evident'.[125] Communications difficulties also occurred due to the electrical disturbance from sun spots as well as difficulties in the communications between the brigade headquarters and the RAF at Kuwait New Airport.[126] Even after withdrawal, communications difficulties between London and Bahrain continued.[127]

During the intervention there was little further learning demonstrated in the IC, with one exception – implementing the lesson of working with the US, although this was not without incident. A few days after the operation launched, rumours began to circulate of a secret collusion between Qasim and the British government.[128] After the Iraqi threat of annexation, the IC had repeated its approach to Jordan by providing intelligence directly to the Emir of Kuwait, with daily assessments from Baghdad and Basra passed on by John Christie. It was believed that Britain had good intelligence on Iraq and the Ruler had limited access to gain his own. As a result, these reports soon convinced the Emir of a significant threat and the need to formally request British military assistance.[129] Once Vantage began accusations were made that the threat had been fabricated or exaggerated to create the environment within which Britain could legitimately return to the region. This included allegations that the IC had leaked stories to the Kuwaiti press to create an atmosphere of fear.[130] The rumours were perpetuated by the hosting of the Iraqi Minister of Economy in London at the same time as Iraq was opposing British efforts in the UN. Eventually the rumours led to serious concerns from allies that the British were trying to reassert power and prestige in the region.[131] The US Embassy in Baghdad had been unable to substantiate the claims coming from the FCO of a threat, and on 4 July 1961 the US Ambassador reported that there was still no direct evidence of Iraqi movement in Baghdad and the US Consul General in Basra had also not seen any evidence of troop movements.[132] Instead, American intelligence cited the nature of the road, a dirt track between Basra and Kuwait, as impeding any rapid annexation.[133] A US diplomat in Iraq, Holsey G. Handyside, also noted that there were not enough tank carriers to transport tanks from Baghdad to Basra, nor could they get aboard a river boat and the railroad was 'so decrepit as to be non-operational' with so few flatbeds that the movement of tanks would take three months.[134]

Consequently, despite ongoing intelligence liaison, the US eventually accused the British of intelligence exaggeration. Philip Talbot from the Far East section of the US State Department advised Dean Rusk 'the British have placed more force in and on Kuwait than was justified by the magnitude or even seriousness of the Iraqi threat'.[135] The US delegation to the UN also expressed concerns over the lack of fresh evidence of any Iraqi aggression.[136] Rusk even challenged the Foreign Secretary, Lord Alec Douglas-Home, on the extent of the Iraqi threat and the CIA's Deputy Liaison Officer in London, Carlton Swift, demanded that the raw intelligence be shared.[137] This was embarrassing for the IC and plans were considered to leak the contents of the diplomatic telegrams from Trevelyan to a 'discreet American correspondent' to counteract the accusations. To ensure the correct audience was reached, Dana Schmidt of *The New York Times* was suggested. However, the idea was soon dropped, with reassurance that 'arrangements are being made elsewhere'.[138] Nonetheless, President Kennedy did not approve of the British policy and disagreed with the notion that British presence in the region helped stability. It was on his orders that requests for joint planning of the region's defence were rejected after Vantage had ended.[139]

Other lessons which had been identified by the IC were not implemented, whilst previous difficulties which had never been formally identified reoccurred, demonstrating the importance of learning lessons. Following Musketeer, a number of learning documents identified that the security of intelligence, and issues of security in IC–MoD liaison, were hindering operations. General Keightley had concluded under the subject of 'Intelligence' that 'Security of plans and operations generally proved a serious problem', whilst one Commander noted 'A constant tug-of-war exists between the dictates of security and the need for adequate briefing.'[140] The JIC(ME) had agreed and identified that the virtual exclusion of the MoD command structure had denied any effective role to the Commanders prior to troop arrival.[141] However, issues of security re-emerged as a problem in Vantage. Commander-in-Chief Elworthy identified 'there was an over use of Top Secret classification which led to delays'.[142]

After the Intervention

Following Kuwait, in the FCO, no official history was written about the events. This followed the Prime Minister's express request that official histories 'should be in the political field e.g. Britain's history of de-colonisation; or the independence of India, rather than in the military field e.g. Suez and Kuwait'.[143] However, a debate about what lessons the FCO could identify from the handling of the Kuwait crisis erupted in response to two despatches: one from Alan Rothnie, the Chargé d'Affairs in Kuwait, and one from Sir William Luce.[144]

Rothnie firstly reflected upon the wide acclaim of the British intervention and reported that a member of the ruling family had specifically drawn comparisons between 1961, 1958 and 1956 and concluded that Britain's actions in Vantage had been commendable. He advised 'I would not find one voice raised except in praise of the help which the British Government had accorded the State of Kuwait.'[145] However, he also warned that there were many lessons to be learned. In particular, he identified the importance of Kuwait becoming part of the Arab community and stressed the need for Arab solutions to Arab problems in the future. He advised that this was one of the lessons which had been identified by the Kuwaiti officials, concluding that the country would begin to mark its independence at the expense of the British 'special position' and become a closer part of the Arab community.

In fact, at the time of writing the despatch, Kuwait had already sent economic delegations to seven Arab countries to discuss investment opportunities. In addition, the Emir soon chose to accept the Saudi Ambassador as his first diplomatic representative, despite a request from the FCO for a British appointment.[146] Kuwait was also beginning to establish itself further internationally through diplomatic and goodwill missions and an application for membership of the UN was granted in 1963. To be accepted in these forums Kuwaitis had begun to understand that there was a need for political reform in their country; from autocracy to democracy. Rothnie noted that all such Kuwaiti lessons would have an impact on the way Kuwait conducted its political and economic relationship with Britain. As a result, many of the lessons learned by Kuwait from the crisis would have a greater impact on the FCO than the lessons that they identified themselves. In London, the notes made on the despatch suggested it was well received, describing it as a 'useful, comprehensive' and 'good' despatch.[147]

Sir William Luce took Rothnie's thinking further and reflected upon the lessons which could be identified to inform the wider strategy of Britain in the Gulf. He firstly endorsed Rothnie's summary of the overall operation and added:

> It is indeed remarkable that in this day and age it should be possible for British forces to intervene in defence of an Arab country against another and, in the process, to strengthen Anglo-Kuwaiti friendship without, as I believe, harming British relations with the rest of the Arab world.[148]

However, one of the biggest lessons identified by Luce was that Iraq had the ability to attack with little, if any, warning. For him this meant that a stronger deployment of British forces was needed in the Persian Gulf with the Kuwaiti forces bolstered to withstand an Iraqi attack until British forces arrived. This was due to the FCO's 'inability so far to devise any policy other than the exercise of military power to protect our interests in the area and to meet our treaty and moral obligations', hence his agreement to the stationing of troops in Bahrain. Luce concluded 'there is at present no policy within Her Majesty's Government's grasp which would enable us to withdraw from the Gulf'.[149] This was also identified by the Cabinet and, as part of a paper produced on Kuwait in October 1961, alternative policies to ensure Kuwaiti independence were considered. These included changes in Kuwait's policies towards Arab countries, including rerouting investment in London to other Arab states, and defence by a UN force which was unlikely due to UN existing commitments, particularly in the Congo. It was concluded that there was no practical alternative to maintaining British forces in readiness to come to Kuwait's assistance.[150] Luce's only suggestion for escaping the quagmire was to encourage the US to play a more active role in the region and Kuwait's protection.

Two months previous the FCO Arabian Department had also written a memo on Kuwait which aligned with Luce's view; Britain's position with Kuwait could not be reviewed without reassessing the British position throughout the wider Gulf region. Furthermore, having recently given reassurances to the Ruler, it would be dishonourable to change British policy and would risk Kuwaiti independence which remained important for the balance of payments, maintaining stability in the region and preventing the spread of communism. The memo concluded 'In short, in the Secretary of State's own words, it was of national interest to defend Kuwait on July 1, it still is so. We should act accordingly.'[151]

Notes suggest that whilst Alan Rothnie's despatch was read by at least five recipients, Sir William Luce's despatch was widely circulated within a number of FCO departments before being further distributed to the Head of the War Office, Air Ministry and Admiralty. It sparked a debate inside the FCO which revealed that different individuals had identified different, and often conflicting, lessons from the same intervention. The Arabist Harold Walker dismissed a number of Luce's points stating 'he does not come to any original conclusions' but did agree that 'planning with the Americans is desirable, and although we have tried to achieve this in the past without success and can hardly be sanguine of obtaining better results if we try again, I think we should do so'.[152] Other diplomats objected to Luce's assumption that British military presence in the Gulf did little harm elsewhere in the Arab world whilst others advised that it also affected Africa and Asia.[153] However, all of the FCO officials who commented on the despatch agreed that working with the Americans was an important lesson and that there was a requirement for Britain to continue its commitment to the Gulf, but in a manner which avoided appearing imperial. This was aptly described by P. S. Ziegler as 'a bad job and all that we can do is to make the best of it by making our military presence as inoffensive as possible'.[154]

Cabinet Secretary Norman Brook, however, had identified a different lesson to the FCO diplomats and advised the Prime Minister that maintaining the position with Kuwait was untenable. He wrote to Macmillan 'We are fighting a losing battle propping up these reactionary regimes ... We ought to recognise that our policy in relation to each one of these places is a pretty short-run affair.'[155] The US State Department identified the same lesson and noted 'The West can no longer afford present policy of reliance on British military protection, which seems to be the most attractive one to greedy, short sighted Shaikhs [sic].'[156] The FCO did not catch up with this thinking for a few years. It was not until 1965 that Luce revised his position and suggested Britain should reconsider its military commitment to Kuwait. The Cabinet Official Committee on Defence and Overseas Policy came to a similar conclusion a few months later.[157]

In the MoD, as well as the AORG reports and subsequent exercises, many other lessons were identified through a variety of methods. As part of the standard process, the Commander-in-Chief produced a full report on the operation, with lessons identified for the future.[158] This was considered by the Chiefs of Staff and referred to the Joint Planning Staff.[159] In addition, the report noted that the Commander-in-Chief's subordinate Commanders were providing their own reports identifying lessons on matters of single service concern and detailed reports were being written on joint matters including medical and communications 'through the normal channels'.[160] The Royal Navy and RAF, for example, learned the limits of their hardware in strategic mobility and the Army revealed concerns over the adaption for their forces in terrain, language, culture and climate. They also felt that the balance of mobility and force size had not been achieved and in an effort of self-preservation wanted a larger force with more armour.[161] Furthermore, even the US Continental Army Command used the British experience in Kuwait to draw lessons for better air support operations.[162]

Elworthy's report identified a number of lessons for the future including that greater direction was required from the government. He also identified the failings of relying on local cooperation as promised accommodation, storage facilities and transport did not emerge. In part, this was because the original resources had been promised by Sheik Mubarak Abdullah – who had recently been relieved of his office – and his successors wished to demonstrate changes in policy.[163] Nonetheless, Elworthy identified the benefit of developing a 'Goodwill with the Kuwaitis' scheme. As there had been no operational role for the Psychological Warfare Unit during Vantage, they developed and issued a pamphlet on the customs and susceptibilities of the Kuwaitis. These were given to all Commanding Officers with the aim of encouraging cultural awareness and understanding to foster a positive relationship.[164] Elworthy also identified the need for tactical loading of aircraft so that men and equipment would arrive together. This led the Director of Land Air Warfare to request further lesson identification and implementation on this issue by the School of Land and Air Warfare.[165]

The War Office held its own debriefing and a meeting specifically to identify the lessons of Vantage, distribute them to relevant Commanders and delegate lesson implementation.[166] In addition, a working party was established to examine Vantage and draw upon 'various post-mortem reports' to produce a report for distribution on the lessons to be learned.[167] Lesson implementation was then pursued by both the War Office and the Minister of Defence.[168] A member of the War Office wrote to General Officer Command MELF 'I wish to ensure that follow up action is taken on certain of the lessons learnt during Vantage' before listing such lessons.[169] The Minister of Defence pursued information on the actions from the AORG findings from the Defence Council, whilst even a year later Minister for War, John Profumo, was still attending meetings on Kuwait and following up on lessons.[170]

However, the distribution of identified lessons was restricted and the extent to which the MoD was prepared to admit faults outside its own walls revealed a barrier to learning. Even eighteen months later John Profumo's Private Secretary explained that documents needed to be treated in 'a "need to know" circle within the War Office to avoid any subsequent embarrassment' and it was decided that the AORG report 'will not be distributed to other Government Departments in view of the criticisms it contains'.[171] In addition, the MoD took criticism from outside the department very personally; the Director of the Royal Artillery called accusations relating to the heat casualties by the Labour MP George Wigg 'a slur on the good name of the British Army'.[172]

Lesson identification also occurred due to the ongoing Iraqi threat to Kuwait after the operation ended, which forced the revision of plans for intervention in the future. These drew upon many lessons from Vantage. For example, throughout the operation communications difficulties had persisted due to the electrical disturbance from sun spots and the revised intervention plan noted 'although communications between London and Bahrein [sic] have been improved, they are by no means certain when conditions are adverse'.[173] Consequently, authorisation was delegated to the Commander-in-Chief to carry out necessary attacks, without the go-ahead from London if necessary.

To inform the revised plans, a working party was established by the Chiefs of Staff Committee to report on the operation. It identified that relying on a plan that required a four day warning period had been a major weakness of the previous Kuwait contingency plan.[174] As a result, the new plan, codenamed Operation Sodabread, implemented the lesson by reducing the warning period to thirty-six hours.[175] In 1967, the MoD used the Kuwait contingency plan, by this time codenamed Operation Livid, as the basis of a war game to identify further lessons on optimum force position and build-up in a limited war.[176]

Beyond the initial reflex to draw lessons from the operation, the MoD also went on to write a number of official histories from which further lessons could be identified. Although the Joint Service In-House Historians deemed Kuwait as 'Essentially a Deployment Operation, not justifying more than a monograph' the Naval Historical Branch produced a history summarising the operational aspects and the Army Historical Branch produced a factual narrative of the operation following the chronology of events.[177] Air Chief Marshal Sir David Lee also included Kuwait as a chapter in his works, *Flight from the Middle East*, for the Air Historical Branch and specifically identified a number of lessons including on the availability and readiness of forces and details of the air transport plan.[178]

Overall, the MoD saw Vantage as a success in two ways. Firstly, it demonstrated that the MoD had implemented a number of lessons identified since Suez. In Parliament, on 5 March 1962, the Minister of Defence, Harold Watkinson, confidently concluded 'there were lessons to be learned, and they have been learned.' He made specific reference to the unified command of joint service operations and the new mobile task force concept. Secondly, testing the implementation of lessons in Kuwait provided the opportunity to identify weaknesses and to argue for further investment into the development of new policies within the 1962 Defence White Paper. Watkinson told Parliament that the operation's identified lessons had been the basis of 'much of our future planning'.[179] In the debate over the 1962 Defence White Paper the Secretary of State for War also explained that further conflicts were expected in the Middle East but that Britain had proved its ability in Kuwait.[180]

Macmillan was also pleased and wrote in his diaries 'It afforded an admirable example of the effective use of a small British force if its deployment was rapid and timely.'[181] Both Rothnie and Luce also reported to the FCO on how impressed they were with the British forces behaviour. Rothnie wrote 'our forces have left behind them a fund of goodwill which has done much for Anglo-Kuwaiti relations and, as has often been said, the British servicemen has been his country's best ambassador'.[182] Even the Americans viewed the military operation as a success. The Secretary of Defence, Robert McNamara, cited the example of Kuwait as an illustration of Britain's value in the region to the Senate.[183] In addition, the Military Attachés of Turkey, Holland, Sweden and Persia all expressed their admiration for the operation.[184]

This success was, as with Jordan, partly down to good fortune. The close proximity of HMS *Bulwark* along with 42 Commando at the crucial time was lucky. There was also the good fortune of a half squadron of tanks afloat in the Gulf on HMS *Striker* on the way to Aden. The initial deployment of such a small force had left those on the ground exposed and vulnerable and, to make matters worse, the numbers of troops were announced by global media sources making Qasim's need for external intelligence negligible. Trevelyan, aware of this threat, wrote swiftly to the FCO:

> Two sources have suggested to us, on the basis of BBC announcement giving details of numbers of troops and tanks landed, that we only have very small forces in Kuwait . . . This impression may be dangerous and encourage Qasim to think he can have a bash and get away with it.[185]

British forces were therefore fortunate that they did not land in a hostile environment and that the military attack did not materialise. The Commandos were the only complete major land unit in Kuwait until 3 July 1961, when an Iraqi attack seemed possible on 1–2 July. Had hostilities erupted they would have had to have formed 'hastily prepared positions on unfamiliar ground and with inadequate communications between units'.[186] In addition, air defence was extremely limited and full capability did not arrive until HMS *Victorious* joined the operation ten days after the initial landing. The eventual large deployment of forces meant that had a crisis emerged elsewhere in the world at the same time the MoD would have been at a loss. British forces were also lucky to be relieved of their duties by the ALSF; the ALSF was forced to remain in Kuwait for another sixteen months until a successful Iraqi coup against Qasim allowed for its final withdrawal in February 1963.

Once British troops withdrew from Kuwait, the JIC continued to assess that Qasim had not abandoned his claim to the country and provided six-week updates to the Chiefs of Staff.[187] Reconnaissance flights over the Iraq–Kuwait border continued, only reducing to bi-weekly intervals in 1964 and ending in 1968.[188] The JIC also continued to report on tank movements and provide intelligence assessments of the Iraqi force and its movements, with an update on Iraqi intentions every four to six weeks.[189] The ongoing intelligence requirements for Kuwait and Iraq, as well as the imminent threat to British interests, forced some internal reflection into the handling of the operation and what lessons could be identified for the future. As early as August 1961 the JIC report, 'Iraqi threat to Kuwait during the next twelve months', offered a re-evaluation of previous assessments and identified that collection capabilities had been, and continued to be, unable to provide the required warning period for British intervention.[190] A Cabinet memo on 2 October 1961 also admitted that the experience had revealed 'difficulties in securing accurate intelligence of Iraqi military preparations'.[191] However, instead of implementing the identified lesson to address the issues of collection, the IC focused upon the issue of providing a warning period. The JIC reassessed scenarios for attack and developed a list of warning indicators for each scenario, but a heavy reliance upon Embassy staff and the Military Attaché continued.[192] By September 1961, the warning indicators had been reassessed again and it was identified that they remained insufficient.[193] Two months later, three attack scenarios had been assessed, but for two of these scenarios it was concluded 'We cannot rely on any warning of these attacks.'[194] To make matters worse, in November 1961, the MoD asked the JIC explicitly to assess the likelihood of an attack as well as Iraq's capability.[195] The resulting paper revealed that the JIC had gained little further intelligence on Qasim and his intentions, offering mixed messages: 'Qasim has in no way modified his claim to Kuwait . . . He is unpredictable and given an opportunity, he could move swiftly without warning . . . we can easily overestimate Qasim's capability for crazy action and under-estimate his peasant cunning.'[196]

Nonetheless, by 5 October 1961 the JIC reassured the Chiefs of Staff that the lesson of the lack of intelligence collection assets had been identified and implemented.[197] Liaison with the Kuwaiti military intelligence was increased, GCHQ hired additional Arab linguists to aid SIGINT and focus was shifted to reporting on Kuwaiti internal affairs, as there were fresh concerns that Qasim would attempt annexation through subversion.[198]

In the meantime, Norman Brook wrote sceptically to the Prime Minister and identified 'Our present intelligence coverage in Southern Iraq is, however, inadequate to enable us to assess accurately whether Iraq is capable of launching an attack on Kuwait.'

Brook also identified that the IC continued to rely upon IMINT as the best source of confirming or denying HUMINT: 'Although steps are being taken to improve our intelligence in Iraq itself, the best and at present the only means of confirming the strength and dispositions of the Iraqi forces in the Basra/Shuaiba/Zubair areas is by vertical aerial photographic reconnaissance.' He went on to advise 'without this information the Joint Intelligence Committee is obliged to use for this purpose unconfirmed information' before identifying 'there are at present no alternative means of obtaining the intelligence needed'.[199]

By the end of November 1961, the situation had not significantly improved and the JIC noted that even the reliance upon IMINT was strained: 'every possible effort is being made to improve our intelligence coverage of the area but the build-up of this coverage takes time'.[200] There were also political difficulties: in October the JIC had proposed another reconnaissance flight over Iraq in an attempt to locate the lost regiment and to inform military planning. However, the FCO was concerned about political embarrassment and delayed the flight by several weeks.[201] When HUMINT reports suggested a new threat of invasion, in December 1961, with GCHQ also reporting anomalies in Iraqi ground communications, the IC were still reliant upon reconnaissance missions alone to collaborate the reports which also continued to be delayed by the required approval process.[202] However, this time the lesson was identified and the IC concluded that for implementation they needed the collection of intelligence to be 'within our control'.[203] Macmillan's Private Secretary, Philip de Zulueta, agreed stating 'It seems inevitable that we shall continue to get alarmist bazaar rumours of Qasim's intention and if we are to avoid politically embarrassing and unnecessary and expensive military movements we must have means to confirm or reject such reports.'[204] The JIC's suggestion for short-term lesson implementation was that the UK Political Resident be delegated to authorise one reconnaissance flight immediately over Iraq should indications suggest an impending attack.[205] Macmillan approved the proposal with a requirement for re-approval every ninety days and a Canberra was permanently stationed in Bahrain for this purpose.[206]

Vantage Learning

Kuwait demonstrated that many lessons from Suez and Jordan had been learned within the FCO. Whilst Suez continued to provide negative identified lessons, of what not to do – appear imperial or intervene without support, especially from the US and regional states – Jordan provided a template of positive identified lessons on how to act throughout a crisis. As a result, Kuwait provided the opportunity to test both positive and negative identified lessons and revealed each as equally useful.

The precedent of Jordan was used as a method of learning for issuing a request for assistance and how to handle the UN. It was also drawn upon during the operation for negotiating the presence of a peacekeeping force to facilitate British withdrawal and ensuring the recovery of costs to protect the British economy. Although this proved to be a successful method of learning during Vantage, many of the personnel in the FCO had remained since 1958 and therefore it was possible for this learning to occur exclusively within the individual sphere with the consequent danger that it might not be retained over time.

Learning in planning and from the operation also revealed a new challenge within the learning process. Where two spheres overlap – in this case the individual and institutional – disagreements can occur over which is the correct identified lesson. Where such an individual remains within a government institution, their beliefs about lessons may be undermined by more senior individuals or those of the institution, with their professional role forcing their acceptance of working within the environment of a contradictory approach. For diplomats, this can cause particular challenges in presenting and defending overseas security policy if it runs contrary to their own ideas.

A number of strategic and operational lessons remained learned within the institutional sphere including the importance of world and public opinion and the importance of the US. All of these were beginning to form part of the best practice of crisis management and overseas military intervention. In the individual sphere, Harold Macmillan demonstrated that the identified lesson of Cabinet and public support also remained learned; both a negative lesson identified from Suez and a positive one from Jordan. However, these lessons were only identified within Macmillan's personal diaries rather than widely distributed or institutionalised for the benefit of future Prime Ministers.

A number of lessons were also forgotten, barriers to learning reoccurred and new barriers emerged. The issue of overflying permissions was an institutional, operational and negative lesson which had been forgotten but also faced a reoccurring learning barrier of the actions of other learners.

Learning by other states also forced new lessons to be identified in the FCO. Officials noted that lessons identified by Kuwait would propel Britain into a different relationship with the Gulf state, and the FCO would have to learn to adjust accordingly. However, the inability to think of viable alternatives or means of implementation to protect British interests revealed a further barrier to learning. Whilst the FCO identified the lesson that alternative policies towards Kuwait were required – to avoid ongoing military protection – officials could not imagine a means by which this would be possible. In fact, Vantage revealed that the FCO was often uncreative and slow to respond to change in the region. It also had a culture of hesitation in implementing strategic lessons which risked disruption in policy elsewhere, preferring to maintain stability and the status quo. As a result, long-term underlying difficulties remained unresolved; the British were on military alert to protect Kuwait again by Christmas and Britain was forced to maintain an expensive base in Bahrain to ensure ongoing military readiness.

Nonetheless, Vantage provided the first example of significant formal and institutional learning after the operation. This, again, was not through official histories or lessons reports but through the internal method of despatches which identified lessons. However, more significantly, the two despatches from Alan Rothnie and Sir William Luce sparked a formal debate about which identified lessons were to be learned. This worked well but also revealed the power of personality and seniority in the learning process within the FCO; it was the despatch from the senior figure, Sir William Luce, which was the most widely debated and distributed.

Learning within the MoD continued in the institutional sphere but was also driven forward, in some cases, by learners in the individual sphere. It had increased since Jordan, despite a similar level of operational success, thus revealing little correlation between the learning process and the success or failure of an operation. Instead, it was arguably the size and timing of the operation which was crucial to the effort and importance placed upon lesson identification – straddled between the end of a five year change in strategy and before the next strategic defence review of 1962. Consequently, in contrast to Fortitude or the response of the FCO to Kuwait, there are a relatively large number of MoD records identifying lessons from Vantage.

The planning of the intervention demonstrated the ongoing attempts to implement the lesson of working with the Americans whilst faced with the continual barrier of an uncooperative ally. However, it also revealed a new method of lesson identification through rehearsal exercises. This method was hugely beneficial as it allowed lessons to be implemented and new lessons to be identified within a safe environment. A similar method was also used after the operation through the war game for Livid.

Once the operation began, many of the identified strategic lessons from Suez were demonstrated as learned. This included air movement and command and control. Joint service working, however, had not been successfully learned and the Commander-in-Chief called upon the institutional sphere – the School of Land and Air Warfare – to study the problem, leaving lesson identification internal. The School implemented the lessons they identified through the formal methods of operating procedures and techniques which acted as a method of lesson retention for the future.

The operation also revealed the role of the media as an external learner in identifying lessons. The lessons identified by the media forced extraordinary and formal methods of further lesson identification, through the AORG, and implementation encouraged by the Under-Secretary of State, James Ramsden. It also led to further internal research, development and testing to identify additional lessons which were widely distributed through lectures.

Once the operation was complete, many reports identifying lessons were produced, as there were after Suez. However, the role of the School of Land and Air Warfare in identification and implementation was re-emphasised and the distribution of lessons was wider than just the Chiefs of Staff. The War Office debriefing ensured lessons were distributed to all relevant Commanders, whilst the working party saw that lessons were learned, pushed forward by an insistent minister. This revealed the importance of an individual driver of learning and a formal body for overseeing lesson implementation. A new method of lesson implementation and retention was also revealed through the revised plans for intervention both before and after the operation.

Overall, much more learning occurred in the MoD from Kuwait than Jordan and even the official histories took greater note of Vantage than Fortitude. In addition, the MoD continued to learn more formally than the FCO and was beginning to reveal itself as a learning organisation through routine reporting, research and development, exercises, schools, lecturing, training and restructuring. However, there were also warning signs of increasing barriers to learning. Whilst the MoD was reflective internally, it was becoming clear that it did not want to distribute lessons across other Whitehall departments or publicly air faults and weaknesses. There was a hostile reaction to external criticism and the ministry was coming under increasing pressure to implement lessons without the necessary finances.

The IC continued to show much less formal or traceable learning than either the FCO or MoD during Vantage. Although this is partly the nature of the work conducted and the availability of archival sources, it is also clear that the IC did not have a culture of lesson identification, nor were 'lessons' part of the routine lexicon. Nonetheless, it is also clear that the IC learned more from Kuwait than it had from Suez or Jordan because the ongoing threat to British interests, before and after Vantage, forced constant reassessment of intelligence. The identification, implementation and retention method of reassessment was internal, routine, formal, strategic and operational but was often led by an external driver through the intelligence requests submitted by the MoD. In part, this is the way in which the IC operates, through the provision of intelligence based upon 'customer' requests, but more could also have been achieved through proactive reassessment.

The results of the reassessments were often limited, with a focus upon lessons identified from the content of the intelligence itself, rather than identification of lessons on how the collection and assessment were conducted and could be improved for the future. When collection weaknesses were identified, the lesson was either forgotten, met with a barrier or was only implemented as a short-term fix. Furthermore, although new assessments adjusted the warning period for aggression, at no point did the IC attempt to identify alternative indicators to allow for an extended warning period.[207]

Other previously identified lessons were also forgotten, including the lesson of security protocol of intelligence, whilst lessons which had not been formally identified – or distributed to relevant learners – caused problems to re-emerge. In the case of security, the lesson being forgotten was unsurprising given that the reports identifying the lesson were created by the MoD (and thus unlikely to have been widely circulated in the IC) or by the JIC(ME) (whose suggestions had been quickly dismissed in London after Suez). Nonetheless, this only seeks to emphasise the importance of lesson distribution across relevant government departments, as well as internally.

Consequently, an examination of the intervention in Kuwait reveals a disparity of learning from history across government, both in comparison to the different institutions and in comparison to the experiences of Suez and Jordan. The operation itself may have been successful – 'Suez in reverse' – but the threat to Kuwait remained. In 1963, after Qasim was killed, Iraq and Kuwait signed 'Agreed Minutes between the State of Kuwait and the Republic of Iraq Regarding the Restoration of Friendly Relations, Recognition and Related Matters'. This agreement formally recognised a boundary between the two nations.[208] However, in 1969, the Research Department at the FCO produced a lengthy memorandum which concluded that Iraq continued to pose a serious threat.[209] In addition, British defence responsibility towards Kuwait remained whilst its power over the state rapidly declined. As a result, the debate over British policy in the Gulf dominated much of the 1960s with full withdrawal of troops from the region announced in January 1968 and completed in 1971. In fact, the unresolved Iraqi threat would remain bubbling under the surface until it re-emerged thirty years later with more disastrous consequences. Britain had not learned to solve the deeper Iraq–Kuwait problem.

5 A Re-Run of Port Stanley – The Gulf 1990–1

> We were lucky in the Gulf conflict because a number of people who were in the department had served in the department during the Falklands conflict and there was a departmental memory over what issues were important and what lessons we had learned.
> *(Margaret Aldred, Director of Defence Policy, 1994)[1]*

Almost thirty years after Vantage, the Gulf War – codenamed Operation Granby – occurred in a very different international context. The recent end of the Cold War had changed the security environment and the events of 1990–1 provided an opportunity to establish a new world order. Nonetheless, many lessons from Vantage – due to similarity of geography, culture, enemy and type of intervention – were still relevant and, as a result, Granby offered the chance for learning to be demonstrated in the long term and in the generational sphere.[2] In addition, the lessons identified from Granby itself would become highly significant when an intervention against the same foe would occur thirteen years later.

During the 1980s, the West and Iraq realigned as allies with Britain and the US supporting the Iraqi President, Saddam Hussein, in his fight against Iran in the prolonged and bitter Iran–Iraq War. The war left Iraq with severe economic difficulties; Iraq's per capita income halved and an estimated $67 billion worth of damage was done to infrastructure and $80 billion was borrowed from other countries, particularly Saudi Arabia and Kuwait. By early 1990, foreign debt servicing and defence costs swallowed seven eighths of Iraq's oil export revenue, which was limited by the Organization of the Petroleum Exporting Countries (OPEC).[3] Iraq's struggling economy, combined with increasing anti-Western propaganda, began to raise suspicions about Saddam Hussein's intentions and by 1990 the JIC had concluded that Iraq had returned to being 'a potential predatory power, whose victims might be Kuwait or Syria'.[4]

During the summer of 1990, tensions between Kuwait and Iraq rose. Kuwait and the UAE were exceeding their OPEC oil quotas leading to the suppression of petroleum prices and, therefore, Iraq's income. Kuwait was also using this economic advantage to place pressure on Baghdad to repay its war loans and to settle their long-standing border dispute. On Iraq's national day, 17 July, Saddam Hussein delivered a speech threatening the Gulf state. Four days later he moved approximately 20,000 troops to the Kuwaiti border. These actions were quickly dismissed by the FCO and IC as sabre-rattling to generate leverage for negotiations at the upcoming OPEC meeting.[5] In addition, Saddam assured his fellow Arab leaders – King Fahd of Saudi Arabia, King Hussein of Jordan and President Mubarak of Egypt – that he had no military intentions and agreed to a meeting with the Kuwaitis in Jeddah to negotiate a solution.[6] OPEC rejected Iraq's proposal to increase oil prices and the Jeddah talks were delayed during which time more Iraqi troops, then totalling an estimated 100,000 men, amassed along the Kuwaiti border.

On 1 August the Jeddah talks began but little was achieved and it was agreed that talks would resume on 6 August. A commitment to participate in these talks soon proved to be a bluff and in the early hours of 2 August 1990 Iraq invaded Kuwait, deposed the Al-Sabah ruling Royal Family and maintained a military occupation of the state as an annexed territory. The same day the UN Security Council adopted resolution 660 – the first of twelve resolutions passed during the Gulf War – condemning the invasion and calling for Iraq's immediate and unconditional withdrawal.[7] On 7 August the US announced that, in response to a request from Saudi Arabia, they would be sending forces to the Gulf to prevent any further Iraqi military action. The next day the British government announced that it would be doing the same, contributing the second largest force to a coalition of thirty-nine nations in the collective defence of Saudi Arabia.

As the weeks went by it became clear that Saddam Hussein had no intention of leaving Kuwait. On 29 November 1990, the UN Security Council gave him six weeks to withdraw before the coalition was authorised to 'use all necessary means' to remove Iraqi troops.[8] The deadline expired on 15 January 1991 and forty-eight hours later coalition air forces began attacks. The whole campaign was concluded within forty-three days, on 28 February 1991, and the responsibility for the demilitarised zone eventually passed from the coalition to UN forces.[9]

The Gulf War saw the largest deployment of British forces since the Second World War. Three times the force involved in the Falklands – 45,759 personnel – and 15,000 vehicles were deployed with 52,661 tons of equipment airlifted and 300,000 tons delivered by over 130 ships. The Royal Navy conducted 3,171 challenges with thirty-six boardings, 1st (BR) Armoured Division covered 290 kilometres in the land offensive, 4,000 sorties and 2,500 support sorties were flown by the RAF and 3,000 tons of weapons were dropped by air during this time. British Special Forces, drawn from all three services and numbering 650, were also committed, in their largest operation since 1945, entering Kuwait and Western Iraq, destroying communication lines and countering the threat of Scud missiles.[10]

The intervention was also hugely significant for Britain for political reasons. The events gave the British government the opportunity to reinforce its role in the world after recent tumultuous international changes and to re-establish its primacy in trans-Atlantic relations. Britain also had a large expat community in Iraq, Kuwait and surrounding countries which needed to be protected: around 50,000 people – the largest group of Europeans living in the region at the time.[11] In addition, there were national interests at stake. The invasion not only created regional uncertainty which could damage British exports to the Middle East but there was concern over the threat of disruption to the world's oil reserves.[12]

Planning the Intervention

Just like Suez, and unlike 1961, the FCO was unprepared for the events of 1990. Primary focus had been on the menace of Iran and Saddam's assurances to Arab leaders had provided false comfort; at the time, the FCO was busy counselling Kuwait on how to handle the Iraqi dispute diplomatically. In fact, the British had been persuaded by the long held maxim that Arab states did not attack each other, ignoring the individual development of Arab nations since the Second World War and the increasing brutality of the Iraqi system. The British Ambassador to Saudi Arabia, Alan Munro, would later conclude that the Iraqi invasion 'at a stroke demolished assumptions about regional amity and balance'[13] whilst the Middle East Heads of Mission would be asked 'Why did we fail to foresee the Gulf Crisis and take preventative action? . . . The beginning of wisdom is to acknowledge mistakes.'[14] The threat from Saddam Hussein was disregarded to such an extent that, at the time of the invasion, the FCO Iraq desk was manned by just one young diplomat.[15] Although the FCO Emergency Unit was put on precautionary alert, both the Foreign Secretary, Douglas Hurd, and Minister of Defence, Tom King, were away on holiday. At the same time, the Prime Minister, Margaret Thatcher, was en route to a conference in Aspen and neither the British nor the US Ambassador to Iraq were in Baghdad.[16] The British Ambassador and Consul to Kuwait were also taken unawares and remained under siege for several months in the Kuwaiti Embassy, surrounded by Iraqi troops, without electricity and water supplies, living off tinned tuna and a vegetable patch.[17]

In the IC, the JIC had not only failed to predict the end of the Cold War but had continued to invest large amounts of its reducing resources into countering the communist threat. As a result, the Middle East had received little attention for some time. There was no formal indicator and warning system for aggression in Iraq or Kuwait and, as a result, when an old threat emerged, the IC found itself lacking in many areas of intelligence.[18] The former Chief of Defence Intelligence, Lieutenant-General Derek Boorman, admitted that the area was 'under-resourced' and any intelligence on Iraq was primarily limited to Baghdad or dedicated to sanction busting.[19] A post-operational report on intelligence during Granby acknowledged that although both Iraq and Kuwait were considered to be high priority for assessment 'Granby was unexpected'.[20]

When Saddam threatened Kuwait in his speech on 17 July it was noted by the IC, but Britain invoked no precautionary measures. The Kuwaitis placed their Army on alert, but there was no request for Western assistance, nor any evidence that the British government tried to persuade the Ruler of Kuwait of its necessity.[21] It was not until two days later that the DIS reported the threat and Defence Attaché staff travelled by car to Kuwait to identify troop movements. The DIS used their information to confirm that all eight divisions of Iraq's Republican Guard were involved.[22] Despite their importance in Vantage it was the Falklands campaign – Operation Corporate – which had led to identification of the importance of intelligence gathering by Defence Attachés.[23] The report on intelligence support for Granby concurred stating 'This intelligence could not have been obtained from any other source' noting that one of the key lessons identified for the IC was 'Attachés can provide a unique source of intelligence on military developments.'[24]

American satellites had also picked up the movement of troops and the US informed their Embassy in Baghdad on 20 July 1990 but did not share the intelligence with the British until four days later.[25] It was only following the American confirmation of movement that the Middle East Current Intelligence Group of the JIC met to produce an assessment of the threat. It assessed that Iraqi military action could not be ruled out 'in the medium term' but the JIC were less optimistic about the timing and circulated a minute to the government indicating that there was a cause for concern.[26]

The next morning, on Friday 27 July 1990, the Chairman of the JIC and Foreign Affairs Advisor to the Prime Minister – Percy Cradock – sent a minute to Thatcher re-emphasising the threat. He also made clear that the Kuwaiti Army would not be able to resist Iraqi aggression and that the emergence of Saddam as a predator in the region would pose a grave threat to British interests.[27] He did not receive a reply to his note and made further inquiries on the morning of Monday 30 July but to no avail. The intelligence warning had not been disseminated and the FCO continued to advise travel to Kuwait was safe, with a flight taking off on the morning of the invasion.[28]

The MoD was even more suspicious and issued a warning on 1 August that an invasion was likely.[29] However, it was no more prepared to react; the expectation of a 'peace dividend' at the end of the Cold War had led the government to reconsider its military expenditure and the MoD had responded with the 'Options for change' defence review.[30] This review proposed creating a 'smaller but better' force, designed primarily for deployment in Eastern Europe, but within a week of its announcement Iraq invaded Kuwait. Consequently, the post-operation learning process became hugely significant for wider strategic and long-term planning. Furthermore, unlike in 1961, no contingency plans were in place. In fact, no serious contingency plans had been considered for high intensity conflicts outside the NATO area in the previous twenty years.[31] Nor had any contingency plans been generated for large scale operations. The Assistant Under-Secretary of State identified to the House of Commons Defence Committee 'We did not have a contingency plan for an operation of this scale, so to that extent we did have to initiate planning from scratch.'[32] The lack of planning soon earned Headquarters British Forces Middle East (HQBFME) the nickname 'Baldrick lines' after the Blackadder character who claimed 'I have a cunning plan.'[33] The lesson identified was not to prepare for specific threats in the future but to focus on a range of capabilities which could meet most situations.[34]

The MoD, therefore, was fortunate to benefit from the period between the commencement of defensive and offensive operations, allowing five months for necessary planning, training and equipment modifications in Saudi Arabia. In addition, the Falklands had provided inshore fighting experience whilst the Royal Navy were extremely familiar with the Gulf region due to the Armilla patrol which had been in the area protecting British interests and shipping since the beginning of the Iran–Iraq war in 1980. There was also good fortune in the availability of forces at short notice, a lesson later identified by Air Chief Marshal Sir Patrick Hine: 'we were fortunate to have a sizeable force, well-trained and immediately available for release from NATO tasks, for Granby. We should not assume that we would always be able to respond similarly in the future.'[35] In fact, Special Forces, due to other tasks, were not able to fully deploy until January 1991.[36]

Nonetheless, there was very little learning explicitly referenced in planning, even though military remnants of the 1961 intervention were still in existence in Kuwait in the form of a training team. As a back-up after British withdrawal from Vantage, and under the British–Kuwaiti defence agreement, a stockpile of tanks had been left with a military mission to oversee their maintenance. By 1990, this mission had become a training team for the Kuwait Army's British supplied armour and after the invasion the members were held hostage by the Iraqis.[37]

There were some differences which reflected change since 1961, but these cannot be directly attributed to a learning process. For example, the operation was planned for the cooler months to avoid the summer temperatures and priority was given for adequate acclimatisation time for the troops.[38] By the end of the operation the House of Commons Defence Committee concluded that excellent general health was maintained amongst personnel through good training in personal hygiene, heat discipline and enforced abstinence from alcohol.[39]

Once the invasion occurred and the FCO overcame the shock, it quickly sprang into action. On 2 August the Emergency Unit was opened, in a blast-proof basement, and the crisis management team formally assembled under the Head of the Middle East Department, Rob Young. The FCO was logistically prepared for the event, with the Unit Manager ensuring the provision of beds, baths and meals for staff working long days.[40] The day began with an assessment of telegrams and draft resolutions from the UK–UN Mission as well as preparing ministers for questions from the media. At 7:30 the Emergency Unit met to discuss the day ahead. This was shortly followed by an inter-departmental briefing between the FCO, Cabinet Office and MoD. At 8:30 a meeting was held between various representatives in the FCO: Middle East, Near East, Defence, UN, Economic Relations, Information and News, as well as the MoD and Cabinet Office. At 9:00 the Foreign Secretary held his own meeting with specific experts. A smaller group also met at 11:00 in the Cabinet Office and a full review of the day was held at 18:00.[41]

On the ground, a similar process was mirrored within the embassies. In Saudi Arabia the Embassy Section Heads – political, press, military, consular, commercial and management – met every day, seven days a week, mid-morning and in the evening.[42] The FCO worked like a well-oiled machine, implementing lessons from responding to a succession of crises, and all the effort fed into the Overseas Defence (Gulf) Cabinet subcommittee which was established to oversee the operation. This in itself was the product of lessons from the Falklands and it was concluded that 'One principle reason that it did [work so well] was that care was taken from the start to take account of the lessons identified in 1982.'[43]

A Crisis Cell was also opened in the Defence Intelligence Centre on 3 August 1990 and the first intelligence summary was issued at 17:30 the next day. By 6 August the cell was manned twenty-four hours and producing two summaries a day.[44] Initially this worked well but as staff increased there was a heavy reliance upon augmentees – personnel assigned as a temporary duty – mainly from the Warsaw Pact and Scientific and Technical Intelligence Directorates.[45] By January 1991, the supply of augmentees was exhausted and the lesson was identified for the future: 'Sufficient augmentees, with clearly defined assignments, must be earmarked to meet all foreseeable crisis requirements.'[46] The DIS later identified 'It is uncertain whether the DIS (even with MoD augmentation) would have the resources to provide intelligence support for two simultaneous crises.'[47] Consideration for opening a second Crisis Cell happened twice during Granby – once due to unrest in the USSR and once due to a confrontation between India and Pakistan.

Similarly, once Iraq invaded Kuwait, the focus of the IC shifted to the Middle East region and the central intelligence machine sprang into action. After Corporate, the IC was criticised for being 'too passive in operation to respond quickly and critically to a rapidly changing situation which demanded urgent attention' and a review of the structure and the position of the JIC Chairman was recommended.[48] This identified lesson was implemented; the JIC was expanded and the central machinery rebuilt, overseen by Percy Cradock. Granby, therefore, provided the opportunity to test the changes under crisis conditions and to demonstrate that lessons had been learned. The Middle East Current Intelligence Group began its morning meeting at 4:00 to produce a daily intelligence bulletin. This would inform the JIC which met at 6:00 to produce a briefing for senior officials at 8:30 who prepared an agenda for the minister's meeting at 10:00.[49]

The quick and decisive response was also led by Thatcher, who, upon hearing of the invasion, immediately instructed two Royal Navy ships to head for the Gulf. Her response was also the implementation of a lesson from history, but again not from 1961. Instead, it was the impact of Suez, an event that occurred three years before she became a MP, and her experience in the Falklands which determined her resolve. In her memoirs, Thatcher described 'Suez syndrome' as a distorted perspective of Britain's place in the world: having previously exaggerated British power, after 1956 Britain exaggerated its impotence, ignoring successes and overemphasising failures. For Thatcher the Falklands campaign changed this state of mind and the Gulf crisis offered the opportunity to reinforce British success:

> The significance of the Falklands War was enormous, both for Britain's self-confidence and for our standing in the world. Since the Suez fiasco in 1956, British foreign policy had been in one long retreat. The tacit assumption made by British and foreign governments alike was that our world role was doomed steadily to diminish. We had come to be seen by both friends and enemies as a nation which lacked the will and the capability to defend its interests in peace, let alone in war. Victory in the Falklands changed that. Everywhere I went after the war, Britain's name meant something more than it had.[50]

Furthermore, Thatcher's opinion on how to handle Saddam Hussein was marred by her experience of living through the Second World War. For her, Saddam, the aggressor, was the new Adolf Hitler, and his annexation of Kuwait was as defiant as Hitler's invasion of Czechoslovakia. Similar to Eden, in opening the two-day debate on the Gulf crisis in the House of Commons, Thatcher identified 'We have bitter memories of the consequences of failing to challenge annexation of small states in the 1930s. We have learned the lesson that the time to stop the aggressor is at once.'[51] Douglas Hurd, on the other hand, preferred the analogy of Korea. He declared 'One way or another Kuwait must be freed. Forty years earlier we had fought a war in Korea to reverse an act of aggression. The same principle, even more blatantly, was at stake here.'[52] It was also the

'Korean precedent' which was agreed to be followed by the FCO in the pursuit of UN resolutions.[53] Consequently, many different identified lessons, from contrasting events of history, were drawn upon in planning the intervention but little reflection was made upon Vantage. In fact, from July 1990–May 1991 the FCO Policy Planning Staff produced fourteen substantive analytical papers on Kuwait, Iraq and the Gulf War, none of which reflected upon the experience in the region thirty years before.[54]

The immediate concern of the FCO was to avoid appearing imperial in Britain's response to the crisis. The quick suggestion of military action – two days after securing UN-imposed sanctions on Iraq – divided the institution similarly to the division of opinion in 1961.[55] The British Ambassador to Saudi Arabia, Alan Munro, identified 'We were ever conscious, perhaps to the point of oversensitivity, of latent Arab resistance to foreign military involvement. The bogey of Western imperialism still sent its echoes down the years from the Arab nationalism of Nasser's Egypt.'[56] He also later reflected 'Conditioned as I [was] by spending much of the past thirty years implementing Britain's withdrawal from direct military engagement in the Arab world this reversal of hallowed policy [took] my breath away.'[57] However, in line with the lessons identified from Jordan and Kuwait, Thatcher insisted that troops could only be sent to Saudi Arabia in response to a specific request from King Fahd.[58] Once the request had been made it was repeatedly emphasised to counteract Iraq's propaganda machine and to portray the British response as appreciated assistance rather than unwanted intervention. By the end of Granby, UK–Saudi relations were closer than ever. Munro wrote to Hurd in January 1991 'our standing has never been higher, and our access at all levels has greatly improved'.[59] Similarly, the British Ambassador to Kuwait, Michael Weston, wrote that 1991 had been 'a good year for Anglo-Kuwaiti relations, which are now better than at any stage since we last saved Kuwait from the Iraqis, in June 1961' and 'there was genuine regret when the last of our fighting troops withdrew at the end of July ... our reputation here now stands higher than at any time for many years'. In fact, the reinvigorated relations led to contracts worth over £500 million for British businesses, despite the British Fire Group taking so long to sign their contract that nearly all of the oil fires were extinguished by the time they arrived.[60]

A further method to avoid appearing imperial was to place a heavy emphasis on the inclusion of other Arab states within the military coalition. The FCO's Policy Planning Staff identified that 'UK military action in the sole company of the US would have serious political implications'[61] and the Granby Coordinator, David Parry-Evans, noted that the 'strategy was to build up the role of the Arabs . . . to make sure that the campaign could not be interpreted afterwards as a Western, anti-Arab, engagement'.[62] Whilst some states were proactive in response – Egypt was the bulwark of the Arab alliance and keen for swift intervention – others had to be convinced.[63] The Assistant Under-Secretary of State – David Gore-Booth – was even sent to Syria, with whom Britain had broken off diplomacy in 1986, in a secret mission to convince the Syrians to take part in the operation.[64] In the end, the only country which remained uncommitted to the coalition was Jordan where there were large protests and burning of British flags in support of Iraq. Nonetheless, Hurd optimistically noted 'But we kept the Jordanians from committing themselves the wrong way even if we could not enlist them as an ally.'[65]

The desire not to appear imperial and to respect local culture had also permeated into implementation by the MoD. As well as planning the operation well before Ramadan, much care was taken to avoid attacks on archaeological, cultural and religious sites. In particular, the Shia holy shrines of Karbala and An-Najaf were regularly photographed to prove that no damage had been caused.[66] Commander-in-Chief General Peter de la Billière, who spoke colloquial Arabic, wrote an information pamphlet for circulation to all troops which included an introduction to the Arabs, their way of life, the importance of religion in Arab culture, tips on how to behave in an Arab society and some basic vocabulary.[67]

The crisis also saw a strong UK–US working relationship, a lesson which had been identified previously but had become increasingly necessary. The Policy Planning Staff declared 'We must keep as close to American decision makers as possible'[68] and it was consistently emphasised that policy should be discussed with allies in Washington before execution.[69] This was made easier by good working relations between Margaret Thatcher and President George Bush as well as between Douglas Hurd and the Secretary of State James Baker. Hurd described the relationship as 'work[ing] together in close confidence as friends'.[70] Anthony Acland, British Ambassador to Washington, noted:

> [the Bush administration] all said to me . . . that when the chips are down there is only one wholly reliable ally in the world, and that is the United Kingdom . . . there were countries which were militarily competent but politically unreliable (I suspect they meant the French), and there were some which were politically reliable but militarily incompetent (like the Egyptians or perhaps, up to a point the Saudis). The only country which was politically reliable and militarily competent was Britain.[71]

In the MoD, working with the trans-Atlantic allies was a necessity because of the coalition. However, one of the most significant lessons identified for the British during Granby echoed those previously identified in 1956: that in the future Britain could not plan major operations without ally support.[72] Implementing the lesson of working together in the past had also earned Britain the privileged position of being the only coalition member to participate in US-led planning. A senior British Brigadier was fully integrated into US Commander-in-Chief General Norman Schwarzkopf's personal planning team of five US officers. A similar arrangement was made for an RAF Wing Commander to be placed within the planning staff of General Horner, Commander of US Central Command (CENTCOM) Air Force.[73] In addition, Air Chief Marshal Sir Patrick Hine, Air Vice Marshal Bill Wratten and de la Billière all helped to prepare and agree the coalition air campaign and Wratten retained the power of veto over all targets.[74] The British Joint Forces Headquarters (JFHQ) in Riyadh was located near to CENTCOM headquarters, allowing close liaison and de la Billière to attend Schwarzkopf's daily briefings.[75] Eventually, around a hundred British officers were placed within the American command system with tactical command passed to American Commanders.[76] Much of the system worked well, facilitated by the use of established NATO procedures and experience. Hine identified:

it is clear that our voice within the councils of the Coalition was much stronger than the scale of our military contribution justified, which reflects the continuation of the special relationship between the UK and the US . . . These ties have been nurtured over a prolonged period and we must do all we can to maintain them in the future.[77]

The only area where joint planning was lacking was between the US and Royal Navies. Although remaining under British command for embargo operations, the Royal Navy was under US command for offensive operations. Three US Navy Task Force Commanders oversaw the operations but with little British consultation. Parry-Evans opined 'the RN's lack of a seat at the planning table for the amphibious phase led to significant US under-estimates of the time that would be required for mine clearance'.[78] The only other time Britain felt excluded from military decision-making was over the calling of the ceasefire. All coalition members were informed rather than consulted and many were surprised at the timing. However, as de la Billière noted, with half a million personnel deployed, 'inevitably, what the Americans did, everybody else really had to go along with'.[79]

Aside from the Americans, the FCO identified the need to gain and maintain broader international and domestic support. It was concluded that this lesson was most likely to be successfully implemented if Britain had specific UN authority and could 'avoid being thought to be acting beyond our UN cover', especially as it was considered that a UK–US led attack without UN authority would produce a backlash from, and in, non-Arab Muslim countries as well as discontent in the British Muslim community.[80] This was, however, in tension with the ideas of Thatcher who was convinced that Article 51 of the UN Charter meant that no further UN authority was required to help the Kuwaitis expel Saddam from their country.[81] Legally, Thatcher was correct but the Americans insisted on pursuing the UN route for legitimacy purposes.[82]

There were also many other diplomatic forums through which Britain negotiated throughout the crisis. These included OPEC, NATO, the European Community (EC) and Western European Union (WEU). Although the EC countries were the first to impose economic sanctions on Iraq, following a special meeting in Rome, the Foreign Secretary later had to block an EC initiative to hold negotiations with Iraq. As the deadline for Iraq's withdrawal from Kuwait approached, a late French initiative, in an attempt to protect France's Iraqi trading relationship, led to a dispute between Paris and London which had to be repaired.

The MoD and FCO also had some difficulties working with coalition nations on the ground. A US CENTCOM report noted 'coalition partners had difficulty keeping pace with the crisis action or time sensitive mode – the learning curve for our planning partners was steep'.[83] In particular, the status of the French forces remained unknown for some time, causing planning headaches whilst their government decided whether to offer outright opposition to Iraq. At a regular meeting of European Union Ambassadors in Riyadh the French Ambassador, Jaques Bernière, bragged that there were more French troops in Saudi Arabia than British troops. 'But Jacques', replied the Italian Ambassador, 'we don't know which way they are facing.' When the French finally committed their forces to the ground assault General Schwarzkopf bemoaned 'going to war with the French is like going duck shooting with an accordion'.[84] However, overall the coalition held. Sweden, who had not taken part in a combat situation since the 1813 Battle of Leipzig, returned to active service and even the Argentineans overlooked past hostilities and arrived to support the British naval flotilla.[85]

Similar to 1958 and 1961, there was also concern over how long support could be maintained, especially given the weight of history. The FCO Policy Planning Staff identified:

> If we became embroiled in a long war, domestic and international opposition would increase even if we had specific UN cover. Comparisons would be drawn with Suez and Vietnam. Parliamentary unity would be threatened. Casualties would mount, and additional deployments would be unpopular.[86]

Consequently, support would be sustained by ensuring the war was as short as possible, achieving defined objectives quickly and efficiently.[87] In addition, the offensive military option was not to be the inevitable option; sanctions, diplomatic negotiations, a coup, assassination, support of alternative leaders and a long-term economic siege backed by a naval blockade were all pursued or considered, and it was hoped that the threat of military action may also be enough to persuade Saddam to reverse his actions.[88]

To help manage domestic opinion, Parliament was recalled from recess for a two day debate on the crisis and a cross-party consensus was managed as it had been by Harold Macmillan. Drawing upon history, Douglas Hurd identified, 'Remembering Suez I felt that it would be wrong to commit British troops to a war denounced by the official opposition' and subsequently 'At home the new Prime Minister and I knew we must do our utmost to keep the opposition on board.'[89] Consequently, a number of meetings took place with Labour leaders and Commons debates were carefully handled, often with orchestrated parliamentary exchanges and Prime Minister's Questions.[90] John Major, who became Prime Minister on 28 November 1990, recalled:

> I sought a cross-party consensus, and was determined to keep Neil Kinnock, as leader of the opposition, and Paddy Ashdown for the Liberal Democrats fully briefed. This was not only prudent in Parliamentary terms, but would also ensure that our servicemen knew there was maximum level of support for the task ahead of them.[91]

He was also aware that history provided no precedent for Granby and further identified the need for good media management:

> This was going to be a different sort of war . . . they were not fighting for home and hearth as in the two great wars of our century. Nor were they fighting for the recovery of a British possession as in the Falklands. They were fighting for something much less tangible: the maintenance of international law.[92]

However, there was a consensus of support and Parliament did not prove difficult despite some hesitation from MPs, such as Denis Healey, who were concerned over the outcome and potential British casualties; this was in stark contrast to President Bush's slim majority in Congress which had to be handled very carefully.[93] In fact, the only time the government suffered significant criticism was over the handling of British citizens in

Kuwait. There were many calls to the FCO complaining that not enough was being done to help British citizens and accusations that this had forced many to attempt their own escape: one forty-nine year old British male, Donald Croskery, was shot dead by Iraqis trying to cross the desert to Saudi Arabia. Criticism increased when British expats were rounded up, detained and used as human shields. Demands for SAS rescue operations were made and a number of elderly statesmen, including former Prime Minister Edward Heath, went against the wishes of the FCO and visited Saddam Hussein to negotiate for the release of the hostages; Heath received equal criticism for negotiating with a tyrant despite returning from Baghdad with a hundred hostages.[94]

In the IC, the predominant difficulty in planning the intervention, echoing the lessons identified from thirty years before, was an ongoing lack of intelligence on the Iraqi President's intentions. With a focus on the Soviet Union, no SIS agents were in a position to obtain access to Saddam Hussein or his close circle of advisers.[95] Furthermore, a combination of a police-state creating fear amongst its population and good Iraqi training in communication security made the ascertaining of intentions challenging.[96] During the Iran–Iraq War the Americans had trained Iraqi military personnel, including providing advice on how to avoid detection by space-based intelligence gathering and ensure secure communications through the use of landlines with fibre-optic cables.[97] Consequently, a system of secure landlines, ironically supplied by a British company, had been installed to allow unmonitored communications and, in the end, the primary source of intelligence on Saddam's intentions came from intercepts of telephone calls made from Saddam to his Ambassador to the UN in New York. These intercepts were relayed from the US National Security Agency to London.[98] Unfortunately, this intelligence was too late to warn of the invasion, by which point the Prime Minister had learned her lesson on Saddam's intentions, 'the important lesson for us was that Saddam Hussein was simply not predictable'.[99] Charles Powell, the Prime Minister's Private Secretary, later identified 'The most difficult type of intelligence to have is that about intentions. In the

Iraqi invasion of Kuwait, we knew where every tank was, but we got his intentions wrong.'[100]

The IC did very little to rectify their lack of knowledge on the dictator or his intentions throughout the campaign, much to the frustration of military Commanders. The Americans knew little more, leaving General Schwarzkopf to state in a briefing that the lack of HUMINT meant he was 'forced to go more by Urint – which is a feeling in the water'.[101] In the end, de la Billière completed his own assessment using a detailed analysis of the Iran–Iraq War and in consultation with the British Embassy in Riyadh. This yielded a character sketch from which key weaknesses were able to be considered and exploited.[102]

However, one lesson on the gathering of HUMINT had been implemented from Corporate. During the Falklands there had been a severe shortage of Spanish speakers but, by the time of Granby, ninety-three British Arabic-speaking personnel and seventy-eight Kuwaiti civilians were deployed to work in hospitals and prisoner of war camps in order to gather as much HUMINT as possible.[103]

Beyond intentions, the IC also had gaps in capability assessments. Whilst there was an existing understanding of the Iraqi Navy and Air Force to conduct maritime operations – as part of intelligence support for the Armilla patrol – little intelligence existed on the strength and efficacy of the Iraqi Army.[104] Any existing intelligence was further confused by the initial appearance of new Iraqi Divisions – a deception by Saddam to persuade the coalition of the existence of a larger Iraqi force.[105] Consequently, the lesson was identified and implemented by establishing thirteen support groups to advise and assist the DIS in the preparation of detailed assessments. By 16 January 1991, 300 new background studies had been issued.[106] However, the process was challenging as a considerable depth of technical knowledge was required on the wide variety of weaponry used by the Iraqis from all over the world. The DIS report acknowledged the lesson to be identified: 'The DIS needs to expand its expertise on weapons systems exported by the west to potential enemies.'[107] The Granby Coordinator went further and suggested that a database of such information should be created to implement the lesson.[108]

One of the specific areas which required immediate assessment was Iraq's non-conventional weapons systems and capabilities in order to inform military requirements for planning. To assess these capabilities, the IC implemented lessons identified from the Iran–Iraq War and Iraq's past use of chemical weapons, as well as existing intelligence assessments, to determine that Iraq had considerable chemical and biological weapons capability and was seeking to develop a nuclear weapon or acquire weapons of mass destruction (WMD) by an extensive procurement network.[109] However, as the campaign progressed, little further intelligence was gathered on these capabilities. Following an International Atomic Energy Agency (IAEA) inspection in November 1990, the JIC noted 'We have no intelligence that would cause us to change our assessment of Iraq's current nuclear capability.'[110]

During the Intervention

Once Granby began, the issue of overflying immediately returned to cause difficulties, a lesson which had been repeatedly identified in past interventions, but implementation was persistently lost between the FCO and MoD. France refused to give priority to RAF flights, whilst Egypt insisted on seventy-two hours' notice for a pre-cleared call sign slot to be allocated.[111] In addition, securing clearance to overfly the Saudis on the way to Bahrain was forgotten until the night of departure. This was exacerbated by the late realisation that the legal status of British forces in Saudi Arabia had not been agreed (this was not finalised until mid-October 1990) and, the night before the launch of the offensive, that Saudi consent had not been given to attack from their territory.[112]

Once British forces landed, the FCO continued to do all it could to avoid accusations of imperialism and implemented this identified lesson by ensuring that Arab culture was respected. Imported magazines had female flesh blacked out, women were forbidden from driving and there was prohibition on pork and alcohol, although local supermarkets tended to stock the basic ingredients for home brewing. Christian worship was done discreetly, on a Friday (the Muslim day of rest) by a Nigerian dentistry lecturer, who was also ordained as a priest, or Army chaplains reclassified as 'morale officers'. The Saudi ban on public music also meant that – despite the presence of nineteen military bands – there were no musical performances and entertainment for off-duty officers was limited to male magicians and comedians; Paul Daniels and Harry Secombe obliged.[113] The FCO and MoD also agreed that it was best that the Prince of Wales make his trip to Saudi Arabia unaccompanied by Princess Diana to avoid negative press around a high profile female and subsequent exploitation of this by Saddam's propaganda machine. Munro stated:

> there were times when we all had to consider what would have been the attitude in 622 – the year of Hijra, when the Prophet Mohammad went from Mecca to Medina – when we tried to decide what line to take ... we did need quite an historical reach-back to back up what was a contemporary war.[114]

In addition, the FCO was careful to manage the media reporting back to Britain, implementing another previously identified lesson. However, the policy was adopted in a new climate; Granby was the first conflict in history in which reporting could no longer be controlled by routing content through military channels because journalists had their own, portable, real-time satellite communications. Ambassador Munro recalled that the strategy was 'maximum briefing material, no matter how trivial, in order to keep the editors' appetite fed'. Much was done by the Embassy in Riyadh to facilitate access for journalists but it was a delicate process and often loopholes or 'blind eyes' had to be negotiated. When the Saudi Embassy in London stopped issuing press visas, journalists were flown by RAF Hercules to Dhahran where they received briefings and were able to observe squadrons on patrol as long as they remained on the airbase. Once they had arrived in the field, difficult journalists were often 'handled'; the unpredictable editor of *The Sunday Times*, Andrew Neil, was promptly sent off to a maritime patrol to divert him out of the way.[115]

From the outset, the MoD had also been keen to manage media relations well. Although this principle had been long established, the lessons specifically referenced only dated back to House of

Commons Defence Committee lessons identified from the Falklands.[116] However, since 1982 a considerable amount of work had been done: plans had been made to meet the PR requirements of all future conflicts with contingency plans including PR annexes. The PR staff had become part of the internal planning process and relationships with editors and senior media staff had been nurtured. A central document had also been produced for quick reference which identified, distributed and retained lessons: 'Proposed Working Arrangements with the Media in time of Tension and War.'[117]

In theatre, over 170 visas were secured for press and over eighty military personnel were responsible for ensuring good relations between the forces and journalists. Tom King held major press conferences in the desert, arriving by tank for added drama, and a number of reporters were attached to major Army formations, Royal Navy ships or RAF detachments.[118] British reporters were fully briefed on the details of the Battle Plan weeks before much of the rest of the military by General Rupert Smith, assessing that a well-informed press – entrusted with confidential information – was less risky than investigative journalists rushing to reveal snippets of discovered information. The generous treatment of the press was appreciated by British journalists as it was in stark contrast to their US counterparts whose military–media relationship 'started at rock bottom and then deteriorated'; a hang-up on both sides from Vietnam.[119]

A further way in which the MoD managed the press was less direct; great care was taken over precision bombing. Targets were diligently selected to minimise civilian casualties and avoid water supplies or sewage installations which could have caused media criticism. Specific military targets were agreed and the care with which the air campaign occurred led the Secretary of State to comment that 'life basically continued in Baghdad normally while key military installations were taken out'.[120]

The good management of the media also improved morale and public support. On 11 January 1991, de la Billière wrote a letter to all of the British newspapers thanking them for their support throughout the campaign. In response the *Daily Star* encouraged the public to bake 'battle cakes', based on a dense fruitcake recipe, to send to the troops.[121] The response was so overwhelming that the delivery of cakes began to hamper the flow of essential military kit.[122] De la Billière later identified:

> In terms of influence on morale, the media are central. If they report adversely, you will get British people either ill-informed or perhaps made fearful, and that will reflect in terms of their communications with the servicemen at the front and have a dramatic impact on morale quickly.[123]

Troop morale was also maintained by the provision of a radio station and a weekly newspaper, *The Sandy Times*.

Throughout the operation FCO and MoD cooperation was successful. Two senior FCO officials were seconded to Joint Headquarters (JHQ) for the duration of the crisis. As in 1961, de la Billière used the Embassy for political advice and senior staff would attend the Embassy's briefing meetings.[124] During the Falklands, de la Billière had identified the need for close cooperation with the FCO's representative on the ground and he implemented this throughout Granby. He later echoed the lesson of Air Marshal Sir Charles Elworthy thirty years earlier by identifying the importance of the close working relationship declaring 'There are important lessons to be reemphasised in this in terms of the necessity of the in theatre British Embassy and military command working closely together in harmony.' The result of clearer communication was a government who supported the military Commanders with 'confidence and firmness'.[125]

Internally, the MoD command structure worked well across the forces but proved more challenging in relation to working with civil servants and ministers. Since 1961, a third tier had been added to the command structure for British operations: HQBFME headed by the Commander-in-Chief, JHQ at High Wycombe commanded by Air Chief Marshal Hine and the MoD under the Minister of Defence, Tom King. JHQ had been added in an endeavour to overcome many of the difficulties previously experienced in operations involving all three services but, although this had been a lesson identified in Vantage, the new system was only implemented from a lesson identified from Corporate twenty years later. Admiral Julian

Oswald noted 'The importance of lessons learnt in 1982 in the Falklands is not lost on people. A lot of good command and control points came out of that campaign and, on the whole, they were well and sensibly picked up.'[126] The relationship between JHQ and HQBFME worked 'excellently' but relations between JHQ and the MoD were often strained.[127] This was partly due to clashes of personality but there was also a feeling that Whitehall bureaucracy was inefficient and lacked urgency.[128] Many at JHQ also felt that there was a disproportionate input by the MoD on decision-making. The Joint Commander reflected 'at times the political imperative (as seen from the MoD) appeared to delay or obfuscate sound military judgement . . . I sometimes felt that I had been given responsibility without the associated authority.'[129] One minister became known as 'the long screwdriver' for too much interference in the construction of the military force, particularly from a naval perspective, leaving the Royal Navy's contribution to Granby less than it would have wished.[130] Following the crisis, this lesson was formally identified and it was recommended that a Defence Secretariat be included within JHQ in the future.[131]

The IC had also been criticised in 1982 by the identification of a failure to work effectively across Whitehall with the FCO and MoD.[132] To implement this lesson Cradock assumed a dual role, attending both the JIC and War Cabinet meetings, and setting up a series of morning meetings to ensure daily intelligence liaison across ministers and intelligence agencies.[133] The Director General of Intelligence, who led DIS, briefed Cabinet daily, paralleling the Chief of Defence Intelligence's briefing to the MoD. He also attended the JIC as well as carrying out briefing tours in the Gulf, sharing intelligence assessments with Egypt, Saudi Arabia, UAE, Bahrain, Qatar and Oman.[134] The implementation of the lesson was successful and after the operation Parry-Evans wrote 'the general assessment by the Cabinet Office of the operation of the Government machinery during the crisis is that it worked well . . . care was taken from the start to take account of the lessons identified in 1982'.[135]

The identified lesson of cost management remained prominent too, despite Thatcher's exclusion of the Chancellor of the Exchequer – John Major and then Norman Lamont – from the

War Cabinet to avoid any objections about money.[136] Early on in the operation, FCO Economic Advisors worked on a paper on the economic consequences of intervention.[137] It was agreed that 'for reasons of cost' Western forces should be temporary and by January 1991 it was recommended that means of securing compensation be taken out of Iraqi revenues.[138] Douglas Hurd recalled:

> A sub-theme of my foreign visits at this time could have become embarrassing. Long gone was the British tradition of financing our allies in time of war. In 1991 we expected well-to-do friends to finance us . . . I begged my way around the world.[139]

In total, Granby cost approximately £2.5 billion of which £2 billion was negotiated in cash contributions from other countries. In addition, assistance in kind – including transport, accommodation, medical services, fuel and food – was received from eighteen different countries.[140] Saudi Arabia, as the host nation, provided much assistance[141] and a post-Granby report concluded the 'benefits of conducting operations from the forecourt of the world's largest petrol station should not be overlooked'.[142]

The problem for the MoD was that the Civil Secretariat, which had previously been used to monitor spending, was abolished in the 1980s. In the first few months of the war the British Army provided credit cards for spending, but it was using them without any form of restriction or accounting. This meant that, unlike other European allies, when the Saudi's offered to pay Britain's bill, only around 70 per cent of costs had been officially recorded and could be compensated. After the intervention the National Audit Office and the House of Commons Committee of Public Accounts considered the MoD's costs and financial management during Granby and a number of lessons were identified; the first troops in Bosnia the following year were accompanied by a Civil Secretariat.[143]

Other previously identified lessons on equipment and logistics were also forgotten. The poor handling of cargo left many troops without sufficient equipment and quickly earned the British the nickname 'the Borrowers'.[144] Some of the equipment which did arrive was unsuitable, as it had been in 1961. Much of the weaponry was designed for counteracting the Soviet threat. Logistics vehicles had also all been procured for operations in Europe and lacked cross-country capabilities,[145] whilst suits were inappropriately designed for hot climates.[146] Puma engine flying hours were reduced from 400 to forty due to sand getting into the engine and causing blade abrasion, something which was of particular concern to Thatcher who recalled the events of 1980 and the failed US–Iranian hostage rescue attempt, Operation Eagle Claw.[147] The Defence Committee identified 'there was no clear basis for provisioning, and several evident deficiencies, such as the absence of desert clothing and footwear'.[148]

Special Forces suffered with particularly poor equipment due to their recent focus on counterterrorism operations. Special Forces aircraft could not support twenty-four hour, all weather, cross-border operations, which prevented deployment. Helicopter support was limited to 30 per cent of the duration and there were difficulties in long range land vehicles as well as a real-time communication system being unattainable.[149] These challenges also occurred during the worst weather conditions in the region for thirty years – including sandstorms, fog and nights so cold that diesel fuel froze – and much has been written about the results of such failings, particularly by members of the now infamous SAS patrol under the call sign Bravo Two Zero.[150]

In addition, the British did not have enough stockpiles of ammunition and £260 million worth of ammunition had to be borrowed from NATO allies. Nor were there enough spares available, blamed largely on years of 'shop window' procurement policy and budget cutbacks. This led to double difficulties with the use of the unreliable Challenger I battle tank. At any one time over 75 per cent of tanks were under repair or out of service – despite Margaret Thatcher summoning the Head of Vickers and the Defence Secretary to swear their reliability for the Gulf. The result was that the MoD made Vickers produce more engines, so that every tank had around four engines spare. In the meantime, engines had to be removed from operational tanks in Germany and sent to the Gulf.[151] The situation was made worse by the political requirement to provide ammunition, spare parts and weapons systems to the Saudis, Kuwaitis, Egyptians and Syrians in order to encourage their participation in the coalition – causing another disagreement between the MoD and JHQ.[152] However, this time a lesson was to be learned and following the end of Granby a Battlefield Equipment Reliability Return system was introduced to monitor equipment and spares in the future.[153]

Besides these lessons, the Gulf War threw up some new challenges, for which there was no historical learning available, due to the advances in technology. In particular, the MoD was not fully prepared for chemical or biological warfare and no relevant defence policy was in place. An Iraqi newspaper had boasted 'Iraq's arsenal contains surprises which will astonish our enemies' and the British were aware of considerable Iraqi chemical and biological capabilities.[154] The IC had also assessed that Saddam was seeking to develop a nuclear weapon or acquire WMD.[155] Many of the IC assessments turned out to be correct with the UN Special Commission (UNSCOM) on Iraq confirming the existence of mustard agents, nerve agents, a programme on anthrax and botulinum toxin and chemical delivery systems in the forms of bombs, artillery, rocket launchers and missile warheads.[156] However, the IC were unable to provide important details surrounding the weapons; no chemical warfare survey had been produced to establish plant locations, nor was there immediate reconnaissance capability to detect locations storing such weapons. In addition, some capabilities were overstated – the Special Commission found no evidence of weaponised biological agents – whilst the effort and scale of progress with nuclear weapons had been understated.

However, the IC warning did enable back channel diplomacy to provide Saddam Hussein with unmistakeable warnings about immediate and catastrophic consequences for Iraq if any such attacks occurred.[157] It also allowed greater precautions to be taken within the military against the risks of such attacks. There had been much research into, and procurement of, protective clothing, detection, immunisation and decontamination equipment as countermeasures. There was also planning to avoid attacking targets which may release radiation, extensive preparations to deal with victims and training for putting on protective clothing and apparatus.[158] In addition, the MoD offered a vaccine to all troops on a voluntary basis. This precaution soon proved to be controversial as three months after the inoculation most immune systems collapsed and there have been many accusations of links between the vaccination and Gulf War syndrome, a chronic multi-symptom disorder. Furthermore, most battlefield vehicles were fitted with a series of seals, air filters and conditioners to protect passengers from outside contamination. However, such measures were less effective on older equipment; on Striker vehicles the gun could not be fired or reloaded without breaking this vital seal.[159] Following the crisis the MoD sought to improve some of the shortcomings in awareness and training for chemical and biological warfare through the revision and extension of relevant training courses.[160]

A new lesson was also identified during the operation, again brought about by rapid changes in technology. On 16 December 1990, three briefcases and a laptop computer containing Britain's war plans were stolen from the boot of a car. The papers were recovered within a few hours but the laptop remained missing until 7 January 1991 when the self-proclaimed patriotic thief returned the item, although it remained in the MoD post room for some time before its significance was realised.[161] The event led to the identification and implementation of lessons; immediately new rules were enforced for the handling of such data and all fixed hard-disk laptop computers were withdrawn.[162]

In the IC, during the intervention, work was done to counteract the lack of HUMINT by relying on IMINT, as had also been the case in 1961. However, although there had been much emphasis in the past on maintaining IMINT, capability was limited and before hostilities began the British were dependent upon US satellite systems. Once hostilities commenced, the MoD also relied upon other American equipment, including two Joint Surveillance and Target Attack Radar System (JSTARS) prototypes, which provided processed, real-time, intelligence on moving targets.[163] This proved invaluable as UK Midge drones were unreliable; Major General Rupert Smith identified to the Defence Committee that the Midge often failed to return or returned with unusable imagery.[164]

Instead, the IC achieved air reconnaissance primarily through six Tornado GR1As, a new addition for the RAF as implementation of lessons identified from the Falklands.[165] However, the IC had a severe shortage of photographic interpreters (PI) and therefore also relied upon US analysis. The DIS identified the lesson for the future: 'Crisis planning must take account of limitations in PI availability and the need to depend in large part on the output of US Agencies.'[166] The lack of up-to-date IMINT was further exacerbated by the difference in grids and reference system datums used around the world; it was during Granby that international agreement was made to use the new World Geodetic System. This rendered all French maps, for example, unusable based on the different Global Positioning System (GPS) receiver settings used by forces.[167]

Similar difficulties occurred in securing intelligence on Battle Damage Assessments (BDA). The IC did not possess appropriate intelligence gathering equipment for BDA and coalition staff became so overloaded with raw intelligence for analysis that the DIS struggled to get tactical BDA in a timely manner.[168] The IC identified two lessons: firstly, that the British were reliant upon the US as the only coalition member with large scale BDA capability and, secondly, that a British BDA methodology was required, aligning with the Americans.[169]

More broadly there was difficulty in the timely analysis, distillation and dissemination of all forms of intelligence. SIGINT, for example, was collected from Nimrod R1s, GCHQ's listening base in Cyprus and the US space borne capability which combined to provide huge quantities of raw data to GCHQ.[170] In addition, the CIA alone sent 215 tons of IMINT to CENTCOM and after five days it was advised that there was not the capacity to handle the deluge of intelligence.[171] As a result, only a small percentage of available intelligence was analysed and even less was disseminated to the field, let alone disseminated in a timely fashion. De La Billière identified to the Defence Committee 'there was so much [intelligence] available in the end that it was very difficult to cope with it and to extract from it the detail which was required at lower command levels'.[172]

Dissemination problems, which were also present throughout Corporate, were compounded by a combination of the lack of secure communication links, document classification and operational security.[173] The DIS noted 'the limited number of secure voice links to US agencies proved a particular hindrance', exacerbated by the American move to a new system which it had previously refused to release to the UK.[174] Many intelligence assessments were classified in a way that required sanitation before being sent to

HQBFME, leaving the Middle East Current Intelligence Group and JHQ knowing more than those in theatre.[175] This lesson had previously been identified during Vantage but was re-identified by the MoD thirty years later.[176] A similar problem also occurred within the coalition where a wide application of US NOFORN (no foreigners) and UK EYES A (UK citizens only) classifications of intelligence caused sharing difficulties and was only solved by a direct intervention from General Schwarzkopf.[177] Following the end of hostilities, there was wide identification of lessons to be learned and procedures for the distillation and dissemination of intelligence were reviewed.[178]

Furthermore, throughout the campaign the IC retained a close working relationship with the US as it had done in previous operations. Early on, the JIC had worked with the CIA to provide estimates on Iraq WMD.[179] Similar to the MoD, working together in the past had also earned the British a privileged position. Air Chief Marshal Sir Patrick Hine confirmed 'The ready availability to us of high-quality US intelligence reflected the mutual trust and rapport established between our intelligence communities over the years.' In addition 'there appeared to be no constraints on the flow of US information'.[180] In fact, the close relationship led the British to believe that they were not only fully informed of national assessments in Washington, but were able to influence that assessment. A British Defence Intelligence Liaison Staff was established in Washington with mirrored Defense Intelligence Agency (DIA) and CIA representatives in London to ensure close communications between the capitals. However, a new lesson was identified: that working with the Americans was not only desirable but had become essential. US agencies had much larger staffs than the UK and the existence of unified geographic Commands meant that – unlike the UK – each had a significant, permanent intelligence component focused on an area of the world.[181] One British analyst advised 'Over 90 per cent of what was in my reports was American material. If we didn't have the Americans, I'd have nothing to write about . . . Without them, we'd be little better than Belgium.'[182]

Working with other ally intelligence agencies during Granby was also important.[183] Early on in Granby 'C', the Head of the

SIS, went to Saudi Arabia to cement the British–Saudi intelligence relationship and compare notes on Saddam with his counterpart Prince Turki. A British Intelligence Corps liaison was also established within the headquarters of the Commander of the Arab Forces and the Saudis ran aerial reconnaissance as part of their contribution to the coalition.[184] Throughout the campaign, liaison visits were made to the Gulf, Europe and Washington. In addition a weekly – and later daily – intelligence summary was released by NATO to Arab allies. The DIS lessons report noted 'European and Arab participation in Coalition forces and the political importance of [redacted] proved the value of connections established by the DIS with many other national intelligence agencies.'[185] Parry-Evans agreed and identified the key lesson was 'The importance of the UK/US intelligence link cannot be overemphasised, but many of our intelligence links with a wide range of countries were of particular value, pointing the need to maintain and foster such links.'[186]

IC psyops also developed during the intervention. Even though psyops had proved of value before Suez, when Iraq invaded Kuwait British psyops capability consisted of one man at the Intelligence Corps training centre. Eventually this number reached twelve, a far cry from the US' 4th Psyops Group of several hundred personnel. Nonetheless, the SIS smuggled videos and cassettes into Iraq which advised that Saddam was leading the country to disaster. A radio station, Free Iraq, was funded which incited people to revolt, but due to Saudi sensitivities had to be broadcast from the air rather than Saudi territory. Instead, a secret radio station in Saudi Arabia masqueraded as Radio Kuwait and broadcast false news, including that Kuwait City had been recaptured by the allies causing a number of Iraqi units to flee prematurely.[187] Psyops were also focused upon Iraqi troops through leafleting which warned against fighting and offered safe conduct passes for those who surrendered. With the decision not to fly into enemy territory before the offensive began, 25,000 leaflets were first sent by hot air balloon. During the war, leaflets were more successfully distributed than they had been in Musketeer; 27 million leaflets were dropped on Iraqi units and many soldiers who promptly surrendered were found clutching a psyops safe conduct pass.[188]

After the Intervention

Since 1961, the FCO had experienced a few changes. The House of Commons Foreign Affairs Committee was established in 1979 to scrutinise FCO policy which encouraged accountability – and in turn self-reflection, including the identification of lessons. However, the committee itself did not offer much in the way of contribution to the learning process. It examined the Gulf War on two occasions: in October 1990 and at the end of the conflict in 1991. The first session acted as a fact-finding mission but did not discuss any lessons from history or attempt to identify lessons from the actions of the FCO.[189] The second session reached a number of conclusions but these were focused upon summarising actions, offering approval to policy or supporting declarations, not reflecting upon lesson identification.[190]

Nonetheless, internally, the FCO had begun to reflect upon interventions. Although the FCO confirmed that no lessons reports were written during Granby, following British withdrawal, a conference was organised with all of the Middle East Heads of Mission to review the recent events.[191] No minutes from the meeting remain[192] but a Chairman's Steering Brief was circulated in advance which identified three lessons from the experience.[193] The first lesson related to Gulf state security, identifying ineffective defence and that non-aggression pacts between regional states alone did not provide security. The historical examples of the 1975 Algiers agreements between Iraq and Iran and the 1989 non-aggression pact between Iraq and Saudi Arabia were particularly referenced. The second lesson focused upon arms control and non-proliferation, identifying that the Gulf Cooperation Council (GCC) would at best provide only partial protection from WMD and long range delivery systems. The third lesson identified was 'that a serious effort must be made to break the Arab/Israel logjam'.[194] During the conflict Iraq had attacked Israel with Scud missiles in the hope of drawing it into the war and recapturing some Arab support.

The Steering Brief also provided a number of key conclusions, one of which remains redacted. The six conclusions identified were: to support the establishment of security arrangements for the GCC, restore stability in Iraq, support the US initiative on the Arab–Israel conflict, continue to improve relations with Iran and Syria, restore the relationship with Jordan and maintain contact with the PLO, and, finally, 'we should begin serious consideration of ways to reduce our dependence on oil'.[195] These identified lessons were subsequently implemented to different extents but there was no follow-up process in place to ensure implementation, further distribution or retention of lessons. Furthermore, there was little else written on learning, and no official history – although the FCO and MoD did cooperate in the publication of a more general history written by the Central Office of Information.[196]

Despite the success of the intervention, there were questions after withdrawal as to whether British forces had done enough. However, the lessons identified from history informed the US and British decision not to depose Saddam. In August 1990, the FCO prophetically assessed that, if Saddam was removed or killed by multinational forces, 'There would be an upsurge of popular nationalist and anti-Western sentiment in Iraq, probably including violence against Western interests. Possibly an upsurge of Islamic fundamentalist sentiment too.' If Saddam stepped down voluntarily it was still considered to be a difficult situation: 'There is no prospect of Western style democratic regime emerging internally in the short-term: there is simply no democratic infrastructure or tradition, and very powerful anti-democratic forces.'[197] Furthermore, the FCO was keen not to become involved in any form of occupation. Margaret Thatcher had long warned of not letting Britain's arm get caught in Iraq's mangle whilst the Foreign Secretary had stressed that the British had no right to decide Iraq's leadership.[198] Alan Munro identified a number of historical lessons which informed all of these decisions:

> there were the lessons of our own experience in the Twenties, Thirties and Forties of an association – tutelage association with the government of Iraq. Iraq is not a homogeneous political society – it is split three ways . . . [If we sought] to establish an alternative government of reconciliation and recovery in Iraq, I rather doubt if we would have got away with it.[199]

There were also other complications: the UN mandate was limited and in a post-Cold War era establishing its legitimacy was vital. Upon reflection, offering a warning of what was to come in 2003, John Major advised:

> If the nations who had gone to war on the basis of international law were themselves to break that law, what chance would there have been in the future of order rather than chaos? What authority in the future would the great nations have against law-breakers if they themselves broke the law and exceeded the United Nations mandate? They would never have trusted us again.[200]

In the MoD, a wide range of post-Granby lessons reports were produced – as they had been in 1961 – with major studies on planning, equipment effectiveness, finances and budgeting, communication and information systems, logistics, withdrawal, intelligence, the use of scientists and military survey as well as a number of more minor papers.[201] Lessons were identified at unit level, passed upwards through the chain of command into overall reports for land, air and sea, endorsed by high command and then by the MoD.[202] For many reports lower ranking servicemen were interviewed, which meant incorporating a new spectrum of experience and opinion into the learning process.[203] 'Wash up' conferences were held, with the RAF hosting a one day event at Cranwell with all Commanders as well as Senior Staff Officers.[204] Furthermore, individual investigations occurred for specific events – including the tragic shooting of nine British servicemen by an American A10[205] – and despatches, including lesson identification, were written by Air Chief Marshal Sir Patrick Hine and Commander-in-Chief Peter de la Billière.[206]

Following the end of hostilities Tom King told the House of Commons Defence Committee:

> There is a very extensive exercise going on, which will continue, to make sure that we have learned the lessons from this whole period of conflict. It is very extensive in that it involves all the services, all the arms, a whole range of different lessons . . . there are going to be some very, very interesting lessons to learn.[207]

The Defence Committee concluded 'The Ministry has gone to some lengths to discover and analyse the lessons of Operation Granby and monitor their implementation . . . the evidence suggests that the arrangements have been broadly effective.'[208] However, noticeably some of the strategic questions about chemical, biological and nuclear war, or the failure of the Kuwaiti defence after thirty years of British training, were not addressed.

The MoD also had lessons identified by external bodies. The National Audit Office examined the movement of personnel, equipment and stores to and from the Gulf and concluded that there were difficulties in handling priorities and tracking freight.[209] In fact, 228 aircraft pallets, worth £680,000, and eighty shipped containers were unaccounted for at the end of Granby, with a further 2,800 containing unknown contents.[210] One RAF Group Captain drew upon these identified lessons in a plea for more learning from history. Group Captain Neville Parton explained that during the preparation for Operation Torch, in the Second World War, tools and spares were packed into containers with a code placed on the outside. For security reasons the list that identified the code number was included as a secret annex to the operation order, with a limited distribution. As a result, when items landed on the beach, the contents and planned destination of the containers were unknown, leading to weeks of delays for equipment. Twenty years later, in 1961, one report from Vantage identified a long, classified, often incorrect, coding list for containers resulting in over 130 containers being unnecessarily opened to find cooking equipment. By the time of the Gulf War, teams worked for months trying to identify thousands of unmarked containers, making it quicker to get spare parts from Europe than from within the country.[211] Following the National Audit Office identification, the lesson was finally implemented and the MoD announced the introduction of new tracking systems including bar coding and other automatic identification systems.[212]

More generally, the Defence Committee had been scrutinising the actions of the MoD, providing a new method of learning, since 1979. In response to Operation Granby the committee produced two substantial reports focused on lessons: *Preliminary Lessons of Operation Granby* and *Implementation of Lessons*

Learned from Operation Granby.[213] This was an additional learning process which had been used after Corporate and made the identification and implementation of lessons widely available for public reading and scrutiny. Consequently, not only was the input into lesson identification becoming more democratic, through the interviewing of all ranks, so was the distribution of lessons.

The second report revealed that a new process was in place in the MoD to ensure lesson implementation. In March 1991, Air Chief Marshal Sir David Parry-Evans was appointed Granby Coordinator to prepare a work plan detailing all the tasks to be addressed, all the individuals and groups responsible for their progression and target dates for their completion.[214] Parry-Evans produced a full report in December 1991 and in early 1992 a small cell was established to consolidate identified lessons into one document to ensure implementation. All lessons were allocated an 'action manager' who reported to the two-star officer responsible for that area and the Defence Staff monitored progress.[215] A six-monthly audit on the process of implementing equipment lessons was also established and the responsibility for ongoing monitoring of implementation was given to the Director of Defence Policy, Margaret Aldred, who had also been responsible for implementing lessons from Corporate.[216]

The Defence Committee also questioned whether there was any benefit of examining the lessons of implementation from the Falklands. Committee member Bruce George asked:

> We have gone through this process before, inquiring into the lessons of the Falklands, and I wonder if there is any scope for an inquiry into the lessons learned from the Falklands, and I wonder if there is any scope for an inquiry into lessons learned from how to learn lessons . . . Are you satisfied that the process of implementing lessons of the Falklands was adequate, and are there lessons from that exercise that might be helpful in gaining full value for diminished resources in learning the lessons of the Gulf operation?[217]

Unfortunately, nothing further came of the inquiry and there remained no formal process on how to learn lessons for some time. In addition, budgetary restraints continued to hamper lesson implementation. Even learning of the stretch of forces during Granby did not prevent their further reduction, with British forces in Germany reduced from 56,000 during the Cold War to 23,000 by 1994 and the number of tanks reduced from 450 during the Gulf War to 286. Similarly, whilst there was some investment in the RAF – for example in the air transport fleet – reductions in defence spending meant that a number of the lessons identified in Granby would be re-identified in the lessons reports from Kosovo eight years later. These included difficulties with secure air-to-air communications and the reliance on the US leading to a lack of timely BDA.[218]

After 1991 the MoD began incorporating relevant contractors into the learning process, particularly manufacturers of military equipment. Whilst lessons were discussed with manufacturers during deployment, the MoD also invited companies to discuss lessons identified in more detail after the operation to ensure implementation. Furthermore, in July 1992, the MoD attended a supplier's conference and made a presentation specifically on the lessons identified from Granby.[219]

By 1991, the MoD had also become more involved in lesson distribution and identifying lessons from others. Conversations were held with allies on relevant issues and a British lesson identification report was prepared for distribution to both NATO and the US.[220] This relationship was reciprocal and the US Defence Department shared its classified report – which was prepared for Congress – with the MoD.[221] The Granby Coordinator also visited the Pentagon and established principles for the exchange of lessons,[222] whilst NATO identified a number of lessons which were shared with the alliance.[223]

Throughout Granby, the MoD was aware that many of its deficiencies had not been completely exposed due to the Iraqi's lack of fight and swift surrender. This had not been expected as Iraq possessed the fourth largest permanent Army in the world and Saddam had recalled the Popular Army, a militia of several hundred thousand men.[224] In addition, the Iraqi Air Force offered no retaliation and the lack of resistance was aptly illustrated when one unit even surrendered to a surprised group of journalists. In fact, the Iraqi Army became so desperate to prevent further surrenders that they banned the wearing of white items of clothing.[225] In addition, the British forces were again fortunate, as they had been in 1956, 1958 and 1961, to be relieved from any long-term responsibilities, this time by the UN. The deployment of UN troops to support operations meant the coalition was not subjected to protracted fighting, peace-building or stability operations but could withdraw from the region.

Across the IC, at the end of the campaign, the DIS conducted a major study on intelligence support to Granby.[226] In addition, the Granby Coordinator and the Defence Committee identified a number of relevant lessons for the IC resulting in lessons being implemented. Many new strategies were developed and the organisation and procedure of intelligence was revisited.[227] To increase the sharing of intelligence across different users and services, an intelligence division was created within Permanent Joint Headquarters (PJHQ) at Northwood.[228] In addition, to improve the distillation and dissemination of intelligence, all assets were centralised under the Chief of Defence Intelligence, whilst an officer was appointed to coordinate and increase intelligence training including running full scale military exercises.[229]

Nonetheless, as part of the MoD, these reports were focused upon defence intelligence, with only a few lessons identified for the wider IC, and there is little evidence of similar reports or self-reflection across other intelligence agencies. Towards the end of the operation, the IC used identified lessons from the Falklands to assess the likelihood of an Iraqi uprising against Saddam Hussein:

> An assumption that we made, not simply an assumption of convenience, but one of serious calculation, was that – rather as in the case of the post Falklands situation – Iraqi public opinion would have reasserted itself – with support from elements within Iraq's still very powerful Army, and would have overthrown their regime; the Galtieri syndrome if you like.[230]

However, by April 1991 it was clear that a successful uprising was increasingly unlikely and yet there was no reflection upon the assumptions of this assessment.[231] It was not until 2004, when Lord Butler conducted an official review of intelligence on WMD, that assessments were revisited, questioned and lessons identified. One such lesson included that assessments of Iraq's chemical weapon stock had been based upon the false assumption that no weapons had been leftover from the Iran–Iraq War.[232]

The IC also underwent a number of changes following Granby, but these were the result of entering the post-Cold War era – including disputes over IC legality, oversight and fiscal management – rather than lessons identified from the Gulf War. Several reviews quickly got underway; the Cabinet Office's 'Review of protective security', the Permanent Secretary of Defence's 'Review of intelligence requirements and resources', two separate reviews on GCHQ and three on counterterrorism.[233] The Permanent Secretary's review also sparked an internal SIS review leading to a 'Christmas massacre' which saw the comprehensive retirement of MI6's Board of Directors to be replaced by a younger generation.[234] In addition, Britain's first legislative intelligence oversight body was established, the Intelligence and Security Committee, and in 1994 the ongoing existence of MI5 and MI6 was officially recognised in the Intelligence Services Act, bringing forth a new era of scrutiny. As a result, the IC was already involved in implementing much broader lessons, leaving the lessons identified from Granby largely ignored.

Granby Learning

The operation in the Gulf revealed that lessons identified from Vantage had long been forgotten. Although a wide variety of historical events were drawn upon, the events of 1961 were not referenced whereas those of 1982 remained ever present. The FCO also focused upon Britain's history of imperialism and the operation in Korea for lesson identification whilst the Foreign Secretary identified lessons from the experience of Korea and Suez and the Prime Minister drew upon Suez and the Falklands. Thatcher and Bush also regularly analogised Saddam Hussein to Adolf Hitler and warned that a lack of response would be akin to the appeasement of the 1930s. In contrast, by the time John Major arrived to the Premiership he was convinced that history provided few lessons for Granby. Such debates only solidify the idea of subjectivity in learning from history. In the individual sphere, the role of Thatcher and her identified lessons from appeasement, Musketeer and Corporate, in combination with her power of personality were crucial for the British response. The Policy Planning Staff also offered a number of identified lessons on the requirement to limit British action in the region and respect the UN mandate. Unfortunately, a lack of institutional implementation or retention of these lessons would lead them to be easily disregarded by government in 2003.

In the MoD, lessons identified from the last major campaign, Corporate, remained the primary focus, ignoring other relevant experience, including the last major coalition campaign – Korea – or Vantage. In fact, despite the large learning process in place in 1961, many of the same lessons were re-identified thirty years later – including the necessity of working with the Americans and the benefit of working with the local Embassy – or had only been implemented as a result of lessons being re-identified during Corporate. This demonstrated an over-reliance on learning in the individual sphere and resonated with the old maxim that the military were always fighting the previous war.

For the IC, learning from history was limited to the identification of lessons from the Iran–Iraq War to assess Iraq's chemical and biological weapons capability. Some lessons which had been formally identified from Corporate were implemented in the institutional sphere, perhaps because these emerged as part of a public report – the external review conducted by Lord Franks – thus forcing a response. In fact, the analysis of chemical and biological weapons would not be examined again for lesson identification until the IC was forced to respond to the Butler external review conducted in 2004. However, a number of lessons identified from Corporate had not been learned, including issues surrounding the dissemination of intelligence.

The emphasis upon learning from history had, however, begun to change across all three institutions. New external methods of scrutiny, through increased media accessibility and coverage, Parliamentary Committees and extraordinary inquiries, forced attention towards learning lessons and the institutions responded accordingly. In the FCO, post-crisis reflection had begun through the holding of a conference, although there is no evidence of following up identified lessons with implementation or distribution. There is also no record of the conference which would have retained lessons and the Foreign Affairs Committee proved much less concerned with ensuring lessons were identified and implemented than the Defence Committee.

In the MoD, the learning process had developed the most significantly. Lesson identification had been extended to external sources of critique – including the National Audit Office, Committee of Public Accounts and Defence Committee – which each proved rigorous in their approach. There was also an increased emphasis placed upon lesson implementation, by both the MoD and Defence Committee, whilst lesson distribution had extended to the sharing of lessons with allies and relevant contractors. The learning process had also become more transparent through the Defence Committee, and more democratic, by including a range of ranks in the process of lesson identification. However, there was still no formal document within the MoD on how lessons should be learned and economic restrictions for implementation were instilled through the 'Options for change' defence review.[235] Between 1990 and 2002 defence spending reduced by more than 20 per cent – going from around 4 per cent of gross domestic product (GDP) to 2½ per cent.

At the same time, across all three institutions, there was recognition of the importance of history to current operations in limiting or empowering British actions. In particular, all three institutions acknowledged that Britain's history of imperialism required increased sensitivity, whilst a history of working with the Americans had earned the British a privileged position in US-led coalitions.

The Gulf War also led to the identification of new lessons for the future. For the FCO, the most significant new lesson was that Saddam Hussein could not be trusted. For the MoD, the new lessons were that Britain could no longer run large scale operations without ally support and needed to be prepared for operations against an enemy with chemical and biological weapons. In the IC, the new lessons included the limitations of SIGINT when fighting a well trained Army, and that working with the Americans was essential for increasing collection and assessment capability. Many of these lessons would remain important, especially as the operation had not solved the problem of an aggressive Iraq long term. Percy Cradock identified:

> The underlying question remained, however: how to deal with post-war Iraq? We had to recognize that Saddam had survived and was probably there to stay ... Means had to be found to reassure his neighbours, to maintain long-term pressure on him and prevent him developing his more dangerous weapons.[236]

This challenge would be revisited over the next twelve years as, despite the removal of Iraqi forces, Kuwait remained apprehensive and pessimistic about its position.[237] There were also several scares which led to the prompt return of British troops to Saudi Arabia and in the long term the stage was set for the invasion of Iraq in 2003 when the rigour of the lessons identified, implemented, retained and distributed from the Gulf War would be truly tested.

6 Afghanistan Part Two – Iraq 2003–9

> I would stick to how we come up with a military and political plan that is likely to be successful; how we get the necessary support; and how we set it up properly, with Afghanistan as the model.
> *(Jonathan Powell advising Tony Blair before a meeting with George W. Bush, 28 March 2002)*[1]

At 8:46 EST on 11 September 2001 hijacked American Airlines Flight 11 was flown into the North Tower of the World Trade Centre in New York City. A second plane, United Airline Flight 175, hit the South Tower less than twenty minutes later. By 9:40 a third plane had crashed into the Pentagon in Arlington, Virginia, home of the US Department of Defence and less than four kilometres from the White House. A fourth plane came down in Shanksville, Pennsylvania, after passengers overcame the hijackers. These events marked the worst ever terrorist attack on American soil: 2,753 people died in New York, 184 in Arlington and forty in Pennsylvania. The events changed the international environment overnight; security became America's utmost priority and it lost all tolerance for countries posing any form of national security threat. Despite occurring across the Atlantic, the attacks were also felt in Britain. There were sixty-seven Britons killed, more than the Lockerbie bombing or the 7/7 attacks that would take place in 2005.

The hijackers were nineteen members of al-Qaeda and the US' initial response to the attacks focused on Afghanistan, where the leader of the terrorist group – and mastermind of the hijackings, Osama Bin Laden – was believed to be hiding. On 7 October 2001, the war against Afghanistan began with UK and US aerial bombings. However, President George W. Bush soon turned his attention to Iraq. Iraq had long been a thorn in the side of the West, ever since President George H. Bush had called a ceasefire on the Gulf War and refused to depose the regime of Saddam Hussein. The terms of the ceasefire included an Iraqi obligation to destroy, remove or render harmless all of its WMD under the supervision of a UN weapons inspection team (the United Nations Special Commission – UNSCOM), but Saddam remained unco-operative and obstructive throughout the 1990s.[2]

When 9/11 happened, the JIC was quick to assess that Iraq was not involved. However, in the wake of the events, issues of terrorism and WMD became conflated, with concerns raised that Saddam could share his weapons with al-Qaeda. On 29 January 2002, the President addressed the Capitol for the State of the Union Address and accused three states of helping terrorism and seeking WMD, labelling them an 'axis of evil': North Korea, Iran and Iraq. Despite intelligence assessments concluding that Iraq had no significant links to al-Qaeda its card was marked.[3] By October 2002, President Bush had persuaded Congress to move the War on Terror beyond Afghanistan. They authorised the removal of Saddam's regime as a pre-emptive strike to prevent further proliferation and minimise the possibility of any WMD being passed to terrorist organisations. In November, the UN unanimously adopted Security Council Resolution 1441 which demanded Iraq's compliance with the UN Monitoring, Verification and Inspection Commission (UNMOVIC) – the successor of UNSCOM – and Britain commenced contingency planning for a military operation. During the beginning of 2003, British forces began to be deployed. At the same time the UK, US and Spain worked to draft a second resolution to authorise military intervention for non-cooperation, but it soon became clear that France intended to use its veto. Consequently, on 17 March 2003, the British Cabinet agreed to join the US, without a UN mandate, in a military 'coalition of the willing' to topple Saddam from power. This was a coalition of thirty-nine other countries, none of which was Arab.

In the early hours of 20 March 2003 Operation Telic – Operation Iraqi Freedom in the US – began with air strikes. By late evening the ground campaign had also begun with 40 and 42

Commando Royal Marines seizing the Al Faw peninsular. It was the largest military operation since Granby with a similar number of personnel deployed in approximately half the time; 46,000 personnel, nineteen warships, fourteen Royal Fleet Auxiliary vessels, 15,000 vehicles, 115 fixed-wing aircraft and 100 helicopters were all deployed. Although major combat operations ended on 30 April 2003, with the set-up of the Coalition Provisional Authority (CPA) as a transitional government, British forces remained in Iraq for six years trying to build peace, with some members remaining even longer to train Iraqis. In total 148,990 individual Armed Forces personnel were deployed and 179 lost their lives.[4]

Planning the Intervention

Despite considerable discussion of intervention in the run-up to the Iraq War, the FCO was still surprised by the decision and timing of the military operation. Although intense negotiations with the US and UN meant that the events of 2003 were less unexpected than those of 1956 or 1990, the Head of the Defence Secretariat for Iraq, David Johnson, noted 'Many diplomats couldn't believe it would ever come to war, and behaved accordingly.'[5] This was partly because diplomats had worked hard on a policy of 'smart sanctions' – a redesign of sanctions to control military and WMD items, whilst avoiding the negative impact of sanctions on the Iraqi people – and had a firm commitment to achieving a second UN resolution. There was also widespread suspicion that Saddam would become more cooperative towards weapons inspectors once he realised the extent of the rising tensions.[6]

In addition, the FCO had repeatedly warned of the huge risks of intervention. Briefs were presented which identified many of the same concerns raised during Granby: the complexities of Iraqi society, the instinct for revenge, the lack of security and that democracy installation was unlikely to be successful.[7] Even lessons identified from Suez were revisited. The FCO Director of Middle East and North Africa, Edward Chaplin, advised the Foreign Secretary 'we risk a repeat of the Suez debacle, which apart from its short-term effects (e.g. sweeping away the Hashemite regime in Iraq) changed Arab popular opinion towards Britain for a generation'.[8]

Between 2002 and 2003, in an endeavour to identify and implement further lessons from the past, the FCO recalled former Ambassadors to discuss the growing Iraq crisis. They identified two key lessons. Firstly, they advised that British experience in Iraq in the 1920s–30s revealed the tensions within the country which would be unleashed upon intervention. Sir Jeremy Greenstock, the British Ambassador to the UN, later informed the Foreign Affairs Committee 'The Foreign Office understood better than some what Iraq might become . . . clearly, given the way things went, their advice was not heeded.'[9]

These lessons from the past were also echoed by the IC who provided assessments of the risks and costs involved for an operation in Iraq, including the differences with Afghanistan, the strategic impact on Russia, the European Union (EU) and other Middle Eastern countries, the difficulties foreseen within the UN and the increase in the al-Qaeda threat.[10] Even one month before Telic began, the JIC warned of the many difficulties of running a post-Saddam Iraq and identified that UN authorisation would be 'crucial'.[11] Two months later the JIC again highlighted risks and prophetically judged 'Iraqi jubilation at Saddam's fall will dissipate quickly' and 'The Iraqi population will blame the coalition if progress is slow.'[12]

Prime Minister Tony Blair also identified the possibility of sectarian violence. He wrote to Bush in January 2003 'The biggest risk we face is internecine fighting between all the rival groups, religions, tribes etc. in Iraq when the military strike destabilises the regime. They are perfectly capable, on previous form, of killing each other in large numbers.'[13] However, he chose to draw upon his previous experience as guidance and reassured senior Labour figures 'I've had two wars – Kosovo and Afghanistan – and I think I can claim that we got it right.'[14] This ignored the fact that Afghanistan was supported by the UN and was ongoing, with the outcome still uncertain. The Kosovo analogy also failed to recognise a number of crucial differences: the intervention was to halt an ongoing humanitarian crisis – not to force regime change – it was widely supported by the international community – including countries in the region – and it was soon validated by the UN. Blair was not ignorant of these differences, writing to President Bush 'This is not Kosovo. This is not Afghanistan. This is not even the Gulf War' but ignored them in situations requiring persuasion.[15]

The second lesson identified by the former Ambassadors was that the FCO was being bypassed by the Prime Minister as it had been in 1956, which could lead to similarly disastrous results.[16] No10 had installed a small group of foreign policy advisors within the Cabinet Office, reducing FCO input and withholding key information and intelligence from senior FCO officials and ministers.[17] In fact, similarly to Suez, much of the machinery of government was avoided. The Cabinet were not involved in any major decision-making and were kept informed rather than incorporated into the policy process.[18] Likewise, in contrast to the five recorded discussions of the Defence and Overseas Policy Committee (DOP) for the four days of UK–US air strikes to degrade Iraq's WMD capability in 1998 (Operation Desert Fox), no DOP meetings occurred before Telic. In fact, the DOP had held its last meeting on Iraq in March 1999.[19] Instead, planning decisions were made either bilaterally between Blair and the relevant Secretary of State or in small meetings which were often not minuted, against standard protocol. This sidelined the Cabinet Secretary and avoided Cabinet challenge or collective ministerial responsibility.[20] These lessons were later identified by the Iraq Inquiry but are yet to be implemented; no new procedural machinery has been put in place despite calls from the permanent secretaries of Department for International Development (DfID) and the MoD for an oversight committee of ministers.[21]

Effective scrutiny was also not achieved through Parliament or Parliamentary Committees but, unlike Eden and similar to Harold Macmillan, Blair was concerned with securing public and parliamentary support which would be tackled in the same way as Afghanistan.[22] Creating a convincing case for military action became an increasing priority and, echoing Thatcher, included a number of analogies between Saddam and Hitler.[23] However, public opinion remained against Telic with large scale anti-war protests held across the country. In January 2003, a poll in *The*

Guardian suggested public opinion was 43 per cent against to 30 per cent for any intervention but No10 remained convinced that once the war began support for the troops would lead to a 'Blair bounce' in the opinion polls.[24] Blair even famously declared of the protests 'Let the day-to-day judgments come and go: be prepared to be judged by history.'[25]

Parliamentary support was more forthcoming. The Leader of the House of Commons, Robin Cook, drew upon lessons identified from circumnavigating Parliament in 1956 to recommend that the Prime Minister recall the House of Commons for a formal debate. Cook stated 'All I ask is that every morning you remember what happened to Anthony Eden.' Whilst Blair dismissed the comparison, the advice was heeded and the historic decision was taken to ask the House of Commons whether to commit Britain to the Iraq War.[26] The parliamentary vote was held on 18 March 2003 ending 412–149 in favour of intervention. This vote set a historic precedent for all future Prime Ministers to gain parliamentary permission to send British troops to war.

Blair had also identified the importance of international support and, as in past operations, the FCO worked hard to secure it – albeit with little success. The Prime Minister wrote in March 2002 'The persuasion job on this seems very tough. My own side are worried. Public opinion is fragile. International opinion – as I found at the EU – is pretty sceptical.'[27] Between April and July 2002, Blair tried to persuade Bush against unilateral US military action. Communications included the infamous note on 28 July 2002 which began 'I will be with you, whatever' before setting out a strategy for achieving a coalition for action, stressing that 'we need, as with Afghanistan and the ultimatum to the Taleban, to encapsulate our casus bellum in some defining way. This [the UN] is certainly the simplest.'[28] In September 2002, Bush reluctantly agreed and on 8 November 2002 UN Resolution 1441 was agreed, with Saddam announcing his intention to comply five days later. In the meantime, the Bush administration was growing impatient and – on 10 December – Blair learned that the US was planning military action as early as mid-February 2003. Blair wanted to delay military action to allow the inspections process more time and gain further international support for the invasion. On 24 January 2003 he wrote to Bush urging for inspectors to be given until the end of March or early April to complete their task. He also argued for the need for a second resolution to state that Iraq had failed to comply with its obligations, therefore tacitly authorising military action.[29] However, the FCO was fighting a losing battle for another resolution in the UN; German Chancellor Gerhard Schröder had won a second term in 2002 by rejecting military action against Saddam and it soon became clear that France intended to follow suit. Russian President Vladimir Putin was also proving problematic and accused Britain and America of inconsistency in their foreign policy.[30] Similarly, the Arab states were extremely concerned about Western military intervention, despite the FCO's early attempts to offer reassurance, including sending messages to Iran. Saudi Ambassador Prince Turki Al Faisal advised the annual meeting of the all-party Saudi Group 'The view of the Arab world is that this is an exercise in empire building.'[31]

Throughout planning, the one diplomatic relationship which remained unscathed was with the US. Just as the Thatcher–Bush relationship had led the UK–US relationship in 1990, so the Blair–Bush relationship led it in the 2000s with almost daily phone calls. Journalist Michael White drew upon history in an analysis of the situation: 'The fact is, however, that no British prime minister can afford to fall out with the President. The last one who did was Anthony Eden and look what happened to him.'[32] Foreign Secretary Jack Straw agreed. He advised the Iraq Inquiry that there was an 'enduring spectre of Suez over British foreign policy which led to an all-pervasive view that the United Kingdom should so far as possible seek to "stay close" to the United States'.[33] For him 'The spectre of Suez had been by far the most potent influence over successive British government's engagement with the US since the 50s' and when Blair began as Prime Minister he had been advised by Jonathan Powell to 'get right up the arse of the Americans'.[34]

However, the aim was not only to maintain good UK–US relations but to provide the opportunity to influence US policy from the inside, as Blair believed he had done in Afghanistan. The Iraq Inquiry concluded 'The issue of influencing the US, both at the strategic and at the operational level was a constant preoccupation at all levels of the UK Government.'[35] It also identified a deep naiveté in Blair's approach to Anglo-American relations; No10 decided early on that the best way to influence US policy was to 'commit full and unqualified support' in an endeavour to persuade from the inside, but in so doing the Prime Minister immediately resigned his diplomatic leverage. Blair also lacked judgement in assessing the situation and his capabilities as his ideas could not have trumped those of the neo-conservative agenda. The problem, the inquiry concluded, was that 'Mr Blair overestimated his ability to influence US decisions on Iraq.'[36] The 'Lessons' section of the report identified that influence should not be treated as an objective in itself but as a means to an end.[37]

US liaison also extended within the FCO. Foreign Secretary Jack Straw had a good relationship with his US counterpart Colin Powell and the FCO also maintained a good working relationship with the US State Department.[38] The problem for the FCO was that there was a poor relationship with the key ideologues in the White House who were doing much of the operational decision-making. Greenstock later identified this lesson: 'The Blair-Bush relationship was very good. The Powell-Straw relationship was very good. But neither Bush for one reason, nor Powell for another, were actually having much effect on operational decision-making, because Rumsfeld and Cheney were running it.'[39] In particular, Dick Cheney, the Vice President, had been Defence Secretary during the Gulf War and was thought to have been frustrated at Saddam's sanction busting and inspection dodging leading to a personal feeling of responsibility for failing to remove him from power in 1991. Straw later noted 'The whole time I was Foreign Secretary I worried about Vice President Cheney's instincts, and his preoccupation with atoning for his 1991 failure.'[40]

In the IC, working with the US had, by now, become an entrenched lesson and its implementation formed part of a broader intelligence relationship. The SIS Chief, 'C', went to Washington in July 2002 for talks and to share with the CIA a report that Iraq had tried to purchase uranium oxide from Niger. A leaked National Security Agency memo to GCHQ also revealed the ongoing relationship between the two SIGINT agencies,[41] whilst the CIA even offered comment on drafts of an intelligence dossier presented to Parliament.[42] The IC also remained reliant – as they had been in Granby – on the US for intelligence sources and warnings. In the run-up to Telic, the UK utilised US technical intelligence and during the campaign the Americans provided pilotless drones to collect IMINT and SIGINT – a resource which the British lacked.[43]

In the MoD, UK–US military discussions on contingency planning for Telic began in early June 2002, with British officers having been embedded in CENTCOM since September 2001.[44] The lesson of the necessity of working with the Americans was re-emphasised in 2003 when the MoD noted:

> It is probable that any future UK medium – or large-scale war – fighting operation will be fought in a US-led or backed coalition. Working with the US in a coalition brings political, diplomatic and military advantages, including the aggregation of capabilities, flexible war-fighting options and the sharing of intelligence and risk.[45]

The Iraq Inquiry found that, in developing the military options for Iraq, the MoD pursued a policy of influencing the US from the inside. Initially air and maritime forces alone were suggested for the intervention, but the MoD believed that offering a significant military contribution would provide the means of influencing US decisions. It warned the Prime Minister that Britain could be excluded from planning if ground forces were not provided and Blair agreed to the inclusion of ground troops on 31 October 2002.[46] However, in contrast to Granby, the MoD had a considerable lack of impact on US plans. Having committed to an all-service military campaign, the MoD soon became aware that it had used all its leverage. The House of Commons Defence Committee identified 'We are not, however, able to define the areas in which the British made a specific contribution to what was essentially an American campaign plan' and '[b]eing a junior partner in a coalition constrained the British Government in its ability to plan independently for after the conflict'.[47]

In fact, when it became clear that war was approaching, concerns were raised over US post-invasion plans. Straw wrote to Blair voicing fears that the US had a serious 'lacunae in their plan, notably . . . no thought apparently given to "day after" scenarios'.[48] From Washington, the British Ambassador – Christopher Meyer

– identified lessons from recent experience and warned 'Afghanistan has shown that the US is not good at consolidating politically what it has achieved militarily.'[49] Consequently, the FCO began to consider how the UN could contribute to post-conflict assistance, as they had in Fortitude, Vantage and Granby. Many historical examples were debated: 'post WWII models of occupation in Germany and Japan', 'a sort of "Bonn process"', 'a Kosovo model', '"lite" operation on the lines of operations in Afghanistan and Cambodia', 'full UN administration on the . . . East Timor model', and even 'by analogy with the 1991 action in Northern Iraq'.[50] However, as the start of operations drew nearer, the FCO failed to consider post-war strategic planning any further. In part this was because there was an assumption that the intervention would be well executed, UN authorised and take place in a relatively benign environment, but it was also because the focus on achieving a UN resolution, the management of public and parliamentary opinion and the political day to day following 9/11 left little time for post-war strategic planning in either Iraq or Afghanistan.[51] This lesson was subsequently widely identified by witnesses at the Iraq Inquiry.[52]

For the MoD, examining Musketeer, Fortitude, Vantage and Granby offered few relevant lessons for post-war planning. Instead, the British drew upon lessons identified from humanitarian interventions and the Chief of the Defence Staff considered Bosnia as a 'worst case' for the length of an aftermath operation, although the experience of Northern Ireland would have provided an estimate of around thirty years.[53] The Americans went back even further into history, with Powell reassuring UN ministers that the US had considerable experience of nation-building from establishing governance in Germany and Japan post-Second World War. However, unlike in 1958, 1961 and 1990, the 'end state' for military contingency planning was broad and idealistic: 'A stable and law-abiding Iraq, within its present borders, cooperating with the international community, no longer posing a threat to its neighbours or to international security, and abiding by its international obligations on WMD.'[54]

For CPA planning the problem was the opposite; there were no objectives, timelines or end states. As early as January 2003, the

Chiefs of Staff had reported to the Prime Minister that 'aftermath planning was still quite immature' and there was no preparation of MoD CPA staff prior to deployment.[55] The result was a lack of strategic direction, a lesson which the CPA's Senior British Military Representative in Iraq, Sir Freddie Viggers, identified to the Iraq Inquiry: 'we suffered from lack of clarity about Ends, Ways and Means. The plan emerged piecemeal and was prone to dislocation by breaking news and by events.' Furthermore, 'Everything was a priority – security, the rebuild, creating the political architecture, capture Saddam, stop the sabotage and smuggling, sustain flows of vital supplies to nations, get the economy going, remove the weapons (tons, of all types)', and all of which was to be completed whilst the CPA remained perpetually understaffed 'by quality and quantity'.[56] Mark Etherington, principle representative of the CPA in Wasit province, confirmed this analysis. He arrived into post in September 2003 to find he was part of a team of two responsible for governing a population of 970,000.[57]

These difficulties were compounded by the lack of financial support for the reconstruction efforts. The Iraq Planning Unit, in considering the implications of post-Saddam Iraq, advised at the beginning of 2003 'This would be very expensive and could have wider resource implications. Ministers urgently need to take a view on this before the military planning assumptions become a fait accomplis.'[58] Initially, it seemed as if the lesson of protecting the British economy had been unlearned as in advance of the war, the Chancellor of the Exchequer, Gordon Brown, advised that he would not rule out any military options on the grounds of cost. The first comprehensive estimate of costs was only produced by the Treasury a month before Telic began and was not sent to Blair or other ministers leaving the Cabinet to agree to Telic without any idea of affordability.[59] However, a Special Reserve had been created in 2002 in preparation for Telic and once the conflict phase of the operation was complete concern for British finances led to restrictions in funding for reconstruction efforts.[60] This had a negative impact and David Johnson later identified 'it is absurd to spend billions on a short, sharp war and then try to run an area the size of France with hardly two pennies to rub together'.[61] Telic eventually cost £9.24 billion.[62]

Although very few senior Commanders in Telic had served in the Gulf War,[63] there had been considerable local operational experience in the Royal Navy and RAF since Granby (working with the US as part of Operation Resinate to patrol an Iraqi no-fly zone and the Armilla patrol, to enforce UN sanctions). Lessons from these experiences were considered 'of particular value' during planning.[64] Similarly, recent exercises were drawn upon for lessons, particularly Exercise Saif Sareea II in Oman in 2001, which informed the implementation of a range of modifications to the Challenger II battle tank and the successful establishment of a Joint Forces Logistics Command Headquarters.[65] At the end of 2002, the British also participated in the US-run Exercise Internal Look in Qatar, which rehearsed the set-up and running of a headquarters for a major coalition campaign. Other exercises which proved of benefit for learning included those with British and American Marines in autumn 2002, 1 (UK) Armoured Division in Kuwait in April 2002 and NATO's Allied Rapid Reaction Corps. Each provided soldiers with important high intensity conflict training.[66]

In addition, there were some key strategic decisions which demonstrated that lessons from 1961 and 1991 remained learned. In particular, the initial operation was planned for the cooler months and there was adequate time for troops to acclimatise, with a programme in place to help those who were deployed from other weather extremes. The Desert Rats, for example, went from training on the northern German plains at -4°F (-20°C) to the desert at 86°F (30°C). However, the speed of operational requirements meant that the lesson was soon unlearned; when one division replaced another in the height of summer, heat casualties rapidly increased. From 15 July to 9 September 2003 over 800 personnel were treated for heat-related issues, 200 were returned to the UK and one soldier tragically died.[67] This lesson was quickly re-identified and after 2004 better training combined with improved air conditioning in accommodation and some vehicles implemented the lesson.[68]

Overall, MoD planning for Operation Telic was extremely challenging. Troops and resources were already stretched with deployments in Sierra Leone, Northern Ireland and the Balkans as well as Afghanistan and around 19,000 personnel committed to providing a replacement fire-fighting service during a union strike.[69] As a result, when planning was taking place over Christmas 2002, personnel joked that Telic was an acronym for 'Tell Everyone Leave Is Cancelled'. This pressure also increased over time and the 2010 *Strategic Defence and Security Review* later identified:

> We must also confront the legacy of overstretch ... UK forces were deployed at medium scale in both Iraq and Afghanistan. This exceeded the planning assumptions that had set the size of our forces and placed greater demands both on our people and on their equipment.[70]

However, this lesson was identified before proposing restructuring the Armed Forces to deploy around 30,000 troops for a limited time – two thirds of the force sent to Iraq in 2003.[71]

The IC was also instrumental in the planning of the Iraq War.[72] The IC had monitored Iraq since Granby and particularly its WMD programme. After the Gulf War, the Cabinet had agreed to commit resources to counter-proliferation with a special Current Intelligence Group within the JIC focused upon the topic. MI6 also set up a new unit and recruited expertise from the DIS to monitor the FCO Non-Proliferation Department's 'countries of concern' including Iraq. The result was regular JIC reporting on Iraq's WMD programme with at least twenty-two separate assessments produced from 17 April 1991 to 9 September 2002.[73]

Nevertheless, the lessons that the IC had identified from the Gulf War had a negative impact upon the assessment of Iraq's WMD programme during this time. Post-Granby, it was revealed that the intelligence agencies had greatly underestimated Saddam's WMD activities and the lesson identified was to not be deceived in the same way again. Its implementation resulted in over-compensation and an inquiry, later established under the Chairmanship of Lord Butler, into intelligence on WMD concluded that there was 'a tendency for assessments to be coloured by over-reaction to previous errors. As a result, there was a risk of over-cautious or worst case estimates, shorn of their caveats, becoming the "prevailing wisdom"'.[74] Even when UNMOVIC failed to find WMD – after inspecting around 500 sites in Iraq – no re-evaluation of intelligence assessments occurred.

In mid-2002, the JIC took the unprecedented decision to jointly publish an intelligence assessment with the government on Iraq's WMD programme.[75] This document became known as the 'September dossier' and was eventually attacked for overstating the imminence of the Iraqi threat, with journalist Andrew Gilligan famously claiming that the document had been 'sexed up'. The Butler inquiry advised that the dossier was unprecedented in three ways: firstly, the JIC had never produced a public document before; secondly, no government case for international action had previously drawn on a JIC publication; and thirdly, the authority of the IC had never before been used in such a public way.[76] In so doing, the usually secretive work of the IC was exposed for the first time and, when questions over the wording of the assessment began to be scrutinised, it quickly placed the IC under new public criticism and pressure to reflect upon lessons to be learned including over the independence of the Chair of the JIC, John Scarlet. This was a lesson that echoed back to the era of reorganisation under Patrick Dean.

Inside Iraq, the availability of HUMINT had not developed since 1991. The Prime Minister, in the foreword to the September dossier, stated 'Gathering intelligence inside Iraq is not easy. Saddam's is one of the most secretive and dictatorial regimes in the world.'[77] However, as identified in Granby, part of the reason for the lack of HUMINT was that the UK and US had become over-reliant on the intelligence gathered from UN weapons inspectors and had not replaced the resource once they left Iraq in 1998. Instead, defectors and exiles – who had their own agenda – were interrogated as primary sources for HUMINT. In the end the British only had five main HUMINT sources and each were ineffectively validated.[78] As a result, little further understanding of Saddam Hussein, or his intentions, had developed since 1991. Instead, it was incorrectly assumed that Saddam's policy had been to seek WMD before Granby and therefore his policy would be to seek WMD afterwards too.[79]

During the Intervention

As Telic became a reality, two intelligence groups were established within the central intelligence machine, implementing lessons from managing the war in Afghanistan. The 'inner group', chaired by the Prime Minister's Foreign Policy Advisor included all of the intelligence agencies but the 'wider group', chaired by the Overseas Development Secretariat, included representatives from DfID, the Metropolitan Police and the Treasury.[80] Similarly, the structure of the FCO changed to accommodate the complexity of the operation. In February 2003 an interdepartmental unit, the Iraq Planning Unit, was set up to coordinate government policy across Whitehall. In March, two Emergency Units, a policy unit and a consular unit were opened, working twenty-four hours a day.[81] The rapid response was the result of implementing lessons from 9/11, the war in Afghanistan and the threat of an India–Pakistan war, where the lesson had been identified that the handling of emergency operations required improvement.[82] To implement the lesson a new database was created, with details of volunteers who could be deployed at short notice.

In Iraq itself, members of the FCO were seconded to the Office for Reconstruction and Humanitarian Assistance (ORHA) – the predecessor of the CPA – in Baghdad, Basra and seven of the eighteen Governorates. The British Office in Baghdad was quickly opened using a containerised Embassy that could accommodate four people and, implementing a lesson identified from Afghanistan, by June a newly developed 'flat pack embassy' had arrived. This was a self-supported container (in terms of electricity and water) which could house up to forty people.[83] However, despite the immediate response, the 2004–5 FCO annual report identified that there were many more lessons to be learned as teams in Iraq had to work under extreme conditions including unbearable heat and a lack of infrastructure.[84] When the new Consulate opened in Basra, in July 2004, it suffered almost daily mortar attacks and was sealed off by twelve foot high concrete walls where the only way in or out was by military helicopter. Fifty members of staff were protected by sixty former Ghurkhas and a company of soldiers, with Black Watch troops guarding the area. At night, everyone had to wear body armour.[85] The challenging environment meant that FCO postings were reduced to the maximum of a year, leading to a much higher turnover of staff and a frequent loss of lessons.

At the same time, tour lengths in the MoD were also limited to six months, due to the high intensity of operations. There was also very limited time allocated for handover, again causing lessons to be forgotten and personnel only seeing snapshots of operations, rather than gaining a strategic overview. This lesson was later identified by Major General Richard Barrons, Assistant Chief of the General Staff, who admitted that the reduced tour lengths caused 'relatively few members of the British armed forces [to have] a genuine understanding of the full ebb and flow of the land campaign'.[86] In contrast, the US Army had twelve to fifteen month tours and the British had been on two year resident tours in Northern Ireland.

To compound the problem of lessons being lost within departments and across personnel, cross-Whitehall relations were difficult and deteriorated as the campaign progressed. The FCO struggled to coordinate with DfID, leaving each with different missions and aims. Coordination between the MoD and other Whitehall departments was similarly difficult and this was combined with a failure to prioritise the operation within Whitehall. There was also no single minister in charge of Iraq which made it difficult for those on the ground to manage multiple lines of reporting and accountability. Lieutenant General Chris Brown later identified

> the FCO maintained its traditional broad remit; DFID was at least initially focused on Millennium Goals – it did not see its role as "bailing out" the military's mistakes, and the [cross-departmental] Stabilisation Unit has seen Afghanistan as its focus from its inception.[87]

The new Foreign Secretary, David Miliband, identified this lesson in 2008: 'We need better integration, particularly between MoD, DfID and FCO . . . we need to think more radically about joining up at all levels.'[88] However, two years later, the lesson had still not been implemented. In 2010 the House of Commons Public Administration Select Committee identified 'Cross-departmental collaboration is variable, analytical resources are underutilised, and different departments understand and discuss strategy in different and incompatible ways. Departmental collaboration therefore falls short.'[89] The Iraq Inquiry concluded that a lead minister should have been appointed to coordinate across departments and the House of Commons Public Administration and Constitutional Affairs Committee (PACAC) suggested that the appointment of a Secretary of State, akin to the Brexit Secretary, would have implemented this lesson.[90]

The relationship with the US also remained challenging throughout Telic. In Baghdad, the UK Special Representative, Jeremy Greenstock, sat in an office next to the US Ambassador, Paul Bremer, and assumed charge of the CPA in his absence. Greenstock, advised that UK opportunities to influence CPA policy was hampered by the dominating Bremer and he later described the feeling of 'sitting in the second carriage, not driving the engine' of post-war planning.[91] The Iraq Inquiry noted the inability of the UK to influence the policy of de-Ba'athification, over which it had a number of misgivings, or to influence the US to produce an Iraqi-wide approach to the reform of the Iraqi Security Forces. It also stated that Britain was excluded from discussions on oil policy, decisions on how to spend the Development Fund for Iraq and the creation of the Iraqi Central Bank as an independent body. In addition, UK approval was also not sought for the CPA's 'Vision for Iraq' and 'Achieving the vision' strategic documents, with the FCO only became aware of the documents once they were at advanced stages of drafting. However, Britain held the status of joint occupying power and was therefore equally liable for any CPA decisions. In an endeavour to manage the legal risk, London proposed a Memorandum of Understanding but Washington would not agree. The Iraq Inquiry report identified 'the US had little incentive to give the UK an influential role . . . and the UK lacked the will and leverage to insist'. In the end the British were so concerned about their lack of influence that Whitehall made the strategic decision to minimise the number of staff sent to CPA headquarters in Baghdad. The aim was to reduce the risk of personal liability and the appearance of UK responsibility for the decisions being made.[92]

The situation was similar in the MoD. Despite many planned operations in the Gulf and Iraq, and embedded staff in the predominantly US-manned Coalition headquarters, UK–US relations on the ground did not run smoothly and suffered from a lack of military liaison on both sides. As a result, Multinational Division

South East (MNDSE) tended to turn to Whitehall or Northwood for assistance rather than effectively communicating with Multinational Corps Iraq (MNC-I) in Baghdad. A report on the land campaign later identified that this was compounded by a lack of understanding on how best to engage the US and the British complained that the US Commander, General Rick Sanchez, never visited, called or installed a secure phone link to Basra.[93] The British Chief of Staff, Colonel Tanner, declared 'Despite our so-called "special relationship", I reckon we were treated no differently than Poland.'[94]

Over time the UK–US relationship disintegrated further as the British disappointed their allies. After committing wholeheartedly to going into Iraq, dedication to the operation slowly eroded. By 2004, Lieutenant General John McColl, Britain's Senior Military Representative in Iraq, reported back to London that the UK refusal to deploy further troops had 'chipped away at the US/UK relationship'.[95] In the summer of 2006, General Mike Jackson reported 'The perception, right or wrong, in some – if not all – US military circles is that the UK is motivated more by short-term political gain of early withdrawal than by the long-term importance of mission accomplishment.'[96] The Iraq Inquiry supported this view and concluded that British attention was focused upon Helmand Province, with Iraq increasingly viewed as drawing resources from the primary theatre of war in Afghanistan. In 2007, the difference between the two allies came to a head when Bush announced 'the surge' strategy – the decision to send a further 28,000 American troops to Baghdad and Al Anbar Province – whilst, in contrast, the UK was planning its withdrawal. Overall, the Iraq Inquiry concluded 'US and UK strategies for Iraq began to diverge almost immediately after the conflict . . . by early 2007 the UK was finding it difficult to play down the divergence, which was, by that point, striking.'[97] When the Iraq Inquiry report was released, the Chairman, Sir John Chilcot, gave a statement in which he highlighted one clear lesson for the future: the UK had to re-evaluate its relations with the US.[98]

Telic also presented challenges in communication and information systems. As in Granby, there were considerable problems of integration and not all British systems were either compatible with

US systems or able to handle the volume of information traffic. An analysis of the land campaign identified this lesson stating 'there was considerable electronic fratricide between UK ECM and UK, US and Iraqi communications'.[99] At the tactical level, this lesson was quickly identified and implemented when the ageing short-range radio was replaced in 2004 with considerable success, leading the US Marines to purchase 5,000 of the same sets.[100]

The IC also experienced challenges in communication, particularly of dissemination of assessed intelligence. Similar to Granby, there was inadequate connectivity between coalition partners due to both a lack of reliable communications and ongoing classification incompatibilities.[101] For example, all of the information on the US digital intelligence network was classified NOFORN (no foreigners) – at times leaving British pilots flying American planes and unable to access pilot and maintenance manuals. When SIGINT collected by the British was given to the US for analysis the reports produced were also classified NOFORN, forbidding the IC to access its own intelligence. Having identified this lesson, Blair complained to Bush who signed a directive to remove the NOFORN restriction for Britain and Australia but, as the US digital intelligence network contained years of intelligence and information, the Pentagon had to create a separate network for British and Australian access. Consequently, the lesson took some time to implement.[102]

As well as difficulties in sharing intelligence across allies, there was a failure to effectively deliver intelligence down to the lowest levels of tactical decision-making – brigade, battlegroup and sometimes company or squadron – due to over-classification and a lack of flexible dissemination protocols.[103] Similarly, there was difficulty in sharing intelligence up the chain of command, particularly in centrally collecting tactical intelligence from company and battlegroup levels.[104] There was even a failure to effectively distribute intelligence across the wider IC with the DIS, PJHQ and theatre intelligence structures all requiring greater fusion.[105] The Butler report identified the lesson of 'unduly strict "compartmentalisation" of intelligence' and that the DIS needed further integration into the wider IC.[106]

Despite difficulties, the MoD did have some initial successes in Telic; the approach to Basra was a military victory with joint

UK–Iraqi patrols conducted within a week and the Royal Navy successfully cleared mines from the Umm Qasr waterway. In addition, in contrast to 1961 and 1991, the RAF were so keen to secure overflying rights that a duplication of effort emerged, with some individual officers taking it upon themselves to personally task embassies with gaining approval rather than following the official command structure.[107] This was in stark contrast to the FCO's failure to gain permission from Turkey for British forces to enter Iraq from the north with the US 4th Infantry Division – forcing troops to be transported an additional 3,000 miles into Kuwait and push into the less peaceful Basra region of southern Iraq. Lessons identified from Afghanistan on how to maintain rifles in dusty conditions were also implemented.[108]

However, in a repeat of the events of 1961, approximately £14 million worth of ammunition had to be discarded due to being stored unprotected in high temperatures. Radars, communication and information systems, unmanned air vehicles and airfield navigation aids were all less reliable in the hot and dusty conditions and, in some cases, the air conditioning – used to implement the lesson of the importance of keeping equipment cool – caused condensation which effected sensitive electrical equipment.[109] There were also reports that the temperatures in the back of the Warrior vehicle were potentially fatal.[110] The journalist John Humphreys identified 'sitting in the back of a Warrior is like travelling in an oven on tank tracks. It gets to 140 degrees in summer. You can cook a leg of lamb at that temperature.'[111] Additionally, some equipment was delayed because of political concerns in 2002 that early preparations by industry would suggest to the international community that military action was inevitable when diplomacy was still being pursued.[112] Difficulties with equipment logistics also persisted, despite the re-identification of these lessons. Personnel arrived in theatre before much of the desert clothing, resulting in a mixture of green and desert camouflage, as planning assumptions had only ensured sufficient equipment for 9,000 personnel.[113] There was also a shortage of nuclear, biological and chemical protection suits and detection equipment and, as there had been in Granby, there were shortages of ammunition, with some soldiers only having five rounds each.[114] The equipment shortages had tragic consequences as the first British casualty of the war, Sergeant Steven Roberts, died due to his unit not having enough body armour, whilst the June 2003 murder of five Royal Military Police Red Caps resulted in a Board of Inquiry into their lack of ammunition and communication systems.

Once supplies were dispatched, further delays occurred due to ongoing equipment identification and tracking failures.[115] The National Audit Office reported that poor asset identification and tracking had been identified from the Second World War, 1961 and 1991, as well as more recent operations including Operation Resolute and Lodestar in Bosnia-Herzegovina (1995–8), Operation Besemer in Macedonia (2001) and Exercise Saif Sareea II in Oman (2001) but the lesson had not been implemented.[116] It also identified that the difficulties were so extreme that frontline units would often send teams back down the supply chain to find their required items. In one example, 1 (UK) Armoured Division sent a team back from Kuwait to the Defence Stores and Distribution Agency depot in Oxfordshire to locate required items.[117] The failings quickly re-earned the British the same nickname that they had held thirteen years before – 'the Borrowers'. The House of Commons Defence Committee identified in its report:

> We are in no doubt that one of the key lessons to emerge from Operation Telic concerns operational logistic support and, specifically, the requirement for a robust system to track equipment and stocks both into and within theatre – a requirement which was identified in the 1991 Gulf War.[118]

There were also initial challenges with the command structure leading to lessons being identified and implemented during the operation. The three UK Contingent Commanders were under the tactical control of the US, based on NATO and Gulf region interactions of the past. For Air and Maritime, for whom there had been ongoing US operations in the area, this worked well but for Land there was an additional level of command – the US 1st Marine Expeditionary Force – between UK Land Contingent HQ and US Land Component HQ. Similarly to Granby, operational command of UK forces remained with the Chief of Joint

Operations, Lieutenant General Sir John Reith, through PJHQ to the National and UK Contingent Commanders in theatre. This did not mirror US command structures, resulting in some confusion and complexity. However, the lesson was quickly identified and doctrine updated by the end of 2003.[119] The Defence Committee also identified the same lesson and recommended a more adaptable command structure to ensure working in greater parallel with the US in the future.[120]

In continuing to implement the previously identified lesson of media management, the method of embedding journalists – learned from Granby – was expanded in Telic. Around 700 journalists were embedded within coalition forces, including 153 within British units. The MoD considered this process to be highly successful as 90 per cent of the reporting during the combat phase from embedded journalists was classed as positive or neutral.[121] However, the initial establishment of PR operations was slow. There was a shortage of trained PR personnel in the Press Information Centres in Qatar, Kuwait, Bahrain and the headquarters of 1 (UK) Armoured Division, leaving positions to be filled by regulars and reserves leading to a delay. Once the centres were up and running there was a continual battle to sufficiently brief officers in order for them to answer questions from journalists who were monitoring twenty-four hour media coverage. The problem was also mirrored in London where the speed of questions from reporters outran the speed of information reaching the top of the Defence chain of command. The result was the need to make regular parliamentary statements at short notice leading to a huge demand on the MoD for information. David Johnson wrote 'it is hard to overstate the number of vexatious and pointless requests ("exactly how many Iraqi tanks were in that column that just left Basrah?" was a No10 classic)'.[122]

Once the combat phase was over, PR became even more demanding as experienced media personnel returned to the UK, including many embedded journalists. For those journalists who remained in theatre, the difficult security situation hampered any positive reporting and the absence of a coherent UK and coalition strategic narrative caused further difficulties, especially as UK and US strategy diverged after 'the surge' in January 2007. The MoD identified the lesson: 'Planning for similar operations in future should take into account, from the outset, media demands during the transition to the post-conflict phase.'[123] Additionally, in June 2003, the MoD participated in a Royal United Services Institute (RUSI) seminar with journalists, broadcasters and academics to identify lessons on how PR campaigns could be handled better in the future.[124]

In conjunction with managing UK and international media, information operations (Info Ops) were being run to communicate with the local population. Britain had identified the benefit of Info Ops in Bosnia where the British had their own radio station which had become the most popular in the country. Whilst the broad idea was replicated in Iraq, many of the lessons on how to conduct such operations were ignored. General Dutton identified in 2006 'I still do not think that we have got Info Ops right ... We have not got the same level of coordination as was demonstrated in the Balkans.'[125] This was not surprising given the failure to deploy professionals to theatre and the approach of conducting Info Ops from the top down with restrictive direction from the MoD.[126] The conclusion was 'Info Ops were appalling. It is a subject that is treated like some form of magical pixie dust that can compensate for any holes in the tactical plan; Info Ops consistently failed to deliver.'[127]

Despite some examples of lesson identification and implementation during the campaign, there were criticisms that the MoD was slow to identify lessons at the strategic level. Since 1991, the learning process had developed with strategic identified lessons originating primarily from the Directorate of Operational Capability (DOC), operational lessons from PJHQ and tactical lessons from Front Line Commanders. Each was managed on a bespoke database and, in addition, Land, Sea and Air each had a separate system. This provided a compartmentalised approach to lesson learning which was compounded by three changes in IT systems and locations during the first few years of Telic.[128]

Having identified this lesson, in 2006, the DOC introduced the Defence-wide Lessons Management (DwLM) system. DwLM incorporated a new lessons database – Defence Lessons Identified Management System (DLIMS) – which was universal in allowing input into the lesson identification process by all ranks and across all environments.[129] The system then ensured that each identified lesson was assigned a method of implementation and a gatekeeper to oversee the process. Lessons remained 'open' until the gatekeeper provided a written statement detailing its implementation, after which it was digitally retained in the Defence Lessons Library, remaining accessible for reference.[130] This was a rigorous, institutionalised procedure but, by making the input more democratic, it became increasingly time-consuming for the lessons teams to process identified lessons. At the same time, the Operational Training and Advisory Group (OPTAG) – who conducted pre-deployment training – visited theatre regularly to identify lessons for implementation in training the next wave of troops. However, they too could not keep up with the changing situation on the ground and the overall slow turnaround of lessons created an inability to examine wider trends and patterns. In fact, due to the overwhelming amount of information being collected, DOC was forced to stop capturing any new strategic or operational lessons in Iraq between 2007 and 2009.[131]

Consequently, British reaction in Basra was slow and lacked dynamism and recent experiences – in the Balkans, Sierra Leone or the latter stages of Northern Ireland[132] – led the MoD to treat Iraq as a stability operation for too long.[133] The 2002 Strategic Defence Review, the 2003 Defence White Paper and the 2005 Defence Strategic Guidance all failed to recognise the need for counterinsurgency and updated doctrine on stabilisation and counterinsurgency, *JDP 3-40*, was not published until the end of 2009, too late for Telic.[134] Similarly, from 1997 to 2008 middle ranking and junior Army officers received limited counterinsurgency education or training whilst the Royal Navy and RAF received none at all. In contrast, the US counterinsurgency doctrine developed quickly; in particular, the Commanding General of Multi-National Force-Iraq (MNF-I), the American David Petraeus, searched the history of counterinsurgency warfare to inspire his 2006 issued field manual *FM 3-24*.[135] In 2005, he also made the study of counterinsurgency history compulsory at the US Army's advanced training colleges resulting in T. E. Lawrence's *Seven Pillars of Wisdom* and David

Galula's *Counterinsurgency Warfare* becoming bestsellers at bookshops near US Army bases.[136]

In the IC, the lessons identified from Granby regarding language requirements had not been implemented, leading to an ongoing lack of HUMINT. Whilst English speaking Iraqi civilians and third party nationals were hired, the exodus of many educated Iraqis, combined with intimidation from militias, meant that there were not enough interpreters for one to be available for each patrol and there remained a lack of local expertise to understand customs and dialects, or to localise coalition information campaigns.[137] This problem was compounded by a failure to learn from the example of General de la Billière in Granby and to provide troops with basic cultural training in order to gain the trust of the local population for HUMINT.[138] It was not until 2007 that the MoD implemented this lesson and produced 'Iraq: cultural appreciation booklet' providing information on Iraqi history, culture, religion and language for personnel in theatre.[139] A post-operational analysis of land operations concluded 'The language and cultural understanding capabilities deployed on Op Telic by the Army were never adequate'[140] and the first DOC lessons report identified: 'Humint is an invaluable resource and [redacted] that should be accorded appropriate priority and resourcing.'[141] To implement this lesson, in 2005, the DIS developed its language capability and the Defence School of Languages was enhanced to improve Iraqi linguistic capabilities. The DIS also began working with GCHQ to share an understanding of the different Iraqi dialects.[142]

SIGINT collection had improved slightly since Granby, particularly as the Iraqi leadership used an old system of communication which had been manufactured by a British company, Rascal. There was also some additional SIGINT success through mobile units accompanying UK land forces, 14th Signals Regiment and Royal Marines Y Squadron. However, the lessons identified around the distillation of intelligence were not successfully implemented.[143] The scale of operations, technology and global communications meant that the amount of raw intelligence which was collected was overwhelming. The MoD quickly re-identified this lesson:

> In an operation of this scale and complexity a vast amount of information has to be processed and interpreted ... a need to service the requirements of rapid, decisive and multi-layered campaigns, has the potential to test severely even the most sophisticated intelligence organisations.[144]

Psyops operations also persisted with leaflets dropped on the Iraqi Army prior to hostilities. However, Britain had not implemented lessons from Granby and continued to be unable to disseminate leaflets in a non-benign environment due to the lack of modified aircraft.[145] Therefore, the UK remained heavily reliant on US capabilities to cover well populated areas.

After the Intervention

On writing his memoirs on the run-up to the Iraq War, the British Ambassador to the US, Christopher Meyer, reflected 'Hindsight usually follows failure' and for the first time the FCO started to embrace the idea of learning lessons.[146] Its 2003–4 annual report included a small 'lessons learned' section on the impact of Telic on visas in the region.[147] The House of Commons Foreign Affairs Committee supported this development – 'We particularly welcome the new "lessons learned" sections and recommend that they be developed and made more specific in future reports'[148] – and consequently the 2004–5 annual report included a specific 'lessons learned' section on Iraq, which identified staff successes and the need to improve project management, staff recruiting and training.[149]

The partly FCO manned and owned Stabilisation Unit went further and produced a lesson identification report, albeit that it was published too late to inform policy during Telic. This report utilised Iraq as a case study to provide policy-makers and practitioners with lessons on how to operate in complex stabilisation environments.[150] At the end of Telic the UK also formed a 1,000 strong civilian standby capacity managed by the Stabilisation Unit to improve capability further, although criticisms of its effectiveness remained following the 2011 intervention in Libya.[151]

The Foreign Affairs Committee also began to embrace the idea of learning lessons and produced a series of seven reports on the foreign policy aspects of the War on Terror, including lessons identified from Iraq. It additionally published one-off reports, including *The Decision to go to War in Iraq* and *Global Security: The Middle East*, which identified an array of lessons as a result of discussions with officials from the UK, US, UN, France and NATO.[152] There was also a newfound concern for monitoring FCO progress which forced some consideration of lesson implementation by the Foreign Secretary in his response to committee reports.[153]

However, despite the new agenda, FCO lesson identification was limited. Just as in 1956 there were concerns over the publication of memoirs and after controversy following the publication of Meyer's book – without FCO approval – Jeremy Greenstock was asked by Jack Straw not to publish his account of events until after the publication of the Iraq Inquiry report.[154] The annual reports were also criticised as they were written for public consumption and accused of being 'PR jobs' with a lack of transparency over how lessons were drawn and offering little self-criticism. For example, in 2004, the FCO's key identified lesson from Iraq was 'in such an environment every single member of staff must be prepared to make 100% commitment'.[155] In addition, no details were provided as to how lessons would be implemented, compounded by the misnomer of identified but not implemented lessons headed as 'lessons learned'.

The Foreign Affairs Committee reports also suffered a number of failings. The first report focused upon the decision to go to war in Iraq and endeavoured to establish whether the FCO had presented accurate and complete information to Parliament in the run-up to Telic. The foremost sources for this analysis were papers provided by the government on the assessment of the Iraqi regime and its WMD and as a result the report focused upon the use of intelligence rather than diplomacy and foreign policy. There was no investigation into why alternatives to war were not sought or why the previous Iraqi policies of containment and smart sanctions had been abandoned. In addition, reports were limited by the committee's lack of access to information. They even accused the government of failing to satisfactorily answer their questions.[156]

Those witnesses who were called for evidence were the most senior officials, mainly promoted by the government and towing the ministerial line, often leaving committee conclusions as little more than a summary of events. When the former FCO official, Carne Ross, appeared as a witness before the committee in 2006 – for a broader report on active diplomacy – he advised that despite being closely involved in Iraq policy for many years, and having been a central part of the drafting of British policy in the UN Security Council, he had never been asked to testify to any committee. He concluded 'I take that as an example of that absence of scrutiny.'[157]

The few lessons that were identified by the reports were not given priority within the FCO for implementation. Carne Ross, also advised:

> what Parliament or this Committee said about our policy was, at best, insignificant . . . Inside the FCO, the recommendations of the FAC [Foreign Affairs Committee] are given little attention. The FCO will politely pretend otherwise, but it is in reality able to carry on its business without fear of significant intrusion.[158]

Mark Etherington argued that the root cause of the FCO's inability to learn was cultural. He told the Iraq Inquiry that the FCO was likely to perpetuate mistakes because of a disinclination for self-criticism and an avoidance of questioning key assumptions by taking comfort in meaningless statistics – spend, speed and numbers of people deployed:

> The argument is often made that the UK has learned from its mistakes in Iraq and moved forward. There is limited evidence of this . . . We still lack the ability – and inclination – dispassionately to consider our errors, identify and act upon the requisite lessons and move on. This has constrained debate, education and our national performance. Lacking this rigour, we tend to turn self-referentially inward; and risk viewing criticism as a threat . . . One fears that a measure of arrogance, complacency and hubris has long prevented us learning.[159]

In contrast, extensive and routine lesson identification reports and processes, which had been in place in the MoD in 1991, remained in 2003 and had been further expanded. New methods of identifying lessons – including developing relationships with academics – had developed and the DwLM formalised the process further by renewing the emphasis upon the implementation of lessons, albeit slowly. Internally, specific 'lessons learned' reports continued to be submitted through the chain of command.[160] Telic had a specific lessons team assigned to identify lessons and retain those identified by others. They also produced two summary reports for public reading whilst the Land Warfare Centre – which united with the Army lessons staff in September 2009 – collected an archive of post-tour reports and interviews and held a lessons conference in January 2010.[161] In addition, DOC produced three volumes of reports identifying lessons and the Vice Chief of the Defence Staff commissioned four special reviews to identify lessons on logistics, consignment tracking, combat identification and nuclear, biological and chemical warfare.[162] The MoD also continued to identify lessons from serious incidents through Boards of Inquiry and further internal inquiries, including the Aitken report on the deliberate abuse and unlawful killing of Iraqis.[163] Although the volume of lesson identification documents produced seem overwhelming, many of the lessons were subsequently implemented as part of Operation Entirety – the endeavour to resource, structure and prepare land forces for counterinsurgency in Afghanistan and hybrid operations elsewhere.

As in 1991, the National Audit Office and House of Commons Defence Committee complemented the process by providing external lesson identification and monitoring lesson implementation throughout the campaign. The National Audit Office conducted a full investigation of the operation and the Defence Committee ran an inquiry – visiting units, organisations, the CPA and interviewing witnesses – to produce the report *Lessons of Iraq*.[164] In compliance with the European Convention on Human Rights, the MoD also held a number of external inquiries for issues related to torture and abuse: the Baha Mousa and Al-Sweady inquiries as well as investigations carried out under the Iraq Historical Allegations Team and the Iraq Fatalities Investigation. Each of these inquiries included the requirement to identify lessons for the future in their terms of reference.[165]

Lesson distribution and identification from others had also extended since Granby. The Defence Medical Services reports from Iraq revealed that lessons identified from the National Health Service (NHS) had been implemented.[166] Lesson distribution also worked particularly well with the intergovernmental body of the Stabilisation Unit, which had its own lessons team, and by the end of Telic it was fully integrated into DLIMS.[167] Across the rest of Whitehall there was an inconsistent approach. The MoD IT system was incompatible with the FCO's, making lesson distribution more difficult, compounded by cultural differences in the classification of information; the FCO system did not accept documents above 'confidential' whilst many MoD documents were assigned the higher classification of 'secret'.[168] There was also mutual lesson distribution with coalition allies and NATO. The lessons team at the MoD's Development, Concepts and Doctrine Centre (DCDC) had the IT capacity installed to distribute identified lessons with ABCA nations (Australia, Britain, Canada, America) resulting in greater connectivity with those countries than across Whitehall.[169]

However, there remained a number of challenges. Many of the Boards of Inquiry were marred by accusations of being cover-ups,[170] an internal lessons report was suppressed to avoid distribution[171] and – without embedded lessons teams in theatre – post-event investigations relied upon an audit trail.[172] The new democratic input into the lessons process also caused difficulties. Soldiers often felt uncomfortable submitting lessons which reflected badly on themselves, their unit or their Commanders.[173] When lessons were submitted, an increasingly haphazard lessons process developed and an investigation into abuse and unlawful killings in Iraq similarly concluded that the lessons process was flawed by its subjectivism.[174]

In the IC, exposure from the September dossier led to new, public, methods of scrutiny and lesson identification. This became even more fervent when WMD failed to be found – despite searches, reward schemes for informers, the digging up of tarmac and the use of ground-penetrating radar.[175] Initially, the Foreign Affairs Committee supported the decision to publish an intelligence assessment describing it as a 'welcome innovation'.[176] However, the dossier had created a sense of IC advocacy for government policy.

John Williams, Chief Spokesman and Media Advisor to the FCO commented to the Iraq Inquiry that his lesson for the future was that 'producing papers like the dossier was the wrong approach, because the media had come to see them as productions'.[177]

The Foreign Affairs Committee were quick to examine the lead-up to war after the invasion, investigating whether the government had presented 'accurate and complete information to Parliament' and publishing a report in July 2003 which included a number of lessons for the IC.[178] This inquiry was transparent, hearing oral evidence from a number of witnesses and considering a variety of issues surrounding the dossier including: its use of language, concluding that it was too assertive; accuracy, which was considered to be too early to judge; and the charges that it had been 'sexed up', which the committee denied. However, it also concluded that the IC had been tainted by the production of an additional dossier in February 2003, which became known as 'the dodgy dossier', even though this was produced by Alistair Campbell's Iraq Communications Group and had not been cleared for publication by the JIC.

However, the IC did not facilitate the external lesson identification process. The Foreign Affairs Committee complained of a lack of access to intelligence material and individuals for interview. The committee wrote to the Cabinet Office Intelligence Coordinator, the Chairman of the JIC, the Chief of Defence Intelligence, the Head of SIS and the Director of GCHQ without receiving one reply. The committee declared 'We regard the Government's refusal to grant us access to evidence essential to our inquiries as a failure of accountability to Parliament.'[179] Blair justified the lack of cooperation by confirming that full cooperation would be given to another inquiry, run by the Intelligence and Security Committee.[180] This did not appease the committee who noted that the Intelligence and Security Committee was appointed by, and reported directly to, the Prime Minister.[181]

The Intelligence and Security Committee had similar objectives to the Foreign Affairs Committee, to 'examine whether the available intelligence, which informed the decision to invade Iraq, was adequate and properly assessed and whether it was accurately reflected in Government publications'.[182] The report was published in September 2003 and included the identification of some lessons, including recommending a process for individuals to record formal concerns on draft JIC documents. However, the criticisms of the September dossier by the Intelligence and Security Committee were temperate. In discussing the repetition of the headline grabbing claim that Saddam's WMD could be ready for deployment within forty-five minutes – without the context that this assessment only referred to battlefield chemical and biological munitions – the committee merely stated 'This was unhelpful to an understanding of this issue.' The failure of the MoD to disclose that a number of staff had raised concerns about assessments in writing to their line managers was labelled simply 'unhelpful'.[183]

It also seemed unlikely that the lessons of the Intelligence and Security Committee would be taken any more seriously by the IC than those identified by the Foreign Affairs Committee. The JIC still withheld eight relevant papers from the inquiry and, whilst the government welcomed the Intelligence and Security Committee report, the IC failed to respond to the committee's questions and recommendations until five months later.[184] When the response arrived, the committee was equally unhappy with the outcome: 'The Committee is not satisfied with the Government's Response. It emphasised only four key conclusions whilst either rejecting or failing to address fully many of our other conclusions and recommendations.'[185]

While the Intelligence and Security Committee was conducting its inquiry, a series of events led to the death of Dr David Kelly on 17 July 2003. Dr Kelly was a MoD biological weapons expert who had been revealed as the source for a claim that the September dossier had been 'sexed up'. The controversy surrounding Dr Kelly's sudden death led the Secretary of State for Constitutional Affairs to request an urgent judicial inquiry into the surrounding circumstances presided over by Lord Hutton. However, the inquiry provided more of a narrative of events than a focus upon identifying lessons.[186]

On the same day that Hutton's report was published, a former top US weapons inspector, Dr David Kay, testified to the US Senate Armed Services Committee that Iraq did not possess WMD and that the programme had begun to be dismantled as early as 1991. At the same time, there was an ongoing inquiry by the US Senate Select Committee on Intelligence into America's pre-war assessments of Iraq and there was mounting pressure on the British Prime Minister to announce a similar inquiry. Consequently, in February 2004, a fourth inquiry, headed by Lord Butler, was established. The inquiry was given a broad remit to review intelligence coverage of WMD as well as the accuracy of intelligence on Iraqi WMD and its use by the government. The inquiry was still limited by working to a tight timetable, having to conclude before other important pieces of evidence – including the report of the Iraq Survey Group – became available. However, unlike the Foreign Affairs Committee and Intelligence and Security Committee, the Butler inquiry was provided access to all JIC assessments and members of the IC for interview. The result was a plethora of identified lessons.[187]

When the report was presented to Parliament, the Prime Minister announced four lessons were to be implemented immediately, including that an SIS officer was to be appointed to oversee the implementation of all Butler lessons.[188] On 15 November 2004, Jack Straw announced that a wider lesson implementation programme had commenced and that the Security and Intelligence Coordinator, Sir David Omand, would establish a special implementation oversight committee, the Butler Implementation Group.[189]

The Butler Implementation Group tasked study teams to provide implementation plans and present the results the following year.[190] These were reported to ministers and the government subsequently published its own report which revealed a number of lessons had been implemented.[191] These included new procedures and resources to oversee SIS validation of HUMINT, greater cross-government intelligence coordination through the creation of a new IT system, the expansion of the Assessment Staff and a new Professional Head of Intelligence Analysis.[192] Furthermore, according to Cabinet Secretary Gus O'Donnell and National Security Advisor Peter Ricketts, Butler lessons were further institutionalised by being given 'significant weight' in the intelligence sections of the 2010 *Strategic Defence and Security Review*.[193] Nonetheless, whilst the government report demonstrated that a number of lessons from the Butler inquiry had been implemented, other identified lessons were ignored. The 216 page Butler report only resulted in an eleven page implementation report, which did not address Butler's recommendations one by one as was the usual government response format.[194]

The Intelligence and Security Committee was requested to monitor the ongoing progress of lesson implementation and included a specific 'Butler implementation' section in its own annual report until 2006. It revealed a number of implementation failures, including concerns over the slow arrival of the new IT system and the merging of the positions of the JIC Chairman and the Security and Intelligence Coordinator.[195] Other lessons implemented from the Butler review quickly became unlearned. The role of the Professional Head of Intelligence Analysis was held until August 2007, when the holder retired, and the post remained vacant until March 2009 when the government subsumed it again into the JIC Chairmanship.[196]

The Butler report also recommended that 'lessons-learned processes' be continued by the JIC.[197] Although this did not occur regularly, two examples emerged: on 13 July 2004, a Current Intelligence Group assessment reflected upon the accuracy of past intelligence by reviewing the possible links between al-Qaeda and Saddam Hussein; and the Challenge Team were tasked with reviewing past papers to see if judgements were correct and to identify lessons for the future.[198]

Throughout the 2000s there were repeated calls for a further, broader, official inquiry into the Iraq War. Initially the government argued that such an inquiry would be a 'huge diversion of effort',[199] that it was the responsibility of Parliament to scrutinise the government over Iraq – not an external inquiry – that any such efforts would divert away from the efforts to improve Iraq and that such an inquiry should not be held whilst troops remained in the country.[200] Many of the arguments against holding an inquiry echoed those of the post-Suez clamour, but MPs made comparisons with the Franks inquiry into the Falklands War as a historical precedent for such an inquiry to take place.

Eventually, under some political pressure, Prime Minister Gordon Brown established the Iraq Inquiry on 15 June 2009 with the huge scope of examining the run-up to the war, the military action and its aftermath, to establish what happened during this time and to identify any lessons to be learned for the future. Under the Chairmanship of Sir John Chilcot – who had also been a member of the Butler inquiry – the evidence hearing began in November of the same year with the report published seven years later, on 6 July 2016.

There were many criticisms of the inquiry from the outset, including the failure to include Parliament in deciding the terms of reference[201] and the committee composition[202] as well as ignoring previous recommendations from the House of Commons Public Administration Committee on how to conduct inquiries.[203] There was also some anger that it was not to be a form of truth and reconciliation process, and it was explicitly stated by the Prime Minister that the inquiry should not attempt to 'apportion blame'.[204] As the inquiry progressed there were also criticisms on the length of time it took to publish[205] – the inquiry ended up taking longer than the war itself – and the cost to the tax payer – a final total of £13,126,900.[206] Nonetheless, the inquiry process was substantial; over 150,000 documents were examined and twenty-one weeks' worth of oral evidence was taken from 180 senior politicians and officials – many in front of a public audience. Although there were arguments between the Cabinet Office and the inquiry committee over what documents could be declassified or included in the final inquiry report, access to government information and individuals was unprecedented.

The final report was damning and wide-ranging, concluding that Iraq had posed no imminent threat, that the war was not a last resort and that Britain failed to achieve its objectives. It was 2.6 million words long, over four times the length of Leo Tolstoy's epic *War and Peace*, and provided a masterful narrative of events supported by evidence; its own official history long before any official history would usually be written. This was not surprising given the inquiry committee included Sir Lawrence Freedman, Emeritus Professor of War Studies at King's College London and the official historian of the Falklands campaign, and Sir Martin Gilbert, an Honorary Fellow at Oxford University and official biographer of Winston Churchill. However, it was less successful in identifying lessons. Whilst the report was scattered with 'findings' throughout its twelve volumes only eleven and a half pages pulled them together as 'lessons'.[207] Additionally, unlike previous inquiries, the report did not offer concrete recommendations as to how any identified lessons could be practically implemented or institutionally entrenched, leaving the implementation decisions down to Whitehall departments.

The report was released during the fallout from Britain's monumental referendum decision to withdraw from the EU. This decision had caused tremors across the political establishment and the Conservative Party were in the midst of a leadership election to decide the next Prime Minister whilst the Labour leader, Jeremy Corbyn, was also facing his own leadership battle. Much of the report's media coverage focused upon blaming Tony Blair for leading Britain into an unsuccessful war and, in amongst a storm of political news stories, reflection upon the findings of the report was brief. The two-day parliamentary debate on the subject opened – after a packed session for David Cameron's last ever Prime Minister's Questions – with only fifty-three MPs. The following day this number had reduced to just thirty-two. In his opening statement the Foreign Secretary, Philip Hammond, noted 'the world's eye will not be focused on our proceedings with quite the laser-like intensity that might have been expected'.[208] However, Hammond suggested that Whitehall departments would look at the report in more detail. Initially, there was some concern that MPs, civil servants and the armed forces had long since identified their own lessons and moved on. In fact, the Foreign Secretary offered one telling remark which suggested that little further lesson identification or implementation would take place:

> The Government, including previous Administrations, have not stood still while waiting for the findings we have before us today. There were a number of important reviews relating to the invasion and occupation of Iraq before Chilcot . . . As a result of each, lessons have been identified and changes have been implemented, so a good deal of the work has already been done.[209]

Nonetheless, following the debate, the National Security Advisor was tasked with conducting a 'lessons learned' investigation across

Whitehall and the MoD held a 'year of Chilcot' with a team focused on identifying themes from the report and how these could implemented.[210] The House of Commons Public Administration and Constitutional Affairs Committee also followed up on this process and conducted their own inquiry to establish lessons to be learned from the Iraq Inquiry process itself, lessons for the machinery of government and how lessons could be implemented.[211] In addition, the Liaison Committee heard evidence from Sir John Chilcot along a similar vein on 2 November 2016. During the questioning Chilcot stated 'the real test will be the take-up of the lessons that we sought to draw and others may indeed find . . . I am reasonably encouraged that the attempt is being made systematically in Government to address those lessons.' He went on to conclude:

> there is a question for Parliament as to how you wish to hold the Government to account for the way in which they do that task and give an account to yourselves, as parliamentarians, of what they have found out, accepted and changed.[212]

However, a year and a half after the publication of the report, no written government response to identified lessons has been issued and no further debate has occurred within Parliament. The risk, therefore, is that lessons from the Iraq Inquiry will not be learned.

Telic Learning

Telic revealed learning from history across all spheres within the FCO but with few references to Granby and none to Vantage. Instead, Suez and appeasement remained ever present and, similar to the Falklands during the Gulf War, the last major intervention in Afghanistan was frequently referenced. In the individual sphere many analogies were utilised, often incorrectly, unwisely or just rhetorically and the importance of No10 decision-making reiterated that the biggest barrier to learning was that lessons could be marginalised by the Prime Minister in the decision-making process.

In the institutional sphere, identified lessons continued to be important for the approach to the UN, whilst the burden of managing Britain's imperial legacy remained in the FCO's strategic approach. However, lesson implementation continued to be ad hoc. Lessons identified from more recent events, including Afghanistan, were implemented but implementation during the operation was slow, leaving the diplomats in theatre to improvise in the individual sphere whilst waiting for the sluggish institutional sphere to catch up. Moreover, as postings in Iraq lasted a maximum of one year – as opposed to the usual two or three years – there was a higher turnover of staff than in normal posts and the frequent changes of personnel translated to a lack of learning continuity.

Lessons identified in the generational sphere also began to be important. FCO past experience in Iraq, from the 1920s through to the Gulf War, informed its understanding of the country and warnings of invasion. Attempts were made to harness individual and generational learning for institutional purposes through the recalling of former Ambassadors for policy discussions, which was a new method of lesson identification and distribution. However, this shift in emphasis towards learning was very limited and did not compare to the reports identifying lessons produced by other departments, including the Stabilisation Unit and MoD; there still was not a learning culture. The Foreign Affairs Committee also revealed a lesson identification agenda but the FCO failed to demonstrate an emphasis upon lesson implementation.

In the MoD, new lessons teams had been created to focus upon the learning process. New methods of identifying lessons – including developing relationships with academics – had developed and the DwLM formalised the process further by renewing the emphasis upon the implementation of lessons, albeit slowly. Externally, the National Audit Office and Defence Committee complemented the process by providing additional lesson identification and monitoring lesson implementation.

Additionally, the MoD had developed its lesson distribution and retention. Distribution occurred across individuals and services (through the Defence Lessons Library), the public and Defence Committee (through published reports) as well as Whitehall and coalition nations (through the dissemination of reports and conferences). The new Defence Lessons Library also ensured that lessons were retained, beyond the updating of doctrine, to inform the planning of operations in the future – albeit that it remains extremely underutilised. Consequently, for the first time, the MoD demonstrated a learning process which encompassed all four stages of the learning process, with the National Audit Office determining the MoD lessons process to be 'comprehensive'.[213]

However, there remained many challenges and Telic revealed that few identified lessons from Vantage or Granby had been implemented or retained long term. Throughout the planning, emphasis remained upon lessons identified from Afghanistan and the most recent operations and exercises, demonstrating reliance upon the individual over the generational sphere. Other generational identified lessons, including the importance of avoiding appearing imperial, had been unlearned. Whilst some lesson implementation was demonstrated in the institutional sphere, in the changes to equipment, this was haphazard and many items continued to be unsuitable. Furthermore, many lessons which had previously been identified in the institutional sphere were either forgotten, re-identified or quickly unlearned, such as the importance of clear military objectives, the necessity of working with the US and heat discipline.

The MoD was also slow to identify and implement lessons during the operation. There were exceptions but these were outweighed by failing to examine strategic lessons until late; too late to inform Telic. This was, in part, due to the overwhelming number of identified lessons that emerged from the operation and through a greatly expanded, more democratic, lessons process.

In contrast, the IC demonstrated little learning from past interventions in any of the spheres of learning during Telic, with two exceptions. Firstly, lessons identified from Granby had led to overestimation in the institutional sphere which had also transcended into the generational sphere. Secondly, in the institutional sphere, lessons identified from Afghanistan were implemented in the central intelligence machinery. Otherwise, many identified lessons were forgotten, including the importance of HUMINT, sufficient language capabilities and methods to deal with the challenges of distillation, dissemination and classification of intelligence.

However, the new publicity of intelligence, since the acknowledgement of the existence of the agencies and due to the September dossier, placed the IC under such scrutiny that for the first time it was forced to reflect upon lesson identification and implementation for the future. The commitment to learning lessons from the Foreign Affairs Committee and Intelligence and Security Committee was negligible but the establishment of the Butler Implementation Group demonstrated that the lessons identified by the 2004 inquiry were taken seriously, with many lessons initially implemented, albeit that several were promptly unlearned. Therefore, the shift in culture to embracing the lessons identified by Butler was temporary and limited with little evidence of many lessons implemented long term. Furthermore, outside the DIS, the process of lesson identification did not continue on an ongoing basis.

There was some initial hope that the Iraq Inquiry – with its wide remit – could help to compensate for the lack of learning in inadequate areas across government. However, its failure to explicitly identify a significant number of lessons, and the lack of subsequent government response or parliamentary debate, suggests that it is even less likely that Chilcot's lessons will be implemented, distributed and retained long term. It also revealed a broader question over the government's reliance on inquiries to ensure that it does not fail history in the future.

7 Failing History or Lessons Learned?

> Rulers, Statesmen, Nations are wont to be emphatically commended to the teaching which experience offers in history. But what experience and history teach us is this – that peoples and governments never have learned anything from history, or acted on principles deduced from it.
>
> *(Georg Wilhelm Friedrich Hegel, 1837)*[1]

In the past, the British government has failed history in a number of ways. Whilst it is clear that learning has developed over time, as has the emphasis placed upon the importance of learning lessons, it is also apparent that the FCO, MoD and IC each learn from history in different ways. Each focuses their efforts to learn on different stages of the learning process, different learners, different stages of an intervention, different levels of policy-making, through different methods and to different extents; there is no consistency for learning from history across government.

Learning from the past is not easy. It is a complex process, with several stages, that develops from 'the acquisition of knowledge' to 'informing policy decision-making' and within, as well as between, each stage – identification, distribution, retention and implementation – there are challenges to be overcome. From 1956 to 2009 the FCO was primarily focused on the lesson identification stage of the process, from internal sources, including the use of despatches. Attempts by the Foreign Affairs Committee to offer external lesson identification were largely ineffective as the FCO did not seek to acquire knowledge from this body. The types of lessons identified were usually strategic, rather than operational or tactical, and there was no routine learning process as there was within the

MoD. Any lesson implementation was ad hoc and lessons were only retained in individual memory and through the informalities of best practice. Despite the existence of in-house historians, no official histories have been written in the FCO on any of the interventions examined in this book and consequently they do not offer a method of retention for the future.

Out of the three government bodies, the MoD had the most comprehensive and substantial learning process, which developed and proliferated over time to cover all four stages of learning with specific lessons teams and systems. The MoD had long written post-operational reports identifying lessons, but implementation also began in earnest, firstly driven by defence reviews after Suez and then by a zealous minister after Kuwait. By Granby, a number of methods had been developed to distribute lessons internally, as well as to the public and suppliers. These methods were further formalised during Iraq through the Defence Lessons Identified Management System which provided a new method to ensure all identified lessons were implemented and retained.

Whilst the MoD identified a large number of lessons internally, including through exercises and war games, there was also an increase in identification of lessons externally from the media, Defence Committee, National Audit Office and Committee of Public Accounts. Unlike the FCO, the MoD tended to be open to lessons identified by these bodies and the Defence Committee developed its agenda to monitor the implementation of such lessons. Consequently, the failure of the MoD did not relate to learning lessons from operations but a failure to learn lessons across operations; treating each operation as individual entities whereby identified lessons were either not transferred or were only implemented in the next major conflict. The result was that future capability improved infrequently and previously identified lessons were regularly re-identified.

In the IC, any substantial lesson identification was conducted externally. Although the IC did not implement the lessons identified by the Foreign Affairs Committee and, to some extent, the Intelligence and Security Committee, larger reviews – those conducted by Lord Franks and Lord Butler – led to identified lessons being implemented. In fact, the IC benefited at the implementation stage by the establishment of the Butler Implementation Group and ongoing monitoring by the Intelligence and Security Committee, albeit that many implemented lessons were quickly unlearned. Similarly to the FCO, lessons were primarily retained through best practise norms and standards, with the Butler report acting as a reference guide. However, they were also retained through significant changes in the institutional structure of the central intelligence machine which proved to be a successful way to ensure lessons remained learned over the long term.

To ensure that the British government does not fail history, the FCO, MoD and IC need to adopt methods to include all four stages of the learning process. To facilitate this process a lessons team must be established for any new intervention – to identify, record and enable implementation of lessons as quickly as possible and to avoid having to establish an audit trail after the operation. After any major event – including military operations – and annually in any event, the FCO, MoD and IC should also conduct a full lessons review and produce a report which clearly identifies lessons and suggests methods of implementation. These reports must avoid the misnomer of 'lessons learned' when the lessons are only identified, as it risks leading to a failure to learn based on the assumption that lessons have been implemented. The language of 'post-mortems' should also be discouraged as it places negativity on the process from the outset and does not encourage cultural embracing of learning where reviews are treated as a current and active part of policy decision-making.

Upon completion of such a report it should be passed to an oversight body to ensure that identified lessons are implemented, at least in the short term. Ongoing, oversight can be conducted internally through lessons management structures and externally through the House of Commons Select Committees – as the Defence Committee does currently – but there is also an opportunity for a cross-Whitehall lesson implementation group. Such a group would have the responsibility of ensuring lessons are implemented, distributed and retained but would also be able to consider methods for cross-departmental efficiencies in terms of time and money.

Learning is further complicated by the number of competing actors and different spheres of learning involved in the process. From Suez to Iraq the FCO focus on learning was in the individual sphere. An appreciation and sensitivity towards history, often borne from a concern and understanding of local environments developed through diplomatic postings, proved beneficial. However, the emphasis on the individual sphere of learning led FCO policy to be more disposed to being driven by the agendas of strong, senior individuals. In particular, lessons identified by the Prime Minister and Foreign Secretary often trumped those of diplomats – most clearly demonstrated in the run-up to the Iraq War – whilst the Prime Minister's Private Secretaries and Cabinet Secretaries also played a significant role. An over-reliance on this sphere resulted in an inconsistent approach across the institution; to overcome subjectivity in the individual sphere, and to create coherent policies, identified lessons must be formally agreed and institutionalised.

However, the use of former Ambassadors in the run-up to Iraq revealed a new emphasis as individually identified lessons were passed into the generational sphere for the first time; the FCO was the only institution to demonstrate any active learning across generations during this time. Learning in this sphere is particularly beneficial for lesson retention as changes in personnel, from retirement and the revolving door of posting rotations within Whitehall, can lead to a loss of corporate memory. In addition, learning in the generational sphere is particularly significant when dealing with the Middle East where many policy-makers stay in power for decades thus retaining lessons for longer than the FCO through individual memory. Generations can be better encouraged to interact through better briefings, handover notes, exit interviews, retaining contacts, conferences, regular meetings and mentoring schemes but other methods of retention can also be better exploited: changes in structure, habit, establishing best practices, education, training and storing formally recorded lessons digitally with well-functioning search engine capabilities. However, these lessons must be regularly updated to ensure contemporary relevance. For Henry Kissinger, the lessons from history should be interpreted by each generation: 'History teaches by analogy, shedding light on the likely consequences of comparable situations. But each generation must determine for itself which circumstances are in fact comparable.'[2] In this regard, context is key as history provides suggestions but must be examined critically to avoid responding to the events of today with the logic of yesterday or injecting present day concerns into historical analysis to result in a biased conclusion. Intellectual honesty and critical thinking are required internally in government and within the media, as well as by the general public, in order that this can be achieved.

In contrast, the MoD focus on learning was in the institutional sphere, through formal methods, with a wide understanding of the importance of the learning process. The MoD also took advantage of regular strategic reviews to place greater emphasis on relevant lessons which provided a bureaucratic imperative to take lesson identification and implementation seriously, even during peacetime. In this sense, lesson identification provided data and rationale for decisions, making them more appealing and persuasive to politicians.

However, focusing on learning in the institutional sphere alone had its limitations. The emphasis on learning is often at odds with the wider MoD culture whereby individuals are trained to have a 'can do' attitude, rewarded for doing the same thing well – rather than questioning its principles – and where loyalty is highly regarded. As Basil Liddell Hart mused '"loyalty", analysed, is too often a polite word for what would be more accurately described as "a conspiracy for mutual inefficiency"'[3] but the problem is compounded when loyalty is measured in terms other than to British security, such as command and departmental or regimental loyalty. In fact, a report by Charles Haddon-Cave – into issues surrounding the 2006 loss of an RAF Nimrod in Afghanistan – identified twelve cultural challenges within the MoD to lesson learning.[4] In any institutional sphere, cultural issues must be combated – including the requirement for a positive professional institutional image, which may be threatened by admitting past difficulties, or a belief that criticism of superiors is a form of dissent. An active encouragement of learning from history and a collaborative approach helps to promote learning as a unified strength rather than a disloyal weakness and more research on operant learning in institutions – rewarding individuals for learning from the past – may also prove beneficial.

The institutional, habitual nature of lesson identification within the MoD also risks removing careful reflection upon lessons and the genuine desire to learn and the quality of lessons identified.

Additionally, the formality of process can lead to a misguided assumption that once a lesson is identified, it will automatically be passed along the conveyor belt to the next stage of learning and responsibility for overseeing its implementation is absolved. The comfort of this formulaic process also leads to the risk of ignoring informal learning that occurs amongst peers and down the chain of command at lower ranks.

From 1956 to 2009, in the IC, little learning occurred in any sphere. This lack of learning was partly due to its culture; whilst the FCO lived with the weight of history, the IC focused on horizon scanning for the future and dealing with the events of the moment. There was, therefore, very little opportunity for reflection on the past. The nature of the IC as a service provider to 'customers' – almost as a consultancy whereby the customer drives the agenda – also meant that lesson identification was primarily driven by customer requests. In the 1970s, the US Intelligence Community Staff commissioned the Product Review Division to conduct reviews on the way it conducted its intelligence.[5] It resulted in a number of lessons being identified and implemented and a similar process may prove beneficial in Britain.

Across all three bodies, the democratic input by learners into the lessons process varied. The FCO process was mainly focused on ministers and Ambassadors, the most senior diplomats. Input into the IC process was mainly by external influences – customers and inquiries. The MoD, over time, developed the most democratic lesson identification process, allowing input by learners across services and ranks. A more democratic process reinforces that learning from history is culturally important to an institution and both a cross-personnel capability and responsibility, albeit leading to new challenges of managing the subjectivity and quantity of data. For example, a brigade tour in Afghanistan would identify approximately 1,000 lessons, which would be distilled to around 300. However, in three months the Land lessons staff can only consider around forty lessons.[6]

As well as examining the learning process and different learners this book has considered learning at different stages of an intervention: before, during and after. In the FCO, the majority of learning from history occurred during the planning of an intervention.

There was also some lesson identification and implementation during operations, but mainly at the early stages. In contrast, whilst the MoD often had the most time to draw upon identified lessons in planning, especially contingency planning, the majority of reflection upon history occurred only after the operation and on that specific operation alone. Learning at this stage was often easier for the MoD because the operation had a defined end point – marked by troop withdrawal – whereas the FCO and IC often continued to work in the area. In the IC, learning was the most limited and was primarily delivered in the form of assessments and reassessments before and during operations. As a result, it was not surprising that the FCO had a longer-term view, although this was limited to only key strategic identified lessons, whilst the MoD reflected upon the lessons identified from the last major operation and the IC identified and implemented very little.

The result was that long-term learning was sporadic. For learning from history to be successful it must occur at the planning stage – reflections from past, relevant, operations – during the operation – to quickly identify and successfully implement lessons whilst the operation is ongoing – and after the operation – to ensure that lessons are learned for the future. Whilst some lessons remained learned from 1956 – managing the media and international, domestic and parliamentary opinion, working with the UN, protecting the economy and the imperative of American support – others were regularly forgotten, unlearned, re-identified or unsuccessfully implemented. In comparison to the learned lessons – which were strategic in nature – these were often operational: in the FCO, forgetting to secure overflying rights was a common theme; in the MoD, issues of logistics and tracking of equipment continued across operations; in the IC, security classification issues reoccurred. In fact, outside the broad strategic identified lessons, lessons from past interventions in the Middle East quickly became forgotten and learning primarily came from the last major conflict: Suez for Jordan, the Falklands for the Gulf, Afghanistan for Iraq. Proximity of time proved more important than proximity of geography or similarity of operation or enemy.

Consequently, in order to improve learning from history, each institution must conduct an internal analysis of its current process for learning from history, with an admittance of any failings. To achieve this, SWOT (strengths, weaknesses, opportunities, threats) analysis can be utilised against each stage of the learning process (identification, implementation, distribution and retention), the three different spheres of learning (individual, institutional and generational) and at each stage of the intervention process (planning, during and after). Each institution would also benefit from studying the others' learning processes in more detail, as well as learning in other countries, before establishing their own revised and improved processes. The analysis should consider that internal lesson identification is a prerequisite to learning, but external identification is also beneficial and should not be ignored. As inquiries are an expensive means of external lesson identification, the House of Commons Select Committees offer a possible option; in comparison to the Iraq Inquiry, the Foreign Affairs Committee's report on Iraq took a year to produce at a cost of £13,000.[7] In addition, the media, think-tanks and academics have a role to play through investigative journalism, the writing of critical histories and engagement with policy-makers. In 2002, several scholars founded a 'History and Policy' website to create a network of historians and provide a resource for policy-makers and journalists.[8] The ambition was to demonstrate the contemporary relevance of history for policy-making, with a belief that history could provide relevant lessons for the present. Such forums provide an important link which could be used to greater advantage. Focus must be given to learning from positive and negative experiences as well as opportunities to challenge historical or analogical assumptions. The government would also benefit from a removal – or at least reduction – of the division of labour between history and learning lessons. Even in the MoD, where there are lessons teams, these are separated from historians whilst historical and lessons analyses are treated as distinct disciplines. The in-house historians, official historians and historical branch historians all offer an invaluable resource for any learning process and should also be further incorporated into policy-making. This is the responsibility of both policy-makers and historians to create a new link and encourage histories to be written with a critical eye and in-depth analysis so that they are relevant for the future.

The learning process requires finance and resources. In particular, the implementation stage of learning can be extremely costly. In an age of budget cuts and austerity measures, investment in history and learning is likely to be a low priority. This was exemplified in 2009 when the Foreign Secretary, David Miliband, accounted that keeping open the FCO library cost £246 per book. Consequently, it was closed, dispersing 60,000 books, pamphlets, reports and documents and over 500 years of Britain's history to other facilities. However, as a result of budget cuts, Whitehall is also experiencing pressure to reform and learning initiatives can offer low cost alternatives to dealing with failures or expensive policy reviews and inquiries which have proved ineffective for long-term learning. An ongoing learning process can help to prevent costly mistakes and investing in the process should form part of the strategic decision-making of budget reviews within each body. Additionally, when resources are tight, focusing upon methods of learning which centre on the overlap of all three spheres of learning, including the holding of conferences, will provide the most efficient results.

Learning from history is also time-consuming and the workload pressure and bottomless in-trays of busy bureaucrats, politicians and service personnel leaves lesson learning perpetually at the end of the 'to-do' list. This challenge has long been known; the political scientists Ernest May and Richard Neustadt advised in the 1980s of the difficulties of getting policy-makers to read history.[9] Even in the learning environment of MoD Staff Colleges, learning is against the clock, with voluminous reading lists and many topics to cover in a short space of time, allowing little opportunity for reflection. This restricts ongoing learning but also significantly impacts learning during planning. When crises occur, decisions have to be made quickly. Consequently, for example, despite the large number of lessons now digitally available in the MoD, there is no time to consult the Defence Lessons Library when a brief is required for a minister within a few hours.[10] Similarly, time is required for lesson implementation and distribution. It is, therefore, important to identify opportunities where time to learn from history can be maximised: during training, lunchtime briefings, diarising and prioritising a regular time slot. In conducting the planning stage of an operation, it is also recommended that a historian, or member of a lessons team, is included. As time is often limited during this phase, inclusion of such personnel will allow historical expertise to be included in discussion or relevant past experiences to be quickly researched for inclusion within the decision-making process.

In addition to the difficulty of allocating time to learn from history, sometimes time must pass after an operation to allow the political environment to be more open to learning from the past. Admitting failure or accepting criticism is always difficult and ministers and civil servants can be extremely sensitive about identifying lessons from past performances. After the 1979 Iranian Revolution the British Ambassador in Tehran, Sir Anthony Parsons, returned to London and ran a series of lunchtime meetings to ascertain how the FCO had failed to predict the recent events. The diplomatic correspondent John Dickie noted 'To have a senior ambassador stand up in front of everyone . . . and admit he made a mistake requires a large measure of courage.' This was an 'exception to the normal ostrich posture in the Foreign Office over learning lessons from mistakes'.[11]

This challenge has become increasingly difficult as manoeuvrings for career promotion rely on success, rather than admitting failure, and as leaders become more aware of creating their own legacy. Winston Churchill not only read history, but was also consciously instrumental in creating his own historical legacy through his speeches and writings.[12] Anthony Eden also repeatedly appealed to history for vindication, convinced that in the course of time history would reveal his actions in Suez to have been correct.[13] Over time, the use of spin doctors and increased media training has resulted in leaders becoming increasingly aware of managing their own image, including through the destruction or withholding of documents from public release. Consequently, if history is politically influenced, so are the lessons which are drawn. However, as this challenge is related to culture, it can be overcome with time and commitment.

Learning from History since Iraq

Despite the challenges to learning from history, events from the past continue to permeate policy debate. As Karl Marx observed

'Men make their own history, but not just as they please. They do not choose the circumstances for themselves, but have to work upon circumstances as they find them, have to fashion the material handed down by the past.'[14] In fact, the spectre of Iraq has long since loomed over foreign and security policy decisions with its lessons pervading current debate, especially in regards to further military interventions in the Middle East region. When Britain withdrew from Iraq in 2009 it left a weak government in place. The 2010 Iraqi elections saw the country without an agreed administration for 249 days and, in 2011, violent civilian deaths totalled 4,087 as US troops completed their withdrawal.[15] In 2012, attacks on Shia Muslim areas of the country sparked fears of new sectarian violence and by the end of the year Sunni Muslims began mass rallies to protest against marginalisation that had begun with the coalition policy of de-Ba'athification. By July 2013, the violence had returned to the levels of 2008 as the sectarian insurgency intensified and, by January 2014, opposition fighters had infiltrated the cities of Fallujah and Ramadi.

Throughout this time, a new insurgent group was emerging. In 2006, al-Qaeda in Iraq (AQI) created an umbrella organisation, Islamic State in Iraq (ISI), which was soon weakened by coalition counterinsurgency operations. However, post-withdrawal, in 2010, ISI gained a new leader – Abu Bakr al-Baghdadi – who rebuilt the group's capabilities. In April 2013, ISI announced a formal merger with forces in Syria to create the Islamic State in Iraq and the Levant (ISIL), before shifting its attention back to Iraq. By June 2014, ISIL had seized Iraq's second city, Mosul, and was advancing towards Baghdad, taking other key cities and towns along the way. It declared the creation of a caliphate and changed its name to Islamic State (known as IS, ISIS or Daesh). To combat this threat, since 2014, Britain has sent over 1,350 military personnel, trained over 52,000 Iraqi soldiers and conducted over 1,340 air strikes. In addition, it has continued to support Iraq financially, providing over £15 million to UN stabilisation efforts, pledging over £169.5 million in humanitarian aid and providing £300 million in loan guarantees.[16]

Consequently, far from increasing security, Telic has facilitated the rise of extremism and continues to be costly. As early as 2005 the JIC assessed that the Iraq conflict had exacerbated the threat to Britain from international terrorism and resulted in increased cooperation between terrorist networks.[17] The displacement of an estimated 4 million people as a consequence of the war – the largest human displacement in the Middle East since 1948, with a further 3.3 million Iraqis displaced by the presence of Daesh – only increased the threat further. In addition, North Korea and Iran, the two other 'axis of evil' nations, took the opportunity to enhance their own WMD capabilities while the West was distracted in Iraq and Afghanistan.[18] This sense of failure had a profound impact on Britain and consequently policy-makers have been keen to stress that there will be 'no more Iraqs' and that the lessons from Iraq have been learned.

The first test for these lessons was during the Arab Spring; this was a revolutionary wave which swept across the Middle East and North Africa, beginning at the end of 2010 in Tunisia and, by the end of 2012, included the toppling of a number of regimes. The government claimed that the lessons identified from Iraq informed its policy decision to avoid direct intervention and, instead, support was offered through an Arab Partnership Initiative and assistance to the Arab League. Focus shifted away from military options and towards diplomatic and economic endeavours and similarly away from Western-led initiatives to working with international organisations, Middle Eastern states and organisations in the region. FCO Minister Alistair Burt advised 'We learnt in Iraq . . . our response to the Arab Spring and our change in approach in Afghanistan have surely shown that we successfully learnt the lessons from the recent past.'[19]

As the Arab Spring sparked turmoil across the Middle East region, a growing crisis emerged in Libya in 2011, with anti-government protesters and rebels clashing with state security forces. As the death toll rose the possibility of a British intervention re-emerged. However, the Prime Minister, David Cameron, was keen to stress that if Britain was to commit to military involvement, the circumstances would have to be different to Iraq. In a debate in the House of Commons he stated:

> I want to deal with the way in which we will ensure that this is not another Iraq ... there will be no foreign occupation of Libya ... However, I would argue that the differences from Iraq go deeper. It is not just that this time, the action has the full, unambiguous legal authority of the United Nations nor that it is backed by Arab countries and a broad international coalition, but that millions in the Arab world want to know that the UN, the US, the UK, the French and the international community care about their suffering and their oppression. The Arab world has asked us to act with it to stop the slaughter, and that is why we should answer that call.[20]

After the passing of UN Security Council Resolution 1973 – authorising member states to take all means necessary to protect civilians – Parliament voted 557–13 in favour of intervention. However, following Cameron's identified lessons from Iraq, fighting in Libya was led by a local opposition movement against the dictator, Colonel Muammar Gaddafi. Consequently, Britain only provided air support – Operation Ellamy – with the Arab League providing further assistance; no British boots were put on the ground. At the peak of the operation, 2,300 British service personnel, thirty-two aircraft and eight warships and attack submarines were deployed. From 19 March to 31 October 2011 over 3,000 sorties were flown, more than 2,000 of which were strike sorties.[21]

Militarily the operation was a success but the intervention has subsequently been criticised. Ellamy suffered from 'mission creep', extending from protecting civilians to supporting the capture and killing of Gaddafi – who had governed the country since 1969 – by rebels. After his deposal, the country descended into chaos; the rebels supported by Britain – the National Transitional Council – murdered Gaddafi and failed to maintain security. After power was handed to the General National Congress (GNC), voters became increasingly dissatisfied and chose to replace the GNC – in June 2014 – with the Council of Representatives. In response, the GNC established a rival government in Tripoli, causing further conflict. In 2015, a UN initiative negotiated the unity of the two camps as the Government of National Accord but this has since been rejected by the Council of Representatives and large parts of the GNC, therefore creating a third government competing for power. There are also many smaller rival groups holding territory across the country, including Tuareg and Daesh forces. The House of Commons Foreign Affairs Committee concluded that the government's policy was not informed by accurate intelligence – including the nature of the Libyan rebellion – that it lacked a clear strategic objective or a post-war strategy.[22] It was clear, therefore, that lessons from Iraq had not been learned.

Protests also began in Syria in 2011 against President Bashar al-Assad's regime. These soon grew into a civil war, deteriorating throughout 2012–13 and causing a refugee crisis, with increasing evidence that Assad was using chemical weapons against his opposition. On 21 August 2013, a chemical attack killed hundreds of civilians causing widespread condemnation. Cameron again began to consider British intervention, especially as President Barack Obama's administration was keen to send retaliatory air strikes and had asked for British participation in a coalition.[23] Parliament was recalled for a vote and, echoing the events prior to Telic, a JIC assessment on Assad's use of chemical weapons was published. The Prime Minister recognised 'the scepticism and concerns that many people in the country will have after Iraq' on the use of intelligence as justification and so the government went to great lengths to demonstrate that lessons had been learned in how to present intelligence to a wide audience.[24]

Efforts were also made to reassure the nation over the intervention itself with Cameron stating 'I am deeply mindful of the lessons of previous conflicts and, in particular, of the deep concerns of the country that were caused by what went wrong with the Iraq conflict in 2003.'[25] However, the failure of Libya made MPs nervous and, on 30 August 2013, Parliament voted 285–272 against joining US-led strikes. Instead, the UK focused its efforts outside the country by condemning the actions of Assad, supporting the High Negotiations Committee of the Syrian Opposition and responding to the subsequent humanitarian crisis in Syria and surrounding countries. However, as the humanitarian crisis worsened, Parliament changed its mind and – in a second vote on 2 December 2015 – chose to support strikes 397–223. The UK has also committed £2.46 billion to the crisis since 2012.[26]

Whilst Iraq has remained present in debates over interventions in the region, there have also been a number of changes in approach to learning from history since Telic. The arrival of a new government, and particularly a new Foreign Secretary – William Hague – in May 2010, led to a number of immediate changes in the FCO. Hague, a part-time historian, regarded learning from history as significant and set a new tone to the culture of the institution by quickly moving the in-house historians from a basement in a satellite building to a newly refurbished office in the main FCO building. He declared:

> Just as one draws on economists and people with specialist knowledge of a particular country, so we should be drawing on the insights provided by our historians. The historians are an obvious resource and they were not appreciated by the last administration. They were languishing in a basement and now the light is shining on their books. It is intended to be a signal to the whole Foreign Office to use them, and to remember the importance of understanding history.[27]

Hague also reopened the FCO library and told the FCO in 2011 'We are putting greater emphasis on cultivating and retaining knowledge throughout the institution; bringing the work of FCO Historians back into the consideration and formulation of policy . . . including regular seminars to learn from history.'[28] These seminars primarily occur internally, as part of an optional lunchtime learning series, but more events have begun to be organised which bring together academics and policy-makers.

To further encourage learning from history, Hague developed a new approach to FCO alumni. He noted when he arrived that when Ambassadors retired from the FCO their accumulated knowledge was being unnecessarily lost. Describing the retired personnel as 'part of the collective memory and intellectual firepower of the organisation', the Foreign Secretary set up a group of former FCO members to consider foreign policy on a global basis.[29] In addition, ex-Ambassadors were invited to participate in regional forums, providing lesson distribution across generations, with the Middle East group meeting every two to three months.[30] Although such meetings provide an ad hoc and less formal method of retaining and distributing lessons, changes in technology mean that they could become increasingly important. As electronic records have replaced paper records, information on policy decision-making has become easier to delete and many staff do not keep drafts of documents, only final versions.[31] This means that the investigation of policy-making to identify lessons, and to establish whether lessons from history were considered, is likely to become increasingly challenging and lead to more reliance on individual and generational memory.

In addition, the FCO's 2015 annual report revealed that some learning processes had been established. In particular, the FCO crisis centre was conducting exercises after every crisis, albeit that these were titled 'lessons learnt exercises'.[32] There was also a less formal process to identify and implement lessons after security breaches, including after the 2014 attack in Kabul and the attack on the US Consulate in Benghazi. Furthermore, the set-up of a new Diplomatic Academy was heralded as a way in which to encourage learning in the generational sphere and may prove to offer an opportune method for lesson distribution.[33] Moreover, the FCO has co-sponsored some doctoral research and experimented with secondments into the department for academic researchers.

The FCO board also recognised the institution's weakness in learning lessons. An internal audit in 2013 identified the 'need to document formally lessons learned, and track the benefits, from completed major projects'.[34] The 2013–14 annual report stated 'We are taking steps to respond to the audit's recommendations.'[35] However, there was no detail as to how this was to be achieved, nor was there any reference to a link with history.

In the MoD, many layers and levels of lessons teams exist, overlapping with knowledge management teams. Lessons are getting increasing prominence – as seen in their own sections on the Army Knowledge Exchange and in the *British Army Review*'s 'Learning in Conflict' special editions – and some association between the historical branches and the lessons teams in the DCDC and at Joint Forces Command have been established. Members of lessons teams have also attended events by the historical branches when the focus has been upon lessons.[36] The history–lessons relationship has been further entrenched in the British Army through the recent establishment of the internal think-tank, the Centre for Historical

Analysis and Conflict Research (CHACR) at Sandhurst. However, the relationship remains ad hoc, disparate and in its infancy, with the historical branches often dismissed as the poor relation and not relevant to contemporary lessons. The Army Historical Branch, in particular, spends most of its time dealing with legal issues rather than writing histories and the separation of services means that joint histories are not written to provide an overarching MoD historical perspective.

Nonetheless, the MoD has recognised the need to study wider patterns of learning across operations of the past. The US military's Joint and Coalition Operational Analysis Division have examined lessons reports from over a decade of operations to ensure that strategic themes are learned and the British military has been placed under pressure to conduct a similar review.[37] The Defence Wide Lessons Board (DwLB) – a lessons management structure – began this process by collating and analysing historical lessons into a broad group of strategic lessons, but more can be done.[38]

In the IC, an annual assessment of accuracy was instigated as a way of identifying lessons across the year, following Butler recommendations, but soon fell by the wayside leaving no ongoing learning process in place. Instead, the most significant change for the IC has been the establishment of the National Security Council (NSC), in May 2010. This was part of an attempt by the government – along with the establishment of at least ten joint units in 2015–16 – to improve cross-Whitehall coordination. It currently includes the Chief of the Defence Staff, the heads of the intelligence agencies and the Chairman of the JIC, as well as relevant ministers and the Attorney General. It also has its own secretariat led by the National Security Adviser. On the first of the two day parliamentary debate on the finding of the Iraq Inquiry the Foreign Secretary, Philip Hammond, stated that the NSC was set up to 'ensure that there is proper, co-ordinated, strategic decision making across the whole of Government ... ensuring that all parts of the national security apparatus are properly joined up across Whitehall and beyond'.[39] However, each weekly meeting commences with an overview of the latest JIC intelligence, forcing greater IC accountability to security policy-makers and more self-reflection on lessons, albeit less formally than through lessons reports.⁴⁰ Hammond went on to claim that the NSC also institutionalised lessons from Iraq on challenging intelligence and planning, ensuring that they would remain learned: 'Having sat on the National Security Council . . . it seems to me highly improbable that the process of conduct of business in relation to this matter through 2002 and 2003, as set out by Chilcot, could be repeated now.'⁴¹ However, this conclusion has been challenged by a number of Parliamentary Committees – especially in relation to NSC failings over the intervention in Libya in 2011 – suggesting that lessons still need to be learned.⁴²

Additionally, in 2009, the government decided to review the programme of official histories produced through the Cabinet Office. This review was conducted by the retired civil servant Sir Joseph Pilling who concluded that the official histories should continue. He also made a number of recommendations for their improvement, particularly noting that the rationale for the programme remained unclear and that a new statement of purpose was required. For him the concept of accountability was central:

> it follows inevitably that it will be possible to learn lessons from histories written with the purpose of accountability in mind. Those with current responsibility in public life ought to be keenest to learn lessons but the lessons will be there to be learned and applied, whether by journalists, scholars or private individuals.⁴³

He also made a number of significant recommendations which are yet to be implemented. In particular, he recommended that subjects for official histories be selected every two years (rather than every eight to ten) to ensure relevance, the profile of the programme be raised and more effort made by civil servants to take advantage of the scheme.⁴⁴

At the same time, another review was conducted into the publishing arrangements of the official history programme by the literary agent Bill Hamilton.⁴⁵ Hamilton also emphasised that the programme was not well utilised and that the histories needed to be communicated in other media as well as print: 'If a central purpose of the Histories is that they should provide lessons learned to practitioners within Whitehall and beyond, the written volume on its own is unlikely to deliver this requirement.'[46] For him, the value of the histories lay as much in the depth of knowledge accumulated by the historian as the book itself and, therefore, the historian should provide consultation services and produce short, digestible briefs for busy policy-makers with reference to the relevant parts of the larger text.[47]

The Freedom of Information (FOI) Act 2000 has also had a significant impact upon learning from history since Iraq. The Act provides access to information held by public authorities by obliging those authorities to publish specific information and entitling the public to request additional information. In some senses, this increased accountability of government and should have forced more reflection upon learning as it allowed for the further scrutiny of the workings of Whitehall. However, in many ways, FOI has had the opposite effect for learning lessons. To avoid voluminous information having to be sanitised for public release, formal reporting has been reduced – including the abandonment of Ambassador annual reviews and valedictory despatches in 2006 – leading to a loss of sources from which to identify lessons and write histories. Furthermore, codewords are widely used in order to avoid being found by FOI searches and informal, face-to-face, briefings – without a written record – are now often preferred. As a result, the lessons of recent experience are expunged or go unreported and each new Head of Department arrives to a *tabula rasa*.[48] In addition, the volume of evidence available to an inquiry akin to the Iraq Inquiry – specifically tasked with identifying lessons – is unlikely to be available again in the future.[49]

Conclusion

Parts of the British government do learn lessons – some of the time – from past experiences of interventions in the Middle East. The emphasis on learning from history has increased over time and there have been further changes, updates and improvements since the end of the Iraq War. Nonetheless, the British government still regularly fails history and more needs to be done to reinforce, complement and improve recent developments. History has current application and is relevant; events occur in a historical context and create the historical context for the future. The difficulty is that historical lessons can be subjective, meaning different things to different people because lessons are interpreted as part of their identification. In addition, in the FCO, MoD and IC, learning becomes irrelevant if the lessons cannot effectively and persuasively be communicated to the ultimate decision-maker – often the Prime Minister. Whilst a better relationship between the FCO, MoD, IC and No10 has begun to develop through the establishment of the NSC, this must be further entrenched.

However, it is not to be assumed that effective learning and communication of lessons will always significantly impact the outcome of future policy. Policy creation is a complex and contested process influenced by many factors including beliefs, political positions, domestic politics, bargaining power and persuasion as well as time and resource restraints. In addition, it is not to be claimed that learning lessons will provide a predicted outcome as there will always be unintended consequences, especially in the multifaceted environment of military interventions.

Within the FCO, MoD and IC, identifying lessons from history will not be easy, but ensuring lessons are learned and stay learned will be even more challenging. History does not, as many historians are quick to point out, offer 'school solutions' but it does provide a database of how to conduct, or not conduct, interventions which can be contextualised to the requirements of today.[50] Certainly, the past should be treated, as L. P. Hartley declared, as 'a foreign country: they do things differently there',[51] but even Basil Liddell Hart conceded 'History can show us what to avoid, even if it does not teach us what to do – by showing the most common mistakes that mankind is apt to make and to repeat.'[52] In fact, whilst many historians would dispute Marx's famous quote that history repeats itself, there are any number of regularities which lead one to align to the often cited Mark Twain maxim that history does not repeat itself, but it sure does rhyme. As Niccolò Machiavelli noted in 1517 'Whosoever wishes to foretell the future must consider the past, for human events ever resemble those of preceding times.'[53]

Notes

The files kept at The National Archives, Kew, which have been used for this book are designated ADM (Admiralty), AIR (Air Ministry), CAB (Cabinet Office), DEFE (Ministry of Defence), DO (Commonwealth Office), FCO (Foreign and Commonwealth Office), FO (Foreign Office), KV (Security Service), PREM (Prime Minister's Office), T (Treasury) and WO (War Office).

Transcripts from the British Diplomatic Oral History Programme Churchill College, Cambridge are designated DOHP. Documents which were declassified or released as part of the Iraq Inquiry are available online at www.iraqinquiry.org.uk. These documents have been appended with TII for clarity of origin.

Finally, documents from the US State Department are published online by the Office of the Historian as a series 'Foreign Relations of the United States'. They are available at history.state.gov/historical-documents and are designated FRUS throughout. Transcripts from the Foreign Affairs Oral History Collection, Association for Diplomatic Studies and Training, Arlington, Virginia, are designated FAOH and are available at www.adst.org. All other documents are provided with a full reference.

Chapter I Learning from History

1. Coleridge, Samuel Taylor [1884] (2005), '18 December 1831', in Samuel Taylor Coleridge, *The Table Talk and Omnia of Samuel Taylor Coleridge*, T. Ashe (ed.), London: George Bell and Sons.
2. Tony Blair, speech to the US Congress, 18 July 2003.
3. <http://www.iraqinquiry.org.uk/the-inquiry/> (last accessed 10 August 2017).

4. This accusation has been repeatedly denied by Sir John Chilcot.
5. David Cameron, UN Assembly address, 25 September 2014.
6. Elton, G. R. (1991), *Return to Essentials*, Cambridge: Cambridge University Press, pp. 114, 4, 9; Taylor, A. J. P. [1957] (2008), *The Trouble Makers: Dissent over Foreign Policy, 1792–1939*, London: Faber & Faber, p. 23.
7. Gowing, Margaret (1978), 'Reflections on Atomic Energy History', *The Rede Lecture 1978*, Cambridge: Cambridge University Press, p. 5.
8. Thucydides [431 BC] (1954), *History of the Peloponnesian War*, translated from Greek to English by Rex Warner, London: Penguin, p. 48.
9. Rowse, A. L. (1946), *Use of History*, London: Hodder & Stoughton Limited, p. 6.
10. Beck, Peter (2006), *Using History, Making British Policy*, Basingstoke: Palgrave Macmillan, p. 26.
11. Hooper, n.d., FO 371/135611.
12. Lord Plowden (1964), 'Report on Representational Services Overseas', FO 366/3197, p. 79.
13. See, for example, Hill, C. R. and P. Beshoff (eds) (1994), *Two Worlds of International Relations: Academics, Practitioners and the Trade in Ideas*, London: Routledge.
14. Response to Freedom of Information (FOI) request made by the author, 28 October 2014.
15. For example newspaper articles see CAB 103/596–7.
16. Woodward, Llewellyn (1970), *British Foreign Policy in the Second World War: Volume 1*; (1971), *Volume 2*; (1972), *Volume 3*; (1976), *Volume 4*; (1976), *Volume 5* all published by London: Stationery Office Books. For more on this see Beck, Peter (2012), 'Locked in a Dusty Cupboard, Neither Accessible on the Policymakers' Desks Nor Cleared For Early Publication', *English Historical Review*, 127/529, pp. 1435–70.
17. Beck, Peter (2013), 'A. J. P. Taylor on the Documents on British Foreign Policy as "a Cover-up for the Foreign Office"', *British International History Group Newsletter*, pp. 19, 4.
18. Cited in Beck, *Using History*, p. 34.
19. Gowing, 'Reflections', pp. 4–5.
20. Tusa, John (2004), 'A Deep and Continuing Use of History', in *History and the Media*, David Cannadine (ed.), Basingstoke: Palgrave Macmillan, p. 131.
21. Churchill, Hansard (Commons), DVII, c24, 4 November 1952; cited by Her Majesty Queen Elizabeth II, Christmas Broadcast, 25 December 1999.

22. See, for example, Ashdown, Paddy (2013), *A Brilliant Little Operation: The Cockleshell Heroes and the Most Courageous Raid of World War 2*, London: Aurum Press; Ashdown, Paddy (2014), *The Cruel Victory*, London: William Collins; Hague, William (2004), *William Pitt the Younger*, London: Harper Collins; Hague, William (2007), *William Wilberforce: The Life of the Great Anti-Slave Trade Campaigner*, London: Harper Press; Johnson, Boris (2014), *The Churchill Factor: How One Man Made History*, London: Hodder & Stoughton.
23. Houghton, David Patrick (1996), 'The Role of Analogical Reasoning in Novel Foreign-Policy Situations', *British Journal of Political Science*, 26/4, pp. 523–52.
24. See, for example, Khong, Yuen Foong (1992), *Analogies at War*, Princeton: Princeton University Press.
25. Thatcher, Margaret (1993), *The Downing Street Years*, London: Harper Collins, pp. 186, 817.
26. Woodward, Bob (2004), *Plan of Attack*, London: Simon & Schuster, p. 337.
27. For more on this see Vertzberger, Yaacov (1986), 'Foreign Policy Decisionmakers as Practical-Intuitive Historians: Applied History and Its Shortcomings', *International Studies Quarterly*, 30/2, pp. 223–47.
28. Schlesinger Jr, Arthur M. (1974), '"Lessons of the Past": The Use and Misuse of History in American Foreign Policy', *The Journal of American History*, 61/2, p. 444.
29. Noon, D. H. (2004), 'Operation Enduring Analogy: World War II, the War on Terror, and the Uses of Historical Memory', *Rhetoric and Public Affairs*, 7/3, pp. 339–66.
30. Mumford, Andrew (2015), 'Parallels, Prescience and the Past: Analogical Reasoning and Contemporary International Politics', *International Politics*, 52/1, pp. 1–19.
31. Butler, 8 March 1960, FO 370/2597.
32. See <https://issuu.com/fcohistorians> (last accessed 10 August 2017), for the latest work.
33. Macmillan, Margaret (2010), *The Uses and Abuses of History*, London: Profile Books Ltd, p. 150.
34. See, for example, AIR 41.
35. Howard, Sir Michael (2006), 'Military History and the History of War', in *Past as Prologue: The Importance of History to the Military Profession*, Williamson Murray and Richard Hart Sinnreich (eds), Cambridge: Cambridge University Press, p. 14.

36. Cited in Liddell Hart, B. H. [1972] (2012), *Why Don't We Learn From History?*, Marston Gate: Amazon, p. 41.
37. Of particular note are the volumes of work produced by F. H. Hinsley. See, for example, Hinsley, F. H. (1979), *British Intelligence in the Second World War, Volume 1: Its Influence on Strategy and Operations*, London: HMSO. For more on releasing information to the public see Aldrich, Richard J. (2004), 'Policing the Past: Official History, Secrecy and British Intelligence since 1945', *English Historical Review*, 119/483, pp. 922–53.
38. Andrew, Christopher (2010), *Defence of the Realm*, London: Penguin; Jeffrey, Keith (2011), *MI6: The History of the Secret Intelligence Service 1909–1949*, London: Bloomsbury; Goodman, Michael S. (2014), *The Official History of the Joint Intelligence Committee: Volume I: From the Approach of the Second World War to the Suez Crisis*, Abingdon: Routledge.
39. A number of which are now declassified and can be found at KV 4.
40. For more on this analogy see Herman, Michael (2008), 'What Can Intelligence Analysts Learn From Historians (and From International Relations Academics)?', background paper, <https://www.nuffield.ox.ac.uk/Research/OIG/Documents/meh%20website%20view%20on%20historians.pdf> (last accessed 9 December 2014).
41. Neisser, Ulric (1967), *Cognitive Psychology*, Michigan: Appleton-Century-Crofts.
42. Piaget, Jean (1972), *Psychology of the Child*, New York: Basic Books.
43. Vygotsky, L. S. (1978), *Mind in Society: The Development of Higher Psychological Processes*, Cambridge, MA: Harvard University Press.
44. Pavlov, I. P. (1960), *Conditioned Reflexes*, New York: Dover Publications.
45. Thorndike, Edward L. (1999), *Education Psychology: Briefer Course*, Florence: Routledge, pp. 69–83.
46. Kant, Immanuel [1781] (1998), *Critique of Pure Reason*, Cambridge: Cambridge University Press.
47. Jonassen, D. (1991), 'Evaluating Constructivist Learning', *Educational Technology*, 36/9, pp. 28–33.
48. Siemens, George (2005), 'Connectivism: A Learning Theory for the Digital Age', *International Journal of Instructional Technology and Distance Learning*, 2/1, n.p.
49. Haas, Ernst B. (1990), *When Knowledge Is Power*, Oakland, CA: University of California Press, p. 3.

50. Ucko, David H. and Robert Egnell (2013), *Counterinsurgency in Crisis*, New York: Columbia University Press.
51. Tetlock, P. E. (1991), 'Learning in U.S. and Soviet Foreign Policy: In Search of an Elusive Concept', in *Learning in US and Soviet Foreign Policy*, G. Breslauer and P. E. Tetlock (eds), Boulder, CO: Westview, p. 22.
52. May, Ernest (1973), *'Lessons' of the Past: The Use and Misuse of History in American Foreign Policy*, Oxford: Oxford University Press; Neustadt, Richard E. and Ernest R. May (1986), *Thinking in Time: The Use of History for Decision-Makers*, London: Collier Macmillan; Jervis, Robert (1976), *Perception and Misperception in International Politics*, Chichester: Princeton University Press.
53. Turner, M. E. (ed.) (2001), *Groups at Work: Advances in Theory and Research*, New York: Lawrence Erlbaum.
54. Jennings, M. Kent, Laura Stoker and Jake Bowers (2009), 'Politics across Generations: Family Transmission Reexamined', *The Journal of Politics*, 71/3, pp. 782–99; Rintula, Marvin (1963), 'A Generation in Politics: A Definition', *Review of Politics*, 25, pp. 509–22.
55. Waddell, Steven J. (2002), 'Six Societal Learning Concepts for a New Era of Engagement', *Reflections*, 3/4, pp. 18–26.
56. See, for example, Nye, Joseph S. (1987), 'Nuclear Learning and US-Soviet Security Regimes', *International Organization*, 41/3, pp. 371–402; Leng, Russell J. (1983), 'When Will They Ever Learn? Coercive Bargaining in Recurrent Crises', *The Journal of Conflict Resolution*, 27/3, pp. 379–419; Reiter, Dan (1994), 'Learning, Realism, and Alliances: The Weight of the Shadow of the Past', *World Politics*, 46/4, pp. 490–526.
57. Huber, George P. (1991), 'Organizational Learning: The Contributing Processes and the Literatures', *Organization Science*, 2/1, pp. 88–115; Levitt, Barbara and James March (1988), 'Organizational Learning', *Annual Review of Sociology*, 14, pp. 319–40; Argyris, Chris and Donald A. Schön (1996), *Organizational Learning*, Wokingham: Addison-Wesley.
58. For a summary of the changing relationship between the Prime Minister's Office and the FCO see Steiner, Zara (2005), 'The Foreign and Commonwealth Office: Resistance and Adaption to Changing Times', in *The Foreign Office and British Diplomacy in the Twentieth Century*, Johnson, Gaynor (ed.), London: Routledge, pp. 13–30.
59. For examples of the impact of organisational culture on learning see Foley, Robert T. (2014), 'Dumb Donkeys or Cunning Foxes? Learning in the British and German Armies during the Great War',

International Affairs, 90/2, pp. 279–98. He also discusses the role of lessons reports for 'horizontal learning' in Foley, Robert T. (2015), 'Horizontal Military Innovation and Lessons Reports', <https://defenceindepth.co/2015/12/09/horizontal-military-innovation-and-lessons-reports/> (last accessed 9 August 2017).
60. Jervis, Robert (1976), *Perception and Misperception in International Politics*, Chichester: Princeton University Press, p. 253.
61. Of particular relevance are Kolb, David A. (1984), *Experiential Learning: Experience as the Source of Learning and Development*, London: Prentice Hall; Levitt and March, 'Organizational Learning', pp. 327–8; Huber 'Organizational Learning'.
62. Cited in Liddell Hart, *Why Don't We?*, p. 15.

Chapter 2 No End of a Lesson – Suez 1956

1. Nutting, Anthony (1967), *No End of a Lesson: The Story of Suez*, London: Constable and Company. For the full story of Suez see, for example, Kyle, Keith (2003), *Suez*, London: I. B. Tauris; Louis, W. M. Roger and Roger Owen (eds) (1989), *Suez 1956: The Crisis and Its Consequences*, Oxford: Clarendon Press; Smith, Simon C. (ed.) (2008), *Reassessing Suez 1956*, Aldershot: Ashgate.
2. The Chief of Staff, Brigadier Hutton, and Chief of Counterintelligence, Sir Patrick Coghill, were also dismissed. Jordan Embassy to State Department, 2 March 1956, FRUS, 'Near East: Jordan-Yemen', 1955–7, volume XIII, document 19.
3. Nutting, *No End*, p. 17.
4. Memorandum, State Department, Washington, 19 July 1956, FRUS, 'Arab-Israeli Dispute', 1955–7, volume XV, document 478.
5. Briefing paper, 'The Suez Canal' paper, n.d., FO 371/119160.
6. UN General Assembly, RES/997(ES-I). This resolution was proposed by the US.
7. Eden, Hansard (Commons), DLXII, c1457–8, 20 December 1956.
8. Evelyn Shuckburgh, Assistant Under-Secretary of State for Middle East Affairs at the FCO, highlighted the legacy of Abadan in Suez and recalled Eden's fear of being called a 'scuttler' or an 'appeaser'. Transcript of Evelyn Shuckburgh, Suez Oral History Project, Liddell Hart Military Archives, King's College London, paper 20, pp. 4–5.
9. Persia was used by the British government to refer to Iran until 1955. Chiefs of Staff (COS) Committee minutes, 23 May 1951, DEFE 4/43, confidential annex.

10. Shatt al Arab is the river upon which Abadan sits. Eden, Sir Anthony (1960), *Full Circle: The Memoirs of Anthony Eden*, London: Cassell and Company, p. 195.
11. Millard, 'Memorandum on relations between the United Kingdom, the United States and France in the months following Egyptian nationalisation of the Suez Canal Company in 1956', 21 October 1957, FO 800/728, p. 2.
12. JIC, 'The Activities of Cairo Radio and Their Impact on the Territories to Which They Are Directed', in COS Committee minutes, 23 July 1956, CAB 158/25, annex.
13. UN Security Council (1951), S/RES/95.
14. Shuckburgh, Evelyn (1986), *Descent to Suez: Diaries 1951–56*, London: Littlehampton Book Services, pp. 305–6.
15. Briefing paper, 'The Suez Canal', p. 4.
16. For a summary of the influence of this time in Eden's career see Kyle, *Suez*, pp. 10–11.
17. Eden, *Full Circle*, foreword.
18. Eden to Eisenhower, 5 August 1956, PREM 11/1098.
19. Gaitskell, Hansard (Commons), DLVII, c513, 2 August 1956.
20. Dooley, Howard, J. (1989), 'Great Britain's "Last Battle" in the Middle East: Notes on Cabinet Planning during the Suez Crisis of 1956', *The International History Review*, 11/3, pp. 499–501.
21. Cabinet minutes, 25 October 1956, PREM 11/1103.
22. Sir Donald Hawley, DOHP 109, p. 14.
23. Ivor Lucas, DOHP 93, p. 3.
24. Sir Richard Parsons, DOHP 101, p. 66.
25. Lord Mountbatten twice drafted his resignation. Flying Officer Kenyon was court martialled for incapacitating his bomber rather than fighting against Egypt. Hennessy, Peter (1989), *Whitehall*, London: Secker and Warburg, p. 164.
26. 'Musketeer' was recommended by the COS Committee as a codename. Although its origins are unknown it may be linked to Churchill's advice to Eden that Attlee's government 'had scuttled and run from Abadan when a splutter of musketry would have settled the matter'. Churchill to Eden, 15 February 1952, PREM 11/91. For more on the origins of codenames see Kettle, Louise (2014), 'Operation Bunnyhug: What's in a Name?', <http://blogs.nottingham.ac.uk/politics/2014/05/26/operation-bunnyhug-whats-in-a-name/> (last accessed 18 August 2017).
27. Keightley, 'Report on HQ AATO – Operation Musketeer', 16 February 1957, WO 32/21899, p. 2.

28. King, 'Airborne Operation – 1956 Pattern', 28 December 1956, WO 32/21899.
29. Howard, 'Report on "Operation Musketeer"', n.d., WO 32/21899, p. 3.
30. Air Chief Marshal Sir Denis Smallwood cited in Sowrey, Air Marshal Sir Frederick B (ed.) (1988), 'Seminar – Suez 1956', *Royal Air Force Historical Society Journal*, 3 (January), p. 32.
31. Howard, 'Report on "Operation Musketeer"', p. 29.
32. Keightley, 'Operations in Egypt', n.d., DEFE 11/137, p. 5.
33. Templer, 'Lessons from Operation Musketeer', n.d., WO 32/16731, annex c.
34. Stockwell, 'Report by Commander 2 (BR) Corps on Operation "Musketeer"', n.d., WO 288/79, pp. 4–5.
35. Hull, 'Lessons from Operation Musketeer', n.d., WO 32/1673, annex a.
36. Ibid., p. 19.
37. Keightley, 'Operations in Egypt', p. 3.
38. Ibid., pp. 33–41.
39. Executive Committee of the Army Council (ECAC), n.d., WO 32/16731.
40. Keightley, 'Operations in Egypt', pp. 3–4.
41. COS minutes, 10 October 1956, DEFE 4/91 cited in Grove, Eric (2008), '"Who to Fight in 1956, Egypt or Israel" Operation Musketeer versus Operation Cordage', in *Reassessing Suez*, Smith (ed.), p. 82.
42. Kyle, *Suez*, pp. 293–4.
43. Article V. A full copy is available in Ibid., appendix A.
44. Smith, Adrian (2012), 'Rewriting History? Admiral Lord Mountbatten's Efforts to Distance Himself from the 1956 Suez Crisis', *Contemporary British History*, 26/4, pp. 490, 497.
45. Lieutenant Colonel Bill Howard disagreed with this analogy. 'Report on "Operation Musketeer"', p. 30.
46. Egyptian Committee, 'Military Operations Force Commanders Outline Plan', 10 August 1956, CAB 134/1217.
47. Bower, Tom (1995), *The Perfect English Spy*, London: William Heinemann, p. 196.
48. The term 'the Nuremberg factor' is used by Kyle, *Suez*, p. 560.
49. COS, 'Situation in Egypt after Musketeer', 25 October 1956, CAB 134/1217.
50. UK national service ended gradually from 1957 with the last intake in 1960.

Notes

51. Aldrich, Richard (1994), 'Intelligence, Anglo-American Relations and the Suez Crisis, 1956', *Intelligence and National Security*, 9/3, p. 548; Bower, *Perfect English Spy*, p. 196.
52. Bower, *Perfect English Spy*, pp. 195–6.
53. JIC, 'Security of Planning for Action against Egypt', 1 August 1956, CAB 158/25; JIC, 'Special Security Procedure "Terrapin"', 12 August 1956, CAB 158/25.
54. The Nasserite movement and Arab threat was the subject of a three day SIS conference in the summer of 1960. Bower, *Perfect English Spy*, p. 236.
55. JIC, 'Egyptian Nationalisation of the Suez Canal Company', 3 August 1956, CAB 158/25.
56. For all assessments during this time see CAB 158/25 and CAB 159/24.
57. JIC, 'Egyptian Nationalisation'; JIC, 'Considerations Affecting Action by Egypt in the Event of Armed Intervention', 7 August 1956, CAB 158/25; JIC, 'The Situation That Might Arise at the Conclusion of the Suez Canal Conference', 25 August 1956, CAB 158/25.
58. JIC, 'The Threat to United Kingdom interests Overseas', 18 October 1956, CAB 158/26.
59. Goodman, Michael (2007), 'The Dog That Didn't Bark: The Joint Intelligence Committee and Warning of Aggression', *Cold War History*, 7/4, pp. 529–51.
60. Dulles, memo, 28 March 1956, CAB 128/30.
61. This is speculative and does not appear to be evidenced in documents. Bower, *Perfect English Spy*, pp. 187–8.
62. Lucas, Scott and Alistair Morey (2000), 'The Hidden "Alliance": The CIA and MI6 before and after Suez', *Intelligence and National Security*, 15/2, p. 107; Kyle, *Suez*, p. 149.
63. Nutting, *No End*, p. 35. There is some debate over whether Eden said 'murdered', 'removed' or 'destroyed' based on differing accounts from Nutting.
64. Corera, Gordon (2011), *MI6: Life and Death in the British Secret Service*, London: Phoenix, p. 80.
65. Kyle, *Suez*, pp. 150–1.
66. Hugh Carless, DOHP 55, p. 12; Sir Terence Clark, DOHP 64, p. 4.
67. Sir Anthony Acland, DOHP 57, p. 5.
68. Keightley, 'Operations in Egypt', p. 4; Joint Planning Staff, report, 11 December 1957, DEFE 11/137, annex, p. 5.
69. Eisenhower, Dwight D. (1965), *Waging Peace 1956–1961*, New York: Doubleday, p. 58.

70. Millard, 'Memorandum', p. 3.
71. Lord Patrick Wright, DOHP 48, p. 14.
72. Keightley, 'Operations in Egypt', p. 4; COS Committee, 11 December 1957, DEFE 11/137, annex, p. 4.
73. The second veto was also used at this time against a similar resolution from the Soviet Union. Dixon to FCO, 30 October 1956, PREM 11/1105; Dixon to FCO, 30 October 1956, FO 371/121746.
74. UN Security Council (1956), S/3721.
75. For more on this see Johnson, Edward (2008), 'The Suez Crisis at the United Nations: The Effects for the Foreign Office and British Foreign Policy Consequences', in *Reassessing Suez*, Smith (ed.), pp. 166–77.
76. Ibid., pp. 173–4, 176.
77. Stockwell, 'Report', p. 43.
78. Keightley, 'Operations in Egypt', p. 4.
79. N.a., 'Operation Musketeer: Narrative of Events', n.d., DEFE 11/137, pp. 3–4.
80. COS Committee, 11 December 1957, DEFE 11/137, annex, pp. 11, 14.
81. JIC minutes, 16 August 1956, CAB 159/24.
82. Anderson, C. C. (1991), 'Suez – 1956', *The Naval Review*, 79/4 (October), p. 358.
83. Kyle, *Suez*, p. 383.
84. Howard, 'Report on "Operation Musketeer"'.
85. Stockwell, 'Report', pp. 26–7.
86. Smallwood in Sowrey, 'Seminar – Suez 1956', p. 31.
87. Lee, David (1989), *Wings in the Sun*, London: HMSO, p. 76.
88. Lee, *Wings in the Sun*, pp. 101–2.
89. Central Office of Information (1960), *Suez in Perspective*, <http://www.nationalarchives.gov.uk/films/1951to1964/filmpage_suez.htm> (last accessed 25 August 2017).
90. Stockwell, 'Report', annex b, p. 15.
91. Lee, *Wings in the Sun*, pp. 103–4.
92. Howard, 'Report on "Operation Musketeer"', p. 29.
93. N.a., 'Ground Lessons', n.d., WO 32/21899, annex e, p. 5.
94. N.a., 'Report on Air Aspects of the Airborne Operation at Gamil Airfield', n.d., WO 32/21899, annex a, p. 2.
95. Ibid., p. 8.
96. COS, 'Part II of General Sir Charles Keightley's Despatch on Operations in the Eastern Mediterranean', 11 October 1957, DEFE 11/137, p. 5.

97. Stockwell, 'Report', annex b, pp. 20–1.
98. COS Committee, 6 February 1958, DEFE 11/137, confidential annex, p. 4.
99. Stockwell, 'Report', annex b, pp. 29–30.
100. Author name indecipherable, 'Report on Operation Musketeer', 4 April 1957, WO 32/21899, p. 10; Howard, 'Report on "Operation Musketeer"', p. 39.
101. Howard, 'Report on "Operation Musketeer"', p. 4.
102. Eustace, memorandum, 15 March 1957, WO 32/21899.
103. Hull, 'Lessons from Operation Musketeer', annex a.
104. Stockwell, 'Report', annex b, pp. 13, 19, 20.
105. JIC minutes, 22 August 1956, CAB 159/24, annex b, p. 19; Lee, *Wings in the Sun*, p. 104.
106. COS, 'Part II', p. 8; COS Committee, 6 February 1958, DEFE 11/137, confidential annex.
107. Hull, 'Lessons from Operation Musketeer', annex c.
108. COS, 'Part II', pp. 4–5.
109. Bloch, Jonathan (1983), *British Intelligence and Covert Action*, Dingle, Co. Kerry: Brandon, p. 123.
110. Stockwell, 'Report', annex b, p. 3.
111. Keightley, 'Operations in Egypt', p. 5.
112. COS Committee, 6 February 1958, DEFE 11/137, confidential annex, pp. 2–3.
113. COS, 'Part II', p. 8.
114. COS Committee, 6 February 1958, DEFE 11/137, confidential annex, pp. 1–2.
115. Cited in Lucas and Morey, 'The Hidden "Alliance"', p. 110.
116. Bower, *Perfect English Spy*, p. 199.
117. Butler, Hansard (Commons), DLX, c1932, 22 November 1956.
118. Macmillan, Hansard (Commons), DCXX, c231, 22 March 1960.
119. Brook to Macmillan, memorandum b, 5 March 1959, PREM 11/2653.
120. Notes on a meeting, 26 April 1967, FO 12/30.
121. Cabinet minutes, 19 December 1956, CAB 195/15; Reid to Trend, 9 May 1966, CAB 103/598; Cabinet Office to Crossman, 14 November 1965, CAB 165/109.
122. Brown to Crossman, 5 October 1966, FO 800/983.
123. Trend to Douglas-Home, 22 November 1963, PREM 11/4282.
124. Douglas-Home to Bligh, 23 November 1963, PREM 11/4282.
125. Bligh, note, 28 November 1963, PREM 11/4282.
126. Gore-Booth, 19 April 1966, FO 370/2913; Gore-Booth to Tower, 26 August 1966, CAB 103/617.

127. Lloyd to Brook, 8 August 1959, FO 800/728.
128. Gore-Booth, 7 March 1966, FCO 12/29.
129. Rennie, 8 April 1967, FCO 12/29.
130. Stewart to Gore-Booth, 5 July 1965, FO 370/2807.
131. Ibid.
132. Gore-Booth to Mason, 13 July 1965, FO 370/2807.
133. Ibid.
134. Millard, 'Memorandum', p. 2.
135. Rowan to Makins, 26 October 1956, T 236/4188.
136. Dooley, 'Cabinet Planning', p. 516.
137. Millard, 'Memorandum', p. 29.
138. Eden, 28 December 1956, PREM 11/1138.
139. Foreign Affairs Steering Committee, 'British Obligations Overseas', 14 April 1958, FO371/135611, pp. 3–4.
140. Ibid., p. 3.
141. Ibid., p. 12.
142. Butler, 'A New Perspective for British Diplomacy', 24 May 1963, FO 371/173334.
143. Ibid.
144. Foreign Affairs Steering Committee, minutes, 30 July 1963 and 23 August 1963, FO 371/173334; Ticknell, note, 14 June 1963, FO 371/173334.
145. Sir Mervyn Brown, DOHP 18, p. 12.
146. Young, John W. (1997), *Britain and the World in the Twentieth Century*, London: Arnold, p. 172.
147. Author name indecipherable, 'Report on Operation Musketeer'.
148. Edwardes Jones to the Under-Secretary of State, 27 November 1956, WO 32/21899.
149. Bray to Edwardes Jones, 18 December 1956, WO 32/21899.
150. Kearney to Air Ministry, 28 February 1957, WO 32/21899.
151. Stubbs to War Office, 2 January 1957, WO 32/21899.
152. Minutes, 29 January 1957, WO 32/21899.
153. Loose minute, 4 February 1957, WO 32/16731.
154. Exham, 'Lessons from Operation Musketeer', 4 February 1957; Howard, 'Report on "Operation Musketeer"'; Author name indecipherable, 'Report on Operation Musketeer', all at WO 32/21899; Stockwell, 'Report'.
155. ECAC, n.d., WO 32/16731.
156. Thompson, loose minute, 9 June 1957, WO 32/16731.
157. Keightley, 'Operations in Egypt'; COS, 'Part II'.
158. Lee to Hardy, 15 October 1957, DEFE 11/137.

159. COS Committee, minute, 22 January 1958, DEFE 11/137.
160. COS Committee, minute, 3 October 1957, DEFE 11/137.
161. Langley, 21 January 1957, WO 32/21899; COS Committee, 6 February 1958, DEFE 11/137, confidential annex.
162. Loose minute, 3 May 1957, WO 32/21899.
163. Powell to Sandys, 28 June 1957, DEFE 7/1736.
164. Macmillan to Brook, 25 July 1957, PREM 11/1130.
165. Trend, minute, 28 March 1963 and Mountbatten to Scott, 5 April 1963, both in CAB 164/1357.
166. Working Party on Joint Service In-House Histories, note, 2 March 1973, DEFE 24/649.
167. Enclosure 1 to COS, 13 April 1973, DEFE 24/649.
168. Stevens to Head of Air Historical Branch, 29 November 1978, DEFE 71/242.
169. Stevens to Head of Air Historical Branch, 22 November 1978, DEFE 71/242.
170. For more on this review see Rees, Wyn (1989), 'The 1957 Sandys White Paper: New Priorities in British Defence Policy?', *Journal of Strategic Studies*, 12/2, pp. 215–29.
171. Powell, 2 January 1957, DEFE 7/982.
172. Eden to Head, 28 December 1956, PREM 11/1138.
173. Ibid., p. 3.
174. Keightley 'Operations in Egypt', n.d., DEFE11/137, paragraph 12; MoD (1957), *Defence: Outline of Future Policy*, London: TSO, p. 2.
175. Dickson to Minister, 25 June 1957, DEFE 11/137.
176. Author name indecipherable, handwritten note, 25 March 1957, WO 32/16731.
177. JIC minutes, 16 November 1956, CAB 159/25.
178. JIC minutes, 28 November 1956 and 12 December 1956, CAB 159/025.
179. Kyle, *Suez*, p. 149.
180. Bower, *Perfect English Spy*, pp. 200–1.
181. JIC minutes, 30 November 1956, CAB 159/025.
182. See, for example, JIC, 'Soviet Policy in Light of the Situation in the M. E. and Satellites', 6 December 1956; 'Soviet Penetration in the Middle East', 1 January 1957, both in CAB 158/26.
183. Cooper, minute, 26 February 1957, received under FOI; JIC(ME), 28 January 1957, received under FOI.
184. JIC(ME), 28 January 1957, received under FOI, annex.
185. Cooper, minute, 26 February 1957, received under FOI.

186. Secretary to Dean, 22 August 1957, received under FOI.
187. Lucas, W. Scott (1999), 'The Missing Link? Patrick Dean Chairman of the Joint Intelligence Committee', *Contemporary British History*, 13/2, p. 123.
188. Kirkpatrick, Ivone (1959), *The Inner Circle*, London: Macmillan and Co., p. 262.
189. Dickie, John (1992), *Inside the Foreign Office*, London: Chapmans, p. 236.
190. Author name indecipherable, handwritten note, 28 November 1956, WO 32/21899.
191. Cooper, Chester L. (1978), *The Lion's Last Roar: Suez 1956*, New York: Harper and Row, p. 70.
192. Beck, Peter (2009), '"The Less Said about Suez the Better": British Governments and the Politics of Suez's History, 1956–67', *English Historical Review*, 124/508, p. 609; Cabinet meeting documents and conclusions, 5 May 1967 and 27 May 1967, PREM 13/1556; Lloyd to Eden, draft letter, n.d., FO 370/2554.
193. Gore-Booth to Mason, 13 July 1965, FO 370/2807.
194. Smith, Adrian (2013), 'Resignation of a First Sea Lord: Mountbatten and the 1956 Suez Crisis', *History*, 98/329, p. 125.

Chapter 3 More like Korea – Jordan 1958

1. Macmillan, Harold (1971), *Riding the Storm: 1956–1959*, London: Macmillan and Co., p. 506.
2. Cabinet Defence Committee minutes, 14 July 1958, CAB 131/19.
3. See, for example, Barrett, Roby (2008), 'Intervention in Iraq 1958–1959', *The Middle East Institute Policy Brief*, 11 (April), p. 3.
4. Tal, Lawrence (1995), 'Britain and the Jordan Crisis of 1958', *Middle Eastern Studies*, 31/1 (January), p. 42; Dann, Uriel (1991), *King Hussein and the Challenge of Arab Radicalism: Jordan 1955–1967*, Oxford: Oxford University Press, pp. 81–2.
5. Macmillan, *Storm*, p. 512.
6. Parsons, Anthony (1986), *They Say the Lion*, London: Jonathan Cape Ltd, p. 36 Eden, Sir Anthony (1960), *Full Circle*, London: Cassell, p. 349.
7. Amman to FCO, 28 July 1956, PREM 11/1422.
8. Ormsby-Gore, Hansard (Commons), DLXV, c33–4, 18 February 1957.

9. Parsons, *The Lion*, p. 36.
10. Stevens to Rose, 9 June 1958, FO 371/133895, p. 2.
11. Middleton to Rose, 2 April 1958, FO 371/134155.
12. Mason to FCO, 16 July 1958, PREM 11/2380/276.
13. For more detail see Kettle, Louise (2016), 'Learning to Pull the Strings after Suez: Macmillan's Management of the Eisenhower Administration during the Intervention in Jordan, 1958', *Diplomacy and Statecraft*, 27/14, pp. 45–64.
14. Eisenhower, Dwight D. (1956), *Waging Peace*, New York: Doubleday and Company, p. 120.
15. For more detail see Jones, Matthew (2003), 'Anglo-American Relations after Suez, the Rise and of the Working Group Experiment, and the French Challenge to NATO, 1957–59', *Diplomacy & Statecraft*, 14/1, pp. 47–79.
16. COS Committee, note, 16 October 1957, DEFE 6/43.
17. Washington to FCO, 8 November 1957, PREM 11/2521; memorandum of a conversation, White House, 13 May 1958, FRUS, 'Lebanon and Jordan', 1958–60, volume XI, document 30.
18. Earlier in 1958 the FCO had complained of 'dilatoriness' in US Middle East policy. Laskey to Bishop, 3 April 1958, FO 371/132330.
19. N.a., 'Wrong Together', *The Spectator*, 18 July 1958, p. 78.
20. N.a., 'Ike and Macmillan', *The Washington Post*, 7 June 1958, FO 371/133823.
21. JIC, 17 March 1958, CAB 158/32.
22. Memorandum of a telephone conversation between Eisenhower and Macmillan, 14 July 1958, FRUS, 'Lebanon and Jordan', 1958–60, volume XI, document 131; Cabinet Defence Committee minutes, 14 July 1958, CAB 131/19.
23. Blackwell, Stephen (2009), *British Military Intervention and the Struggle for Jordan: King Hussein, Nasser and the Middle East Crisis, 1955–1958*, London: Routledge, pp. 91–4; COS Committee minutes, 19 November 1957, DEFE 4/101.
24. N.a., 'US-UK Precautions against Coups d'état in Jordan and Lebanon', 10 October 1957, PREM 11/2521.
25. Cabinet Defence Committee minutes, 14 July 1958, CAB 131/19.
26. Eisenhower, *Waging Peace*, p. 272.
27. Macmillan, *Storm*, p. 511.
28. Cabinet conclusions, 16 July 1958, CAB 128/32; Macmillan, *Storm*, p. 519.
29. FCO to Washington, 6 December 1957, PREM 11/2521.

30. FCO to Washington, 15 July 1958, PREM 11/2380.
31. FCO to Amman, 16 July 1958, PREM 11/2380.
32. FCO to Washington, 15 July 1958, PREM 11/2380.
33. Wilson to Macmillan, 16 July 1958, PREM11/2380.
34. Memorandum of a telephone conversation between Macmillan and Dulles, 16 July 1958, FRUS, 'Lebanon and Jordan', 1958–60, volume XI, document 184.
35. FCO to Amman, 17 July 1958, PREM 11/2380.
36. Macmillan Diaries, 14 and 17 July 1958, The Bodleian Library.
37. Nutting, Anthony (1958), *New York Herald Tribune*, 20 July 1958.
38. Macmillan Diaries, 16 July 1958, The Bodleian Library.
39. COS to Minister, 6 December 1957, DEFE 32/5.
40. Pearson, 'Operation "Fortitude" Appreciation and Outline Plan', July 1958, WO 305/5597; Wilson, notes, 16 July 1958, PREM 11/2380.
41. See, for example, Joint Planning Staff, 'Action That May Be Required If Military Situations Develop Which Threaten the Position of Our Forces in Jordan', 11 August 1958, DEFE 5/50; FCO to Amman, 4 August 1958, PREM 11/2380.
42. Pearson, 'Outline Plan'.
43. Ibid. The nicknames for the Royal Palace and British Embassy were 'Brown Hen' and 'Town Crier' respectively. The nickname for the US Ambassador's residence was 'Ding Bat'. Operation Order 6/58, 5 October 1958, WO 305/5597, annex e.
44. Pearson to Chaplain, 13 October 1958, WO 305/5597.
45. Cabinet Defence Committee minutes, 14 July 1958, CAB 131/19.
46. Maclean, Donald (1970), *British Foreign Policy since Suez*, London: Hodder & Stoughton, p. 187.
47. FCO to Washington, 18 July 1958, PREM 11/2380.
48. Symon to de Zulueta, 28 July 1958, PREM 11/2416.
49. Atkinson to COS Committee, 'Reorganisation of the JIC', 7 October 1957; Dean to Dulles, 25 June 1957, both in CAB 163/9.
50. Bromley, note, 12 February 1958; JIC, 'Joint Intelligence Organisation, BDCC (ME) after 1st April 1958', 5 February 1958, both in CAB 158/31.
51. JIC, 20 March 1958, CAB 158/32.
52. Bower, Tom (1995), *The Perfect English Spy*, London: William Heinemann, p. 232.
53. Cabinet meeting minutes, 7 July 1958, CAB 130/153.
54. JIC, 'The Situation in Iraq and Jordan', 14 July 1958, CAB 158/33.
55. See, for example, Glubb to Rose, 24 March 1958, FO 371/134116.

Notes

56. Bower, *Perfect English Spy*, p. 234.
57. JIC, 'Nationalist and Radical Movements in the Arabian Peninsular', 10 February 1958, CAB 158/31.
58. For discussions on this conference see FO 371/133895.
59. JIC, 'Likely Soviet Reactions to United States/United Kingdom Military Intervention in the Lebanon', 22 May 1958, CAB 158/32.
60. JIC, 'The Situation in Iraq and Jordan', 14 July 1958, CAB 158/33, annex.
61. N.a., 'Middle East Crisis – 1958', n.d., WO 216/930.
62. JIC, 8 August 1958, CAB 158/33; Mason to FCO, 16 July 1958, PREM 11/2380.
63. See, for example, Ashton, Nigel John (1997), 'A Microcosm of Decline: British Loss of Nerve and Military Intervention in Jordan and Kuwait, 1958 and 1961', *The Historical Journal*, 40/4, p. 1074.
64. Memorandum of a conference with the President, 16 July 1958, FRUS, 'Lebanon and Jordan', 1958–60, volume XI, document 179, footnote 2.
65. Foreign Affairs Steering Committee, 'British Obligations Overseas', 14 April 1958, FO371/135611, p. 21.
66. Eisenhower, *Waging Peace*, p. 279.
67. Boyle to MoD, 17 July 1958, AIR 20/10110.
68. Johnston, Charles (1972), *The Brink of Jordan*, London: Hamish Hamilton, p. 102.
69. Cabinet minutes, 17 July 1958, CAB 128/32.
70. Rundall to Rose, 22 July 1958, AIR 20/10110.
71. COS Committee, 14 August 1958, DEFE 4/110, annex.
72. Cabinet Defence Committee minutes, 3 October 1958, CAB 131/19.
73. Shattock to FCO, 29 October 1958, FO 371/134024.
74. Johnston, *The Brink*, p. 108.
75. Johnston to FCO, 24 August 1958, PREM 11/2381.
76. Johnston, *The Brink*, p. 108; Johnston, 'Annual Review of Developments in Jordan 1958', 22 January 1959, FO 371/142100.
77. Dulles to Macmillan, 1 August 1958, PREM 11/2399.
78. Jarratt to Bishop, 18 July 1958, AIR 20/10110; Hood to FCO, 17 July 1958, PREM 11/2380; record of a meeting, 27 July 1958, PREM 11/2399.
79. Memorandum of a conversation, 17 July 1958, FRUS, 'Lebanon and Jordan', 1958–60, volume XI, document 188; Macmillan to Eisenhower, 22 July 1958, FRUS, 'Lebanon and Jordan', 1958–60, volume XI, document 214.

80. Macmillan to Eisenhower, 18 July 1958, FRUS, 'Lebanon and Jordan', 1958–60, volume XI, document 193.
81. Eisenhower, *Waging* Peace, pp. 281–2; Eisenhower to Macmillan, 4 November 1958, PREM 11/2389.
82. Cabinet Defence Committee, 9 December 1958, CAB 131/19.
83. Beeley to FCO, 25 July 1958, PREM 11/2380.
84. Dixon to Hayter, 1 July 1958, FO 371/134156.
85. Hood to FCO, 5 August 1958, PREM 11/2381; FCO to Amman, 16 July 1958, PREM 11/2380; FCO to Amman, n.d., PREM 11/2380; FCO to Washington, 15 July 1958, PREM 11/2380.
86. UN General Assembly, A/RES/1237 (ES III), 21 August 1958.
87. See, for example, record of a meeting at the State Department, 17 July 1958, FO 371/133823; Hood to FCO, 19 July 1958, PREM 11/2380.
88. FCO to New York, 2 August 1958, PREM 11/2380.
89. Note to the Prime Minister, 18 July 1958, PREM 11/2380.
90. Roberts to FCO, 1 August 1958, PREM 11/2335.
91. Correspondence on this issue are at PREM 11/2380.
92. N.a. (1958), 'Keep Out!', *The Herald*, 16 July 1958, King's College London Military Archives (KCLMA) Liddell Hart 15/5/496.
93. N.a. (1958), 'Blind Blind Blind', The *Daily Mirror*, 17 and 18 July 1958, KCLMA Liddell Hart 15/5/496.
94. N.a. (1958), '2 to 1 in Favour of Troops Going in', *News Chronicle*, 21 July 1958, KCLMA Liddell Hart 15/5/496.
95. Blackwell, *The Struggle for Jordan*, p. 136; record of a telephone conversation between Macmillan and Lord Hood, 15 July 1958, PREM 11/2388; Lord Hood to FCO, 19 July 1958, PREM 11/2388.
96. Johnston to FCO, 4 August 1958, PREM 11/2380.
97. Headquarters Middle East Air Force (HQ MEAF) to London, 27 July 1958, AIR 20/10110.
98. Sandys, 25 July 1958, AIR 23/8580.
99. HQ MEAF to Air Ministry, 27 July 1958, AIR 20/10110.
100. Johnston to FCO, 8 August 1958, DEFE 11/173.
101. Cabinet minutes, 7 July 1958, CAB 130/153.
102. Johnston, *The Brink*, p. 8.
103. Record of a telephone conversation between Macmillan and Hood, 15 July 1958, PREM 11/2388; Jarratt to Bishop, 18 July 1958, AIR 20/10110.
104. Macmillan, note, 25 August 1958, PREM 11/2381; Cabinet minutes, 25 August 1958, CAB 130/153.
105. Robert V. Keeley, FAOH, p. 17–18.

106. Macmillan, minute, 22 August 1958, PREM 11/2381; Johnston to FCO, 24 August 1958, PREM 11/2381.
107. Macmillan to Minister of Defence, 25 July 1958, PREM 11/2380.
108. See, for example, Cabinet Defence Committee minutes, 23 July 1958 and 5 November 1958, CAB 131/19.
109. Cabinet Defence Committee minutes, 14 July, CAB 131/19; FCO to Amman, n.d., PREM 11/2380.
110. COS, 'Defence of UK interests in the Persian Gulf', 15 July 1958, DEFE 6/51.
111. FCO to Amman, 4 August 1958, PREM 11/2380.
112. Adjutant-General, 'Problems of Reservists', 19 October 1956, WO 32/16713.
113. MoD (1957), *Defence: Outline of Future Policy*, London: TSO, p. 2.
114. Chief of Defence Staff to COS, 7 August 1958, DEFE 11/173; Butler to Chief of the Defence Staff, 11 September 1958, AIR 10/10112.
115. COS Committee minutes, 5 November 1958, DEFE 6/52.
116. Hood to FCO, 17 July 1958, PREM 11/2380; record of a luncheon meeting, 27 July 1958, PREM 11/2399.
117. Cabinet Defence Committee minutes, 24 July 1958, CAB 131/20/35.
118. Cabinet Defence Committee minutes, 6 August 1958, CAB 131/20/42; Macmillan to Dulles, 27 July 1958, PREM 11/2380.
119. London to Washington, 11 August 1958, FRUS, 'Lebanon and Jordan', 1958–60, volume XI, document 26.
120. COS Committee, 15 September 1958, DEFE 5/84.
121. UK/US Planning Group, 'Coordination of UK/US Plans for the Persian Gulf', annex in Joint Planning Staff report, 22 October 1958, DEFE 6/51.
122. Tal, 'Britain and the Jordan Crisis', p. 47; Johnston to FCO, 4 August 1958, PREM 11/2380.
123. Johnston to FCO, 30 July 1958, FO 371/134040.
124. Wilson to Macmillan, 'Military Assistance to Jordan', 16 July 1958, PREM 11/2380.
125. COS Committee minutes, 1 August 1958, DEFE 4/110; FCO to Amman, 4 August 1958, PREM 11/2380.
126. COS Committee minutes, 12 August 1958, DEFE 4/110.
127. Joint Planning Staff, 'Action That May Be Required If Military Situations Develop Which Threaten the Position of Our Forces in Jordan', 9 August 1958, DEFE 6/51.
128. HQ 3 Division and HQ 1 Guards Brigade Group, 'Exercise "Starlight One"', 16 August 1960, DEFE 42/4.

129. Joint Planning Staff, 'Withdrawal of United Kingdom Forces from Jordan', 19 September 1958; 'Plan for the Withdrawal of United Kingdom Forces from Jordan', 22 September 1958; 'Jordan – Planning for Post-withdrawal Period', 9 October 1958, all in DEFE 6/52.
130. Lee, David (1989), *Wings in the Sun*, London: HMSO, p. 144.
131. King Hussein of Jordan (1962), *Uneasy Lies the Head: An Autobiography of H. M. King Hussein of Jordan*, London: Heinemann, p. 172.
132. Johnston, *The Brink*, p. 120.
133. JIC, 'The Outlook for Jordan', 8 August 1958; JIC, 'Likely Soviet Reactions to the Present Western Actions in the Middle East', 21 July 1958; JIC, 'Nasser's Probable Policy and Aims over the Next Six Months', 1 August 1958; JIC, 'Lebanon and Jordan – Infiltration and Subversion by the UAR', 8 August 1958, all in CAB 158/33.
134. Lee, *Wings in the Sun*, p. 144.
135. Johnston to Lloyd, 22 January 1959, FO 371/142100, p. 3.
136. Ibid., pp. 4, 6, 7.
137. Notes, 17–19 February 1959, FO 371/142100.
138. Cabinet Official Committee on the Middle East (COCME), 'Points for a Middle East Policy', part one – 15 October 1958, part two – 19 November 1958, CAB 134/2342.
139. COCME, 'Points', part one, point 16, part two, point 10i.
140. COCME, 'Points', part two, point 30, point 11i.
141. Ibid., point 13.
142. De Zulueta to Macmillan, 10 September 1958, PREM 11/2397.
143. COCME, 'Points', part one, point 25.
144. COCME, 'Points', part two, point 14.
145. Ivor Lucas, DOHP, p. 9.
146. Lord Plowden, 'Foreign Service Review', n.d., FO 366/3197, point 16.
147. Chief of Air Staff to Chief of Defence Staff, loose minute, December 1958, AIR 10/10112.
148. General Headquarters Middle East Land Forces (GHQ MELF), loose minute, 4 November 1958, WO 305/5597.
149. N.a., 'Report of a Study of the Ministry of Defence's Departmental Record System', n.d. DEFE 24/650.
150. Ibid., p. 3.
151. Ibid., p. 12.

152. Joint Service In-House History Working Party, loose minute, 5 March 1973, DEFE 24/649.
153. See, for example, Vice Chief of Defence Staff to MoD, 'History of Indonesian Confrontation Operations 1962–66', terms of reference, 15 August 1973, DEFE 24/649; Operation Fortitude War Diary, WO 305/5597.
154. Lee, *Wings in the Sun*, pp. 140–5.
155. De Zulueta to Macmillan, 10 September 1958, PREM 11/2397.
156. JIC, 'Intelligence Targets', 21 November 1958, CAB 158/33.
157. JIC, 'Consequences in the Middle East of the Anglo/American Withdrawal from Jordan and the Lebanon', 16 October 1958, CAB 158/34.
158. JIC, 'The Threat to Aden and the Aden Protectorate', 17 September 1958, CAB 158/34.
159. JIC, 'The Outlook for the Persian Gulf over the Next Six Months', 21 August 1958, CAB 158/34.
160. Ibid.
161. Cited in De Zulueta to Macmillan, 10 September 1958, PREM 11/2397.
162. Parsons, *The Lion*, p. 42.
163. JIC, 'The Activities and Influence of Cairo Radio', 3 December 1958, CAB 158/33.
164. Jordan General Intelligence Department (n.d.), 'G.I.D. Law and Establishment', https://www.gid.gov.jo/en/Law.html (last accessed 4 May 2013).
165. Joint Service In-House History Working Party, loose minute, 5 March 1973, DEFE 24/649.
166. Macmillan to Selwyn Lloyd, 21 October 1958, PREM 11/2398.

Chapter 4 Suez in Reverse – Kuwait 1961

1. Cited in Alani, Mustafa M. (1990), *Operation Vantage: British Military Intervention in Kuwait 1961*, Surrey: LAAM, p. 233.
2. McMeekin, Sean (2011), *The Berlin-Baghdad Express: The Ottoman Empire and Germany's Bid for World Power, 1898–1918*, London: Penguin.
3. Walmsley, confidential note on Kuwait, 27 June 1961, FO 371/156846.

4. Research Branch, 'Report No.9/62', December 1962, AIR 38/399; in 1961 40 per cent of all crude oil imported by Britain was produced in Kuwait. Verrier, Anthony (1983), *Through the Looking Glass*, London: W. W. Norton and Company Ltd, p. 171; Research Branch, 'Report No.9/62'.
5. Exchange of letters, 19 June 1961, FO 93/137.
6. Trevelyan to FCO, 28 June 1961, PREM 11/3427.
7. Elworthy, 'Report by the Commander-in-Chief Middle East on Operations in Support of the State of Kuwait in July 1961', 30 September 1961, DEFE 5/118, p. 11; Alani, *Operation Vantage*, p. 248.
8. Trevelyan to FCO, 26 June 1961, FO 371/156845.
9. Trevelyan to FCO, 27 June 1961, PREM 11/3427.
10. Trevelyan to FCO, 28 June 1961, FO 371/156873.
11. Trevelyan to FCO, 28 June 1961, PREM 11/3427.
12. Walmsley, 'Formal Assurance to the Ruler of Kuwait', 27 June 1961, FO 371/156845.
13. Johnston to Stevens, 16 March 1961, FO 371/157389.
14. Macmillan to Karachi and Kuala Lumpur, 30 June 1961, PREM 11/3427.
15. Baghdad to FCO, 26 June 1961, FO 371/156845.
16. Luce to Stevens, 16 July 1961, FO 371/156884.
17. FCO to New York, 29 June 1961, FO 371/156874.
18. Defence Committee note, 29 June 1961, CAB 131/26.
19. Henniker-Major to FCO, 13 September 1961, FO 371/156900.
20. Trevelyan, Humphrey (1970), *The Middle East in Revolution*, Boston: Gambit Incorporated, p. 197.
21. Elworthy, 'Report by the Commander-in-Chief', p. 18.
22. Cabinet conclusions, 6 July 1961, CAB 128/35.
23. Beeley to FCO, 2 July 1961, FO 371/156875.
24. Dixon to FCO, 1 July 1961, PREM 11/3428.
25. Commonwealth Relations Office (CRO), 27 June 1961, FO 371/156845; CRO, 30 June 1961, FO 371/156847.
26. See, for example, from Australia, Menzies to Macmillan, 3 July 1961, PREM 11/3428.
27. Atkins to CRO, 1 July 1961, FO 371/156847.
28. FCO to Washington, 29 June 1961, FO 371/156874.
29. Dean to FCO, 30 June 1961, FO 371/156874
30. Ibid.
31. Elworthy, 'Report by the Commander-in-Chief', p. 10.
32. These were 'A Memorandum Respecting British Interests in the Persian Gulf, a Historical Summary of Events in the Territories of the

Ottoman Empire', 'Persia and Arabia, 1907–1928' and a 'Historical Summary of Events in the Persian Gulf Shaikdoms in the Sultanate of Muscat and Oman, 1928–1953', FCO to New York, 3 July 1961, FO 371/156847.
33. UK Mission to the UN to Arabian Department, 17 July 1961, FO 371/156847.
34. Arabian Department, 'United Kingdom/United States Military Planning in the Middle East (Especially Kuwait)', 6 June 1961, FO 371/156694.
35. Defence Committee minutes, 27 April 1961, CAB 131/25.
36. Arabian Department, 'Military Planning in the Middle East', annex a.
37. Note of a Defence Committee meeting, 2 July 1961, CAB 131/26.
38. Macmillan to Holyoake, 30 June 1961, PREM 11/3427.
39. FCO to Washington, 28 June 1961, FO 371/156874.
40. Wells to Samuel, 30 June 1961, FO 371/156670.
41. Maynard, note, 12 January 1962, FO 371/156670.
42. Macmillan, Harold (1973), *Pointing the Way 1959–1961*, London: Macmillan, p. 385.
43. Elworthy, 'Report by the Commander-in-Chief', pp. 5, 6.
44. Ibid., pp. 5, 2.
45. Ibid., pp. 5, 2, 14.
46. JIC minutes, 30 January 1957, CAB 159/26.
47. Joint Planning Staff, 'Defence of UK Interests in the Persian Gulf', 15 July 1958, DEFE 6/51.
48. Joint Planning Staff, 'Review of Operations for Intervention in Kuwait', 17 September 1958, DEFE 6/51; Joint Planning Staff, 'Political and Economic Implications of Military Intervention in Kuwait', 9 December 1958, DEFE 6/52.
49. JIC minutes, 5 August 1958, CAB 158/33.
50. JIC minutes, 6 March 1959, CAB 158/36.
51. JIC minutes, 15 March 1961, CAB 158/42.
52. Bowden to War Office, 6 January 1961, FO 371/157704.
53. Elworthy, 'Report by the Commander-in-Chief', p. 26.
54. Bower, Tom (1995), *The Perfect English Spy*, London: William Heinemann, pp. 235–6.
55. See, for example, Pyman to FCO, 2 July 1961, FO 371/156876; Pyman to FCO, 3 July 1961, FO 371/156876.
56. Trevelyan, *Middle East in Revolution*, pp. 188–9.
57. FCO to Baghdad, 5 July 1961, FO 371/156876.
58. See, for example, PREM 11/3427; FO 371/156876.

59. Holsey G. Handyside, FAOH, p. 51.
60. Elworthy, 'Report by the Commander-in-Chief', p. 7.
61. Trevelyan, *Middle East in Revolution*, p. 189.
62. FCO to Baghdad, 5 July 1961, FO 371/156876.
63. Richmond to FCO, 9 July 1961, FO 371/156880.
64. Elworthy, 'Report by the Commander-in-Chief', p. 5.
65. Trevelyan to FCO, 28 June 1961, FO 371/156873.
66. Trevelyan, *Middle East in Revolution*, p. 188.
67. Trevelyan to FCO, 20 July 1961, FO 371/156851; Chancery Baghdad to Eastern Department, 27 July 1961, FO 371/156852.
68. Bower, *Perfect English Spy*, p. 188.
69. COS Committee, 11 October 1957, DEFE 11/137, p. 8.
70. JIC Secretary to COS, 25 November 1957, DEFE 11/137.
71. MoD, 'Intelligence on Kuwait', 12 January 1962, DEFE 13/268; COS Committee, 'Air Reconnaissance in the Basrah [sic] Kuwait Area', 12 January 1962, DEFE 5/99.
72. Mobley, Richard A. (2001), 'Gauging the Iraqi Threat to Kuwait in the 1960s', *Studies in Intelligence*, 45/5, p. 23.
73. Cited in Ashton, Nigel (1998), 'Britain and the Kuwaiti Crisis, 1961', *Diplomacy and Statescraft*, 9/1 (March), p. 170.
74. R. D. F. (1962), 'Kuwait', *The Naval Review*, 50/1 (January), p. 39.
75. Amery, Hansard (Commons), DCXLIV, c1224, 19 July 1961.
76. FCO to Tehran, 1 July 1961, FO 371/156874.
77. Defence Committee minutes, 30 June 1961, CAB 131/26; Lee, David (1981), *Flight from the Middle East*, London: HMSO, p. 174.
78. Ankara to FCO, 1 July 1961; Ankara to FCO, 2 July 1961, both in FO 371/156876.
79. Ankara to FCO, 2 July 1961, FO 371/156876.
80. Ankara to FCO, 1 July 1961, PREM 11/3427.
81. Lee, *Flight*, p. 175.
82. Brenchley to FCO, 1 July 1961, FO 371/156876.
83. FCO to Washington, 3 July 1961, FO 371/156876.
84. Caccia to FCO, 3 July 1961, FO 371/156876.
85. FCO to Washington, 3 July 1961, FO 371/156876; Caccia to FCO, 3 July 1961, FO 371/156876; FCO to Kuwait, 6 July 1961, PREM 11/3429.
86. FCO to Rome, 3 July 1961, FO 371/156878; Clarke to FCO, 5 July 1961, FO 371/156878.
87. Elworthy, 'Report by the Commander-in-Chief', p. 3.
88. Defence Committee minutes, 18 July 1961, CAB 131/26.
89. COS Committee minutes, 11 October 1957, DEFE 11/137.

90. Elworthy, 'Report by the Commander-in-Chief', p. 3.
91. Lee, *Flight*, pp. 177–8.
92. Elworthy, 'Report by the Commander-in-Chief', pp. 4, 13.
93. Munro, Alan (2012), *Keep the Flag Flying: A Diplomatic Memoir*, London: Gilgamesh, p. 44.
94. Lee, *Flight*, p. 182.
95. Elworthy, 'Report by the Commander-in-Chief', p. 21.
96. Watkinson, Hansard (Commons), DCLV, c45, 5 March 1962.
97. MoD (1963), *Central Organisation for Defence*, London: HMSO.
98. Macmillan, *Pointing the Way*, p. 385.
99. Walmsley, note from the Arabian Department, 14 July 1961, FO 371/156881.
100. Luce to Stevens, 16 July 1961, FO 371/156884.
101. Minute, 'Kuwait and the United Nations', 10 July 1961, FO 371/156883.
102. Note of a Defence Committee meeting, 18 July 1961, CAB 131/26.
103. Department of State to Embassy in UK, 12 July 1961, Department of State, Central Files, 686D.87/7–1261.
104. Anderson, C. C. (1991), 'Suez – 1956', *The Naval Review*, 79/4 (October), p. 358; Macmillan, *Pointing the Way*, p. 385.
105. Macmillan's Diaries, 8 July 1961, The Bodleian Library.
106. Defence Committee minutes, 2 July 1961, CAB 131/26.
107. Macmillan to Home, 12 August 1961, PREM 11/3429.
108. Richmond to FCO, 17 July 1961, FO 371/156882.
109. Monthly diary of events, 25 June – 24 July 1961, FO 371/156824.
110. Elworthy, 'Report by the Commander-in-Chief', pp. 2, 22–3.
111. Ibid., pp. 22, 18, 23.
112. Army Operational Research Group (AORG), n.d., 'Operation Vantage', Report No. 6/61, WO 291/2240, pp. 18–23.
113. R. D. F., 'Kuwait', p. 41.
114. Darby, Phillip (1973), *British Defence Policy East of Suez: 1947–1968*, London: Oxford University Press, p. 248.
115. Elworthy, 'Report by the Commander-in-Chief', pp. 6, 19, 20.
116. Cordeaux, Hansard (Commons), DXLIV, c1216, 19 July 1961.
117. N.a., *Daily Telegraph*, 6 July 1961, WO 32/20372, p. 28; Young, 6 July 1961, WO 32/20372.
118. Watkinson to Douglas-Home, 7 July 1961, WO 32/20372.
119. Profumo to Ramsden, 13 July 1961, WO 32/20372.
120. N.a., note, 17 July 1961, WO 32/20372.
121. Ramsden to Profumo, 25 July 1961, WO 32/20372.

122. AORG, 'Operation Vantage'; AORG, 'Survey of Factors Affecting the Health and Efficiency of Troops on Operation "Vantage"', December 1961, WO 291/2242.
123. Kuwait to FCO, 4 July 1961, PREM 11/3428.
124. Elworthy, 'Report by the Commander-in-Chief', pp. 11, 14, 18–19.
125. Ibid., p. 4. This lesson was also identified in AORG, Report No 6/61, pp. 15–18.
126. Note of a Defence Committee meeting, 3 July 1961, CAB 131/26.
127. Minister of Defence, memorandum, 13 April 1962, CAB 129/109.
128. Beeley to FCO, 6 July 1961, FO 371/156878.
129. Alani, *Vantage*, p. 209.
130. Fletcher, '"The Shambles" at Kuwait', *Tribune*, 16 August 1963; Verrier, *Looking Glass*, pp. 186–7.
131. Beeley to FCO, 4 July 1961, FO 371/156875; Richmond to FCO, 6 July 1961, FO 953/2035.
132. Caccia to FCO, 28 June 1961, PREM 11/3427; Caccia to FCO, 5 July 1961, FO 371/156878.
133. Talcot W. Seelye, FAOH, p. 33.
134. Holsey G. Handyside, FAOH, p. 52.
135. Ashton, Nigel John (1997), 'A Microcosm of Decline: British Loss of Nerve and Military Intervention in Jordan and Kuwait, 1958 and 1961', *The Historical Journal*, 40/4 (December), p. 1078.
136. Caccia to FCO, 5 July 1961, FO 371/156878.
137. Conversation between Home and Rusk, 6 August 1961, PREM 11/3429; Bower, *Perfect English Spy*, p. 237.
138. Richmond to FCO, 6 July 1961, FO 953/2035; Trevelyan to FCO, 11 July 1961, FO 953/2035; FCO to Kuwait, 10 July 1961, FO 953/2035.
139. Bower, *Perfect English Spy*, p. 237.
140. COS Committee minutes, 11 October 1957, DEFE 11/137, p. 8; Commander 2(BR) Corps, 'Operation Musketeer', WO 288/79.
141. JIC(ME)(56)-52, 28 January 1957, received under FOI, annex, point 6.
142. Elworthy, 'Report by the Commander-in-Chief', p. 21.
143. Macmillan, note, 28 November 1963, PREM 11/4282.
144. Rothnie to Home, 8 November 1961, FO 371/156894; Luce to FCO, 22 November 1961, FO 371/156670.
145. Rothnie to Home, 8 November 1961, FO 371/156894.
146. Cabinet conclusions, 19 September 1961, CAB 128/35.
147. Rothnie to Home, 8 November 1961, FO 371/156894.
148. Luce to FCO, 22 November 1961, FO 371/156670.

Notes

149. Ibid.
150. Cabinet memorandum, 2 October 1961, CAB 129/106; Cabinet conclusions, 5 October 1961, CAB 128/35.
151. Arabian Department, 'Memo on Kuwait', 2 September 1961, FO 371/156889.
152. Walker, 9 January 1962, FO 371/156670.
153. Maynard, 12 January 1962, FO 371/156670; Blaker, 17 January 1962, FO 371/156670.
154. Ziegler, n.d., FO 371/156670.
155. Brook to Macmillan, 13 September 1961, PREM 11/3430.
156. Jernegan to Department of State, 28 December 1961, Department of State, Central Files, 611.86D/12-2861
157. Luce to Brenchley, 31 May 1965, FO 371/179839.
158. Elworthy, 'Report by the Commander-in-Chief'.
159. Watkins, note, 18 October 1961, DEFE 5/118.
160. Elworthy, 'Report by the Commander-in-Chief', p. 26.
161. AORG, Report No. 6/61, pp. 248–9.
162. Watkins to Chief of the Defence Staff, 5 February 1963, WO 32/20721.
163. Elworthy, 'Report by the Commander-in-Chief', pp. 4, 18–19.
164. Ibid., p. 23.
165. Weston to School of Land/Air Warfare, 8 February 1962, WO 32/20721.
166. War Office, 'Debriefing of Vantage', n.d., WO 32/20720; meeting notes, 1 August 1961, WO 32/2072.
167. N.a., loose minute, 4 August 1961, WO 32/20720.
168. War Office to General Officer Command MELF, 30 January 1962, WO 32/20721; Assistant Secretary, 2 January 1962, WO 32/20721.
169. War Office to General Officer Command MELF, 30 January 1962, WO 32/20721.
170. Assistant Secretary, minute, 2 January 1962, WO 32/20721; Profumo to Quarter Master General, 29 November 1962, WO 32/20372.
171. Wilson to Secretariat, 14 February 1963, WO 32/20372; confidential note, 8 January 1961, WO 32/20721.
172. Director of the Royal Artillery to Secretary of State for War, 29 October 1962, WO 32/20372.
173. Defence Committee meeting, 3 July 1961, CAB 131/26; Watkinson, memorandum, 13 April 1962, CAB 129/109.
174. COS Committee minutes, 16 October 1961, DEFE 5/116.
175. Watkinson, 'Kuwait', 1 September 1961, CAB 129/106.

176. MoD, 'Notes on the Development of a Limited War Game', January 1967, DEFE 48/737.
177. Joint Service Historians, 'Report by the Working Party of Joint-Service In-House Histories', 13 April 1973, DEFE 11/567, annex c; 'Policy for Official Histories on Defence since World War II', 29 September 1972, DEFE 11/567, annex f.
178. Lee, *Flight*, pp. 165–88.
179. Watkinson, Hansard (Commons), DCLV, c44–5, 5 March 1962.
180. Profumo, Hansard (Commons), DCLV, c612, 8 March 1962.
181. Macmillan, *Pointing the Way*, p. 387.
182. Rothnie to Home, 8 November 1961, FO 371/156894.
183. Darby, *British Defence Policy*, pp. 222–3.
184. Baghdad to War Office, 10 August 1961, FO 371/157704.
185. Trevelyan to FCO, 2 July 1961, FO 371/156876.
186. Elworthy, 'Report by the Commander-in-Chief', p. 24.
187. Cradock, Percy (2002), *Know Your Enemy: How the Joint Intelligence Committee Saw the World*, London: John Murray, p. 207.
188. Mobley, 'Iraqi Threat', p. 26.
189. Cradock, *Know Your Enemy*, p. 207; Minister of Defence, 1 September 1962, CAB 129/106.
190. JIC, 'Iraqi Threat to Kuwait during the Next Twelve Months', 18 August 1961, CAB 158/44.
191. Cabinet memorandum, 2 October 1961, CAB 129/106.
192. JIC, 'Iraqi Threat to Kuwait'.
193. COS Committee minutes, 12 September 1961, DEFE 4/138.
194. JIC, 'Iraqi Threat to Kuwait', 23 November 1961, CAB 158/44.
195. JIC minutes, 9 November 1961, CAB 159/36.
196. JIC, 'Iraqi Threat to Kuwait'.
197. COS meeting minutes, 5 October 1961, DEFE 32/6.
198. Rothnie to FCO, 23 September 1961, FO 371/156891; MoD, 'The Threat to Kuwait', December 1963, DEFE 7/2122.
199. Brook to Macmillan, 18 October 1961, PREM 11/3430.
200. JIC, 'Iraqi Threat to Kuwait'.
201. COS meeting minutes, 5 October 1961; COS meeting minutes, 12 October 1961; COS meeting minutes, 9 November 1961, all in CAB 159/36.
202. JIC to Cabinet Office, 'Assessment of Iraqi Threat and UK Collection Posture', 22 December 1961, PREM 11/4359; Brook to Macmillan, 12 January 1962, DEFE 13/268.
203. Brook to Macmillan, 12 January 1962, DEFE 13/268.
204. De Zulueta to Cabinet Office, 15 January 1962, DEFE 13/268.

205. JIC to Macmillan, 15 January 1962, DEFE 13/268.
206. Brook to Macmillan, 9 February 1962, DEFE 13/269.
207. Neither was Kuwait considered as a case study for Doug Nicoll's examination of the JIC's past warnings of aggression. For more on this see Goodman, Michael (2007), 'The Dog That Didn't Bark: The Joint Intelligence Committee and Warning of Aggression', *Cold War History*, 7/4, pp. 529–51.
208. UN Security Council Resolution S/RES/687 (1991).
209. Research Department Memorandum, 'Kuwait-Iraq Relations', 6 February 1969, FCO 51/49.

Chapter 5 A Re-Run of Port Stanley – The Gulf 1990–1

1. House of Commons Defence Committee (DC) (1994), *Implementation of Lessons Learned from Operation Granby*, London: HMSO, p. 1.
2. A few personnel remained from Vantage, including the British Ambassador to Saudi Arabia, Sir Alan Munro, Commander-in-Chief, General Peter de la Billière and Admiral Sir Julian Oswald, but these were exceptions.
3. House of Commons Foreign Affairs Committee (FAC) (1991), *The Middle East After the Gulf War*, London: HMSO, p. vi; Hiro, Dilip (2003), *Iraq: A Report from the Outside*, London: Granta Publications, p. 32.
4. Cradock, Percy (1997), *In Pursuit of British Interests*, London: John Murray, p. 170.
5. Thatcher, Margaret (1993), *The Downing Street Years*, London: Harper Collins, p. 816.
6. Dickie, John (1992), *Inside the Foreign Office*, London: Chapmans, p. 183.
7. UN Security Council Resolution S/RES/660 (1990).
8. UN Security Council Resolution S/RES/678 (1990).
9. Central Office of Information (COI) (1993), *Britain and the Gulf Crisis*, London: HMSO, p. 41.
10. Parry-Evans, Air Chief Marshal Sir David (1991), 'Report by the Granby Coordinator: Lessons Learned from the Gulf War', DEFE 11/945, received under FOI, p. 31; National Audit Office (NAO) (1993), *Ministry of Defence: Movements of Personnel, Equipment and Stores To and From the Gulf*, London: HMSO, p. 27.

11. Danchev, Alex and Dan Keohane (eds) (1994), *International Perspectives on the Gulf Conflict, 1990–91*, Basingstoke: Macmillan, p. 150.
12. Thatcher, *Downing Street*, p. 817.
13. Munro to Hurd, 5 January 1991, received under FOI.
14. N.a. to Policy Planning Staff (PPS), 15 April 1991, received under FOI.
15. Urban, Mark (1996), *UK Eyes Alpha: Inside British Intelligence*, London: Faber & Faber, p. 145.
16. Munro, Alan (2012), *Keep the Flag Flying: A Diplomatic Memoir*, London: Gilgamesh, p. 226.
17. Munro, *Flag*, p. 236.
18. This lesson was quickly identified and implemented, with a system set up post-invasion. Parry-Evans, 'Report', pp. 24–5.
19. Urban, *Alpha*, p. 145; FAC (1990), *Gulf Crisis*, London: HMSO, p. 38.
20. Defence Intelligence Staff (DIS), 'Intelligence Support to Operation Granby', 1991, received under FOI, p. 1.
21. It was American satellite imagery showing the movement of Iraqi tanks and 100,000 troops to the border of Saudi Arabia which convinced the Saudis to request Western assistance. Thatcher, *Downing Street*, p. 820.
22. Parry-Evans, 'Report', p. 24.
23. Franks, Lord Oliver (1983), *Falkland Islands Review*, London: HMSO, paragraph 313.
24. DIS, 'Intelligence Support', p. 2.
25. Freedman, Lawrence and Efraim Karsh (1993), *The Gulf Conflict: Diplomacy and War in the New World Order*, London: Faber & Faber, p. 50; Urban, *Alpha*, p. 144.
26. Urban, *Alpha*, p. 146; Cradock, *Pursuit*, p. 172.
27. Cradock, *Pursuit*, p. 172.
28. Sir Patrick Hine, speaking at a meeting of the RAF Historical Society (RAFHS), 13 March 2013.
29. Professor Gordon Barrass, cited in 'Britain and the 1991 Gulf War Witness Seminar', *Air Power Review*, Summer 2016, p. 41.
30. King, Hansard (Commons), CLXXVII, c468-86, 25 July 1990.
31. Parry-Evans, 'Report', p. 4.
32. DC (1991), *Preliminary Lessons of Operation Granby*, London: HMSO, p. xiii.
33. DC, *Preliminary Lessons*, p. xiii.
34. Sir Peter Harding, in 'Gulf War Witness Seminar', p. 66.

Notes

35. Hine to Vincent in Parry-Evans, 'Report', annex b, p. 1.
36. Ibid., p. 17.
37. Munro, Alan (2006), *Arab Storm: Politics and Diplomacy Behind the Gulf War*, London: I. B. Tauris, p. 18.
38. Hine, Air Chief Marshal Sir Patrick (1991), 'Despatch by Air Chief Marshal Sir Patrick Hine GCB ADC FRAES CBIM RAF Joint Commander of Operation Granby', *The London Gazette*, 28 June 1991, Second Supplement, p. G47; NAO (1992), *Ministry of Defence: The Costs and Receipts Arising from the Gulf Conflict*, London: HMSO, p. 3.
39. DC, *Preliminary Lessons*, p. xxv.
40. Dickie, *Inside*, p. 182.
41. Ibid., pp. 185–6.
42. Munro, *Arab Storm*, p. 60.
43. Parry-Evans, 'Report', p. 13.
44. DIS, 'Intelligence Support', p. 3.
45. Ibid., pp. 4–5.
46. Ibid., p. 13.
47. Ibid., pp. 4–5
48. Franks, *Falkland Islands*, paragraphs 318–19.
49. Major, John (1999), *The Autobiography*, London: Harper Collins, p. 234.
50. Thatcher, *Downing Street*, pp. 816, 8, 173.
51. COI, *Britain and the Gulf Crisis*, p. 56. For more on this see Danchev, Alex (1994), 'The Anschluss', *Review of International Studies*, 20, pp. 97–106.
52. Hurd, Douglas (2003), *Memoirs*, London: Little Brown, p. 391.
53. Munro, *Arab Storm*, p. 89.
54. All fourteen papers received under FOI.
55. UN Security Council Resolution S/RES/661 (1990).
56. Munro, *Arab Storm*, p. 75.
57. Munro, *Flag*, p. 228.
58. Thatcher, *Downing Street*, p. 818.
59. COI, *Britain and the Gulf Crisis*, p. 59; Munro to Hurd, 'The Kuwait Crisis', 5 January 1990 [sic 1991], received under FOI.
60. Weston to Hurd, 'Kuwait Annual Review for 1991', received under FOI.
61. PPS, 'Iraq: Partial Withdrawal from Kuwait', 12 December 1990, received under FOI, p. 4.
62. Parry-Evans, 'Report', p. 4.
63. Major, *Autobiography*, p. 230.

64. Cradock, *Pursuit*, p. 184.
65. Hurd, *Memoirs*, p. 410.
66. Major, *Autobiography*, p. 236.
67. de la Billière, General Peter (1992), *Storm Command: A Personal Account of the Gulf War*, London: Harper Collins, p. 16.
68. PPS, 'Iraq/Kuwait: Political Consequences of Military Action', 7 November 1990, received under FOI, p. 1.
69. PPS, 'Iraq/Kuwait: the Long Haul', 26 November 1990, received under FOI, p. 5; PPS, 'Gulf Crisis: Strategy after Iraqi Defeat', 24 January 1991, received under FOI, p. 8.
70. Hurd, *Memoirs*, p. 392.
71. Sir Antony Acland, DOHP 57, p. 47.
72. DC, *Preliminary Lessons*, p. ix.
73. Ibid., p. xi.
74. DC (1991), *The Conflict in the Gulf: Minutes of Evidence*, London: HMSO, p. 9; DC, *Preliminary Lessons*, p. xi.
75. de la Billière, *Storm Command*, p. 39.
76. Air Chief Marshal Patrick Hine, RAFHS.
77. Hine to Vincent in Parry-Evans, 'Report', annex b, p. 23.
78. Parry-Evans, 'Report', pp. 63–4.
79. DC, *Preliminary Lessons*, p. x.
80. PPS, 'Political Consequences of Military Action', pp. 2–3.
81. Article 51 focuses on the right of 'individual or collective self-defence if an armed attack occurs against a Member of the United Nations, until the Security Council has taken measures necessary to maintain international peace and security'.
82. Lord Hannay of Chiswick and Lord Powell of Bayswater, in 'Gulf War Witness Seminar', pp. 45, 48–9.
83. United States Central Command, 'Operation Desert Shield/Desert Storm', 11 July 1991, National Security Archive, <http://nsarchive.gwu.edu/> (last accessed 13 October 2017), p. 16.
84. Munro, *Flag*, pp. 231, 252.
85. Major, *Autobiography*, p. 232; Munro, *Flag*, p. 231.
86. PPS, 'Political Consequences of Military Action', pp. 2–3.
87. Parry-Evans, 'Report', p. 3.
88. PPS, 'The Gulf Crisis: a Just War', 2 January 1991; PPS 'Future Regime of Iraq', 30 August 1991; PPS, 'Iraq/Kuwait: the Long Haul', 14 November 1990, all received under FOI.
89. Hurd, *Memoirs*, pp. 393–4, 409.
90. Hurd, *Memoirs*, p. 410; Major, *Autobiography*, p. 224.
91. Major, *Autobiography*, p. 224.

Notes

92. Ibid., p. 234.
93. Lord Powell of Bayswater, in 'Gulf War Witness Seminar', p. 49.
94. Dickie, *Inside*, pp. 188–9.
95. PPS, 'Future Regime', p. 10.
96. For more on specific intelligence lessons see Kettle, Louise (2016), 'Between Franks and Butler: British Intelligence Lessons from the Gulf War', *Intelligence and National Security*, 31/2, pp. 201–23.
97. Aldrich, Richard J. (2011), *GCHQ*, London: Harper Press, pp. 466–7.
98. Urban, *Alpha*, pp. 144, 170.
99. Thatcher, *Downing Street*, p. 823.
100. Urban, *Alpha*, p. 150.
101. Air Marshal Ian MacFadyen, in 'Gulf War Witness Seminar', p. 94.
102. de la Billière, *Storm Command*, pp. 24–5.
103. DC, *Preliminary Lessons*, p. xxiv.
104. DIS, 'Intelligence Support', p. 2. In contrast the CIA had written hundreds of reports during the 1980s which were provided to the US military. CIA, 'CIA Support to the US military during the Persian Gulf War', 16 June 1997, <http://www.cia.gov/library/reports> (last accessed 14 December 2013).
105. Lord Hamilton of Epsom, in 'Gulf War Witness Seminar', p. 77.
106. DIS, 'Intelligence Support', pp. 3, 10.
107. Ibid., p. 15.
108. Parry-Evans, 'Report', p. 84.
109. DC, *Implementation*, pp. ix, 26; DC, *Conflict in the Gulf*, pp. 10–11; Cradock, *Pursuit*, p. 169; for more on this see Kettle, 'Franks and Butler', pp. 13–14.
110. Cited in Lord Robin Butler (2004), *Review of Intelligence on Weapons of Mass Destruction*, London: HMSO, p. 42.
111. Group Captain Jerry King, speaking at a meeting of the RAFHS, 13 March 2013.
112. Munro, *Storm*, pp. 87, 92; Munro, *Flag*, p. 244.
113. Munro, *Flag*, pp. 216, 232.
114. Sir Alan Munro, in 'Gulf War Witness Seminar', p. 63.
115. Munro, *Storm*, p. 361; Munro, *Flag*, p. 247.
116. DC, *Conflict in the Gulf*, p. 3.
117. Parry-Evans, 'Report', p. 20.
118. Hine, 'Despatch', p. G46; DC, *Preliminary Lessons*, p. xxv; DC, *Conflict in the Gulf*, p. 12.
119. Adie, Kate (2002), *The Kindness of Strangers*, London: Headline, pp. 391, 389.

120. DC, *Conflict in the Gulf*, p. 10.
121. de la Billière, *Storm Command*, p. 3.
122. Munro, *Flag*, p. 234.
123. General Sir Peter de la Billière, in 'Gulf War Witness Seminar', p. 99.
124. Munro, *Storm*, pp. 102, 179.
125. de la Billière, in 'Gulf War Witness Seminar', pp. 61–2; de la Billière to Hine, in Parry-Evans, 'Report', annex c, p. 8.
126. Admiral Sir Julian Oswald, in 'Gulf War Witness Seminar', p. 52.
127. Hine to Vincent in Parry-Evans, 'Report', annex b, p. 2.
128. Air Chief Marshal Sir Richard Johns, RAFHS.
129. Hine to Vincent, 20 May 1991, in Parry-Evans 'Report', annex b, pp. 2–3.
130. Admiral Sir Julian Oswald, in 'Gulf War Witness Seminar', p. 53.
131. Parry-Evans, 'Report', p. 16.
132. Franks, *Falkland Islands*, paragraph 317.
133. Major, *Autobiography*, p. 234.
134. DIS, 'Intelligence Support', pp. 6–7.
135. Parry-Evans, 'Report', p. 13.
136. Lord Powell of Bayswater, in 'Gulf War Witness Seminar', p. 78.
137. PPS, 'Gulf crisis', 19 September 1990, received under FOI.
138. PPS, 'Winning the Peace', 31 January 1991, received under FOI, p. 2; PPS, 'Gulf Crisis: Strategy after Iraqi Defeat', 24 January 1991, received under FOI, p. 8.
139. Hurd, *Memoirs*, p. 410.
140. COI, *Britain and the Gulf Crisis*, p. 32.
141. The UK also had an economic interest in protecting Saudi Arabia. It was supplying trade of at least one market (redacted) worth £2.4 billion. Munro to Hurd, 5 January 1991, received under FOI, p. 6.
142. Parry-Evans, 'Report', p. 39.
143. NAO, *Costs and Receipts*; House of Commons Committee of Public Accounts (1993), *Ministry of Defence: The Costs and Receipts Arising from the Gulf Conflict*, London: HMSO; author interview with Sir Alan Munro, 2 July 2017.
144. Air Chief Marshal Sir Michael Alcock, RAFHS.
145. Parry-Evans, 'Report', pp. 5, 69.
146. DC, *Implementation*, p. 33.
147. Group Captain Mike Trace at RAFHS; Thatcher, *Downing Street*, p. 825.
148. DC, *Preliminary Lessons*, p. xiv.

Notes

149. Hine, 'Despatch', p. G44; Parry-Evans, 'Report', p. 57; Hine to Vincent, in Parry-Evans, 'Report', annex b, p. 18.
150. See, for example, McNab, Andy (1993), *Bravo Two Zero*, London: Bantam Press.
151. Lord Powell of Bayswater and Field Marshal Sir John Chapple, in 'Gulf War Witness Seminar', pp. 54, 76; DC, *Implementation*, p. xiv; Parry-Evans, 'Report', pp. 31, 35–6.
152. Adrian Sindall, DOHP 120, p. 60.
153. DC, *Implementation*, p. xiv.
154. Major, *Autobiography*, p. 235.
155. DC, *Implementation*, pp. ix, 26; DC, *Conflict in the Gulf*, pp. 10–11.
156. DC, *Implementation*, p. 26.
157. Major, *Autobiography*, p. 223.
158. DC, *Lessons*, p. xxvi; DC, *Conflict in the Gulf*, p. 11; Adie, *Kindness of Strangers*, p. 384.
159. Parry-Evans, 'Report', p. 46; DC, *Implementation*, pp. xi, x.
160. DC, *Implementation*, p. xii.
161. Parry-Evans, 'Report', p. 30.
162. Ibid., p. 31.
163. DC, *Implementation*, p. 20.
164. The Midge was soon replaced by the Phoenix. DC, *Implementation*, p. 19.
165. Hine, 'Despatch', p. G42.
166. DIS, 'Intelligence Support', p. 13.
167. Ibid., p. 29.
168. DC, *Implementation*, p. 25.
169. Parry-Evans, 'Report', pp. 26, 104.
170. Urban, *Alpha*, p. 159. For more on SIGINT learning see Kettle, 'Franks and Butler', pp. 216–17.
171. Parry-Evans, 'Report', p. 25.
172. DC, *Preliminary Lessons*, p. 16.
173. DC, *Implementation*, p. 23.
174. DIS, 'Intelligence Support', p. 7.
175. Urban, *Alpha*, pp. 159–60.
176. DIS, 'Intelligence Support', p. 6.
177. Parry-Evans, 'Report', p. 29.
178. DIS, 'Intelligence Support', p. 13; Parry-Evans, 'Report', p. 104.
179. Cradock, *Pursuit*, p. 176.
180. Hine to Vincent in Parry-Evans, 'Report', annex b, p. 9.

181. DIS, 'Intelligence Support', pp. 10–11.
182. Urban, *Alpha*, p. 181.
183. For more on this see Kettle, 'Franks and Butler', pp. 221–2.
184. Munro, *Flag*, p. 221; Munro, *Arab Storm*, p. 93.
185. DIS, 'Intelligence Support', p. 11.
186. Parry-Evans, 'Report', p. 83.
187. Urban, *Alpha*, p. 163; Aldrich, *GCHQ*, p. 468.
188. Urban, *Alpha*, pp. 163, 170, 177.
189. FAC, *Gulf Crisis*.
190. FAC, *After the Gulf War*.
191. Response to FOI request, 12 April 2013.
192. Response to FOI request, 30 December 2014.
193. PPS, 'Middle East Heads of Mission Conference: Theme Paper', 25 March 1991, received under FOI.
194. Ibid., pp. 1, 3–4.
195. Ibid., p. 8.
196. COI, *Britain and the Gulf Crisis*.
197. PPS, 'Future Regime of Iraq', 30 August 1990, received under FOI, p. 8.
198. COI, *Britain and the Gulf Crisis*, p. 68.
199. Alan Munro, DOHP 13, p. 18.
200. Major, *Autobiography*, p. 240.
201. Parry-Evans, 'Report', annex e.
202. MoD (1991), *Statement on Defence Estimates*, London: HMSO, p. 26.
203. DC, *Implementation*, p. vi; Parry-Evans, 'Report', pp. 62–73.
204. Air Marshal Sir Peter Harding, in 'Gulf War Witness Seminar', p. 89; for more on RAF learning see Ritchie, Sebastian (2014), 'The Royal Air Force and the First Gulf War, 1990–91: A Case Study in the Identification and Implementation of Air Power Lessons', *Air Power Review*, 17/1, pp. 36–53.
205. DC, *Conflict in the Gulf*, p. 5.
206. Parry-Evans, 'Report', annex e, p. 2.
207. DC, *Preliminary Lessons*, p. 2.
208. DC, *Implementation*, p. viii.
209. NAO, *Movements*, p. 10.
210. Ibid., p. 3.
211. Parton, Group Captain Neville (2006), 'Why Should We Care About History?', *Spirit of the Air*, 1/1, pp. 23–4.
212. NAO, *Movements*, p. 3.
213. DC, *Preliminary Lessons*; DC, *Implementation*.

214. Notice to Directors and Heads of Division in Parry-Evans 'Report', annex c.
215. DC, *Implementation*, pp. 44–5.
216. Ibid., pp. 1, 3.
217. Ibid., p. 3.
218. MoD (2000), *Kosovo: Lessons from the Crisis*, London: TSO, Chapter seven.
219. DC, *Implementation*, p. vii.
220. Ibid., pp. 1, vi.
221. Ibid., p. 37.
222. Parry-Evans 'Report', p. 78.
223. DC, *Preliminary Lessons*, p. xxv.
224. Hine, 'Despatch', p. G37.
225. Munro, *Flag*, p. 252; Urban, *Alpha*, p. 169.
226. DIS, 'Intelligence Support'.
227. Parry-Evans, 'Report', pp. 24, 26.
228. Aldrich, *GCHQ*, p. 469.
229. DC, *Implementation*, pp. 22–3.
230. Sir Alan Munro, DOHP 13, p. 18.
231. PPS, 'Iraq: How Can Things Go Wrong?', 30 April 1991, received under FOI, p. 4.
232. Butler, *Review*, p. 106. For more on this see Kettle, 'Franks and Butler', pp. 213–14.
233. Davies, Philip H. J. (2012), *Intelligence and Government in Britain and the United States: A Comparative Perspective*, e-book: ABC-Clio, n.p.
234. Davies, Philip H. J. (2004), *MI6 and the Machinery of Spying*, Abingdon: Frank Cass, p. 300.
235. DC, *Implementation*, p. 3.
236. Cradock, *Pursuit*, p. 182.
237. FAC, *After the Gulf War*, p. v.

Chapter 6 Afghanistan Part Two – Iraq 2003–9

1. Powell to Blair, 'Crawford', 28 March 2002, TII.
2. UN Security Council Resolution S/RES/687 (1991). For more on this see Hiro, Dilip (2003), *Iraq: A Report from the Outside*, London: Granta Publications, pp. 96–108.
3. McKane to Manning, 18 September 2001, TII.

4. National Audit Office (NAO) (2003), *Ministry of Defence Operation TELIC – United Kingdom Military Operations in Iraq*, London: TSO, p. 1.
5. Johnson to Howard, 'Op Telic – Lessons for the Secretariat', 6 July 2004, TII.
6. Chaplin to Straw, 'Iraq: Military Action', 12 July 2002, TII.
7. Chilcot to Chaplin, 'Iraq: Day-after Issues', 17 January 2003, TII; Straw to Blair, 'Crawford/Iraq', 25 March 2002, TII.
8. Chaplin to Straw, 12 July 2002, TII.
9. Sir Jeremy Greenstock, evidence to the House of Commons Foreign Affairs Committee (FAC) on 'Active Diplomacy for a Changing World', 8 November 2006.
10. McKane to Manning, 'Iraq Stocktake', 18 September 2001, TII; Central Intelligence Group, 'A Review of Intelligence on Possible Links between Al Qaida and Saddam's Regime', 13 July 2004, TII; Dearlove to Manning, 'Iraq', 3 December 2001, TII.
11. JIC, 'Southern Iraq: What's in Store?", 19 February 2003, TII.
12. JIC, 'Iraq: the Initial Landscape Post-Saddam', 16 April 2003, TII.
13. Blair to Bush, 24 January 2003, TII.
14. Mullin, Chris (2010), *A View from the Foothills*, London: Profile, p. 302.
15. Blair to Bush, 28 July 2002, TII; Robin Cook also explicitly denied the comparison between Iraq and Kosovo in his resignation speech. Cook, Hansard (Commons), CDI, c726–8, 17 March 2003.
16. Author interview with Sir Alan Munro, 16 July 2014.
17. FAC (2004), *Foreign Policy Aspects of the War against Terror: Seventh Report of the Session 2003–2004*, London: TSO, p. 5.
18. Sir John Chilcot evidence to the House of Commons Liaison Committee, 2 November 2016, Q49.
19. Chilcot, Sir John (2016), *The Report of the Iraq Inquiry*, London: HMSO, executive summary, pp. 55–6.
20. Sir Jeremy Heywood, evidence to the House of Commons Public Administration and Constitutional Affairs Committee (PACAC), 14 September 2016, Q40.
21. Sir John Chilcot stated that the need for collective responsibility was his most important identified lesson. Evidence to the Liaison Committee, Q112, Q149. For more on the failings of Cabinet see Kettle, Louise (2016), 'Essay by Louise Kettle', in 'Policy Roundtable 1-1 on the Chilcot Inquiry', <http://issforum.org> (last accessed 17 October 2017).
22. Chilcot, *The Iraq Inquiry*, section 3, p. 398.

23. Straw to Blair, 25 March 2002, TII; Blair to Powell, 17 March 2002, TII; Powell to Blair, 19 July 2002, TII; Woodward, Bob (2004), *Plan of Attack*, London: Simon & Schuster, p. 337.
24. The poll was conducted by ICM on a random sample of 1,002 adults by telephone. Travis, Alan (2003), 'Support for War Falls to New Low', 21 January 2003, <http://www.theguardian.com/politics/2003/jan/21/uk.iraq2> (last accessed 25 July 2015); Cook, Robin (2004), *The Point of Departure: Diaries from the Front Bench*, London: Simon & Schuster, p. 270.
25. Ashley, Jackie and Ewen MacAskill (2003), 'History Will Be My Judge', 1 March 2003, <http://www.theguardian.com/politics/2003/mar/01/iraq.foreignpolicy> (last accessed 12 April 2014).
26. Cook, *Departure*, p. 203; Campbell, Alastair (2007), *The Blair Years: Extracts from the Alastair Campbell Diaries*, London: The Random House Group, p. 636.
27. Blair to Powell, 'Iraq', 17 March 2002, TII.
28. Blair to Bush, 'Note on Iraq', 28 July 2002, TII.
29. Blair to Bush, 'Note', 24 January 2003, TII.
30. Campbell, *Blair Years*, p. 694.
31. Mullin, *Foothills*, p. 400.
32. Ibid., pp. 316, 348.
33. Straw, memorandum, January 2010, TII.
34. Straw, Jack (2012), *Last Man Standing: Memoirs of a Political Survivor*, London: Macmillan, p. 371.
35. Chilcot, *The Iraq Inquiry*, executive summary, p. 130.
36. Statement by Sir John Chilcot, 6 July 2016, <http://www.iraqinquiry.org> (last accessed 27 October 2017).
37. Chilcot, *The Iraq Inquiry*, executive summary, p. 130.
38. Denis MacShane, witness statement, n.d., TII.
39. Jeremy Greenstock, DOHP 99, p. 54.
40. Straw, *Last Man*, pp. 364–5, 369.
41. A Mandarin linguist working at GCHQ, Katharine Gun, leaked a memo to the *Observer* from the National Security Agency (NSA) to GCHQ.
42. Rycroft to Manning, 'Iraq: Prime Minister's Meeting, 23 July', <http://nsarchive.gwu.edu/NSAEBB/NSAEBB328/II-Doc14.pdf> (last accessed 10 June 2012); Woodward, *Plan*, p. 202; Aldrich, Richard J. (2011), *GCHQ*, London: Harper Press, p. 518; Intelligence and Security Committee (ISC) (2003), *Iraqi Weapons of Mass Destruction – Intelligence and Assessments*, London: TSO, p. 24.
43. ISC, *Iraqi Weapons*, annex b, p. 51; Aldrich, *GCHQ*, p. 526.

44. Straw to Blair, 8 July 2002, TII; House of Commons Defence Committee (DC) (2004), *Lessons of Iraq: Third Report of the Session 2003–2004*, London: TSO, p. 5.
45. MoD (2003), 'Operations in Iraq: Lessons for the Future', <http://www.mod.uk/DefenceInternet/AboutDefence/CorporatePublications/DoctrineOperationsandDiplomacyPublications/OperationsInIraq/OperationsInIraqLessonsForTheFuture.htm> (last accessed 3 April 2012), p. 36.
46. Chilcot, *The Iraq Inquiry*, executive summary, p. 121.
47. DC, *Lessons*, pp. 5, 19.
48. Straw to Blair, 'Iraq: Contingency Planning', 8 July 2002, TII.
49. Meyer to Cabinet Office, 'PM's visit to Camp David: Iraq', 6 September 2002, TII.
50. Chilcot to Chaplin, 17 January 2003, TII; Stephen Pattison, witness statement, January 2011, TII; Ricketts to Straw, 'Iraq: Resolutions: the "Kosovo Option"', 3 October 2002, TII.
51. Statement by Sir John Chilcot, 6 July 2016; MacShane, witness statement, n.d., TII.
52. John Williams, witness statement, 9 January 2011, TII; MacShane, witness statement, n.d., TII; Sir Freddie Viggers, witness statement, 8 December 2009, TII; Stephen Pattison, witness statement, January 2011, TII.
53. Permanent Joint Headquarters (PJHQ), 15 January 2003, TII.
54. Ricketts to Webb, 3 May 2002, TII.
55. Chiefs of Staff, meeting record, 22 January 2003, TII.
56. Viggers, witness statement, 8 December 2009, TII.
57. Etherington, Mark (2013), 'I waited for instructions, but was told: no one will help', *Sunday Telegraph*, 10 March 2013, p. 21.
58. Iraq Planning Unit, 'Planning for the UK's Role in Iraq after Saddam', 5 March 2003, TII.
59. Chilcot, *The Iraq Inquiry*, section 13, pp. 484–5.
60. Sir Nicholas Macpherson, witness statement, 15 January 2010, TII.
61. Johnson to Howard, 6 July 2004, TII.
62. Chilcot, *The Iraq Inquiry*, section 13, p. 445.
63. Three exceptions were Air Component Commander, Air Vice Marshal Glenn Torpy, Deputy to the Head of Office for Reconstruction and Humanitarian Assistance, Major General Tim Cross and Commander of 16 Air Assault Brigade Brigadier 'Jacko' Page. MoD, 'Brief Biographical Details of the Senior UK Commanders Involved in Operation Telic', n.d., <http://webarchive.nationalarchives.gov.uk> (last accessed 24 March 2014).

Notes

64. MoD, 'Lessons', p. 53.
65. NAO, *Operation TELIC*, pp. 13–14; Lieutenant General Chris Brown, 'Operation Telic Lessons Compendium', n.d., <http://www.mod.uk/NR/rdonlyres/F0282A90-99E5-415E-B3BC-97EAD7D7873A/0/operation_telic_lessons_compendium.pdf> (last accessed 12 June 2012), TEL.N.19.
66. MoD, 'Lessons', p. 54.
67. DC, *Lessons*, p. 44.
68. N.a. (2010), *Operations in Iraq January 2005-May 2009 (Op Telic 5–13): Analysis from the Land Perspective*, <https://operationtelic.co.uk> (last accessed 31 October 2017), p. 11.
69. PJHQ, 'Record of COS Briefing to the PM', 15 January 2003, TII.
70. Cabinet Office (2010), *Securing Britain in an Age of Uncertainty: The Strategic Defence and Security Review*, London: TSO, p. 15.
71. Ibid., p. 19.
72. Straw to Blair, 25 March 2002, TII; Blair to Powell, 17 March 2002, TII; Powell to Blair, 19 July 2002, TII; Woodward, *Plan*, p. 337.
73. Butler, Lord Robin (2004), *Review of Intelligence on Weapons of Mass Destruction*, London: TSO, pp. 42–74.
74. Ibid., p. 103.
75. Prime Minister's Office (2002), *Iraq's Weapons of Mass Destruction: The Assessment of the British Government*, London: TSO.
76. Butler, *Review*, p. 76.
77. Prime Minister's Office, *Iraq's Weapons*, p. 3.
78. These include the infamous defector codenamed Curveball. FAC (2003), *The Decision to go to War in Iraq*, London: TSO, p. 9; Butler, *Review*, pp. 99–102, 152.
79. Butler, *Review*, p. 151.
80. Manning to Blair, 'Iraq', 12 September 2002, TII.
81. Lord Jay Ewelme, witness statement, 21 June 2010, TII.
82. FCO (2004), *Departmental Report 1 April 2003–31 March 2004*, London: TSO, p. 55.
83. FAC (2003), *Foreign Policy Aspects of the War against Terror: Second Report of the Session 2002–2003*, London: TSO.
84. FCO (2005), *Departmental Report 1 April 2004–31 March 2005*, London: TSO, p. 208.
85. North, Richard (2009), *Ministry of Defeat*, London: Continuum, p. 56.
86. Barrons, Richard (2010), 'Foreword' in n.a., *Analysis from the Land Perspective*, p. i.
87. Brown, 'Compendium', footnote 68.

88. To add further to the loss of individual lessons in the FCO there were three Foreign Secretaries during the Iraq War: Jack Straw (June 2001–May 2006), Margaret Beckett (May 2006–June 2007) and David Miliband (June 2007–May 2010). David Miliband, 'Speech at the FCO Leadership Conference', 4 March 2008, <http://ukingermany.fco.gov.uk/en/news/?view=Speech&id=4616832> (last accessed 27 December 2011).
89. House of Commons Public Administration Select Committee (PASC) (2010), *Who Does UK National Strategy?*, London: TSO, p. 19.
90. Chilcot, *The Iraq Inquiry*, executive summary, p. 135; PACAC (2017), *Lessons Still to Be Learned from the Chilcot Inquiry*, London: HMSO, p. 30.
91. Greenstock, Jeremy (2016), *Iraq: The Cost of War*, London: William Heinemann, p. 423.
92. Chilcot, *The Iraq Inquiry*, executive summary, pp. 90–2.
93. N.a., *Analysis from the Land Perspective*, pp. 3–1, 3–6.
94. Gilligan, Andrew (2013), 'We must face the truth: Britain was humiliated', *Sunday Telegraph*, 10 March 2013, pp. 20–1.
95. McColl, 'Iraq up to and beyond January 2006 – Defining a UK Position', 23 September 2004, TII.
96. Cited in Chilcot, *The Iraq Inquiry*, executive summary, p. 103.
97. Ibid., p. 124.
98. Statement by Sir John Chilcot, <http://www.iraqinquiry.org> (last accessed 27 October 2017).
99. N.a., *Analysis from the Land Perspective*, p. 7.
100. MoD (2003), 'Operations in Iraq: First Reflections', <http://www.mod.uk/defenceinternet/aboutdefence/corporatepublications/doctrineoperationsanddiplomacypublications/operationsiniraq/operationiniraqfirstreflections.htm> (last accessed 3 April 2012), pp. 24–5; MoD, 'Lessons', p. 10.
101. MoD, 'Reflections', p. 15.
102. Woodward, Bob (2006), *State of Denial*, London: Simon & Schuster, pp. 318–19.
103. N.a., *Analysis from the Land Perspective*, p. 2–13.
104. Ibid., pp. 6, 2–1, 2–3.
105. Brown, 'Compendium', TEL2.A.07.
106. Butler, *Review*, pp. 153, 158.
107. Johnson to Howard, 6 July 2004, TII.
108. MoD, 'Lessons', p. 28.
109. MoD, 'Lessons', pp. 44–5.

110. DC (2006), *UK Operations in Iraq: Thirteenth Report of the Session 2005–2006*, London: TSO, p. 18.
111. Cited in North, *Ministry of Defeat*, p. 159.
112. Chilcot, evidence to Liaison Committee, Q129.
113. MoD, 'Reflections', p. 25.
114. Gilligan, 'We must face the truth', p. 21.
115. MoD, 'Lessons', p. 40.
116. NAO, *Operation TELIC*, p. 36.
117. Ibid., p. 20.
118. DC, *Lessons*, 16.
119. MoD, 'Lessons', p. 9.
120. DC, *Lessons*, p. 7.
121. MoD, 'Lessons', p. 59.
122. Johnson to Howard, 6 July 2004, TII.
123. MoD, 'Lessons', pp. 59–60.
124. MoD, 'Reflections', p. 16.
125. Cited in N.a., *Analysis from the Land Perspective*, p. 7–1.
126. Ibid., p. 7–11.
127. Staffords, cited in Ibid.
128. MoD, 'Defence-wide Lessons Management', received under FOI; Brown, 'Compendium', Chapter 9.
129. Private information.
130. Ibid.
131. Melvin, Major General Mungo (2011), 'Learning and Exploiting the Lessons of War', *The British Army*, p. 85.
132. From the mid-1980s the theatre in Northern Ireland was mature with successful policing, specialised counterterrorism operations and, from 1994, Irish Republican Army (IRA) ceasefires.
133. N.a., *Analysis from the Land Perspective*, pp. 4–5, 1–3, 1–4.
134. DCDC (2009), *Security and Stabilisation: The Military Contribution: Joint Doctrine Publication 3–40*, Bicester: DSDA.
135. Petraeus, David and James F. Amos (2006), *Counterinsurgency: FM 3–24*, Washington: Paladin Press.
136. Macmillan, Margaret (2010), *The Uses and Abuses of History*, London: Profile Books Ltd, p. 153.
137. Those in the British Army with an interest in languages were more attracted to learning Pashtu or Dari for Afghanistan. N.a., *Analysis from the Land Perspective*, p. 1–8.
138. DC, *Lessons*, p. 8; Brown, 'Compendium', TEL.0.59, TEL.0.61.
139. MoD (2007), 'Iraq: Cultural Appreciation Booklet', <http://www.gov.uk/government/uploads/system/uploads/attachment_data/

file/16869/iraq_cultural_appreciation_booklet.pdf> (last accessed 30 March 2014).
140. N.a. (2010), *Operations in Iraq: January 2005-May2009 (Op Telic 5–13): An Analysis from the Land Perspective*, released under FOI, pp. 7–10, 4.
141. Brown, 'Compendium', TEL.0.210, TEL.0.211.
142. ISC (2006), *Annual Report 2005–2006*, London: TSO, p. 9.
143. Aldrich, *GCHQ*, pp. 524–6.
144. MoD, 'Reflections', p. 15.
145. Brown, 'Compendium', TEL.0.239, TEL.0.240.
146. Meyer, Christopher (2005), *DC Confidential*, London: Orion, p. 278.
147. FCO, *Report 2003–2004*, p. 131.
148. Cited in ibid., p. 14.
149. FCO, *Report 2004–2005*, p. 212.
150. Stabilisation Unit (SU) (2010), 'Responding to Stabilisation Challenges in Hostile and Insecure Environments: Lessons Identified by the UK's Stabilisation Unit', <http://www.stabilisationunit.gov.uk/attachments/article/520/Top%20Lessons%20from%20Stabilisation%20and%20Conflict.pdf> (last accessed 10 August 2012).
151. N.a., *Analysis from the Land Perspective*, pp. 5, 11; Crispin Blunt during Chilcot, evidence to Liaison Committee, Q41.
152. FAC, *Decision*; FAC (2007), *Global Security: The Middle East*, London: TSO.
153. See for example FCO (2004), *Second Report from the Foreign Affairs Committee Foreign Policy Aspects of the War Against Terrorism Session 2003–2004: Response of the Secretary of State for Foreign and Commonwealth Affairs*, London: TSO.
154. Meyer, *DC Confidential*; Greenstock, *Iraq*. Greenstock's book was also delayed by the FCO clearance process. To avoid the same problem Sherard Cowper-Coles submitted his manuscript to the less stringent Cabinet Office for approval. Private information. Cowper-Coles, Sherard (2012), *Cables from Kabul*, London: Harper Press.
155. FCO, *Report 2004–2005*, p. 212.
156. FAC (2005), *Foreign Policy Aspects of the War against Terror: Sixth Report of the Session 2004–2005*, London: TSO, p. 41.
157. FAC (2006), 'Active Diplomacy for a Changing World: the FCO'S Strategic Priorities', oral evidence, 8 November 2006, <http://www.publications.parliament.uk/pa/cm200607/cmselect/cmfaff/167/6110801.htm> (last accessed 20 June 2012).

158. FAC 'Active Diplomacy'.
159. Mark Etherington, witness statement, 12 August 2010, TII.
160. MoD, 'Lessons', p. 3.
161. Ibid., MoD, 'Reflections'.
162. NAO, *Operation TELIC*, p. 4.
163. Aitken, Brigadier Robert (2008), 'The Aitken Report: an Investigation into Cases of Deliberate Abuse and Unlawful Killing in Iraq in 2003 and 2004', <mod.uk/NR/rdonlyres/7AC894D3-1430-4AD1-911F-8210C3342CC5/0/aitken_rep.pdf> (last accessed 20 May 2012).
164. NAO, *Operation TELIC*; DC, *Lessons*.
165. Article two; Gage, Sir William (2011), *The Baha Mousa Public Inquiry Report*, London: TSO, p. 1; Forbes, Sir Thayne (2014), *The Report of the Al-Sweady Inquiry*, London: TSO, p. 5; <http://www.gov.uk/government/groups/iraq-historic-allegations-team-ihat> (last accessed 5 July 2015).
166. Defence Medical Services (DMS), 'Director General Medical Operational Capability Report', 20 February 2006, TII, pp. 5–19.
167. MoD, 'Lessons Management', received through FOI, p. F-4.
168. Private information.
169. Ibid.
170. Fairweather, Jack (2011), *A War of Choice*, London: Vintage, pp. 187–8.
171. Brown, 'Compendium'.
172. Ibid., TEL0.77; Johnson to Howard, 6 July 2004, TII.
173. Private information.
174. DMS, 'Capability Report', pp. 5–18; Aitkin, 'Aitkin Report', p. 22.
175. Attlee, Hansard (Lords), DCCXI, c1250, 18 June 2009.
176. FAC, *Decision*, p. 7.
177. Williams, witness statement, December 2010, TII.
178. FAC, *Decision*, p. 7.
179. Ibid., pp. 8, 49.
180. Blair, Hansard (Commons), DMVI, c147, 4 June 2003.
181. FAC, *Decision*, p. 8.
182. ISC, *Iraqi Weapons*, p. 5.
183. Ibid., pp. 44, 27, 30.
184. ISC (2004), *Annual Report 2003–2004*, London: TSO, p. 25; Prime Minister's Office (2004), *Government Response to the Intelligence and Security Committee Report on Iraqi Weapons of Mass Destruction – Intelligence and Assessments*, London: TSO.
185. ISC, *Annual Report 2003–2004*, p. 25.

186. Hutton, Lord Brian (2004), *Report of the Inquiry into the Circumstances Surrounding the Death of Dr David Kelly C. M. G.*, London: TSO, p. 1.
187. Butler, *Review*, pp. 156–60.
188. Blair, Hansard (Commons), DMXXIV, c195, 20 July 2004.
189. Straw, Hansard (Commons), DMXXVI, c54WS, 15 November 2004.
190. ISC (2005), *Annual Report 2004–2005*, London: TSO, p. 25.
191. Cabinet Office (2005), *Review of Intelligence on Weapons of Mass Destruction: Implementation of Its Conclusions*, London: TSO.
192. Ibid., pp. 4, 7, 9.
193. Gus O'Donnell and Peter Ricketts, written evidence, 28 January 2011, TII, p. 6; Cabinet Office, *Securing Britain*.
194. None of the identified lessons on policy, links between al-Qaeda and the Iraqi regime, the forty-five minute claim or mobile biological weapons labs was acknowledged.
195. ISC, *Annual Report 2003–2004*, pp. 34, 7.
196. ISC (2008), *Annual Report 2007–2008*, London: TSO, p. 36.
197. Butler, *Review*, p. 146.
198. Central Intelligence Group, 'A Review', TII; O'Donnell and Ricketts, 28 January 2011, annex b, TII, p17.
199. Straw, Hansard (Commons), CDXI, c673, 22 October 2003.
200. Beckett, Hansard (Commons), CDLI, c171, 31 October 2006.
201. Parliament had debated the terms of reference for the 1982 Franks Inquiry. Cameron, Hansard (Commons), CDXCIV, c26, 15 June 2009.
202. No one on the committee had legal experience nor was there a senior politician (one from each party was represented on the Franks inquiry) or a military representative.
203. PASC (2005), *Government by Inquiry*, London: TSO; PASC (2008), *Parliamentary Commissions of Inquiry*, London: TSO; PASC (2009), *The Iraq Inquiry*, London: TSO.
204. Brown, Hansard (Commons), CDXCIV, c24, 15 June 2009.
205. This was due to the scope of terms of reference and evidence, agreeing the publication of sensitive documents, illness of a committee member, the Maxwellisation process (although Sir John Chilcot has claimed this did not cause delays), security clearance and limitations of resource and capacity. Suggestions of an interim report were also ignored. Lord Bridgwater, Hansard (Lords), DCCXI, c1236, 18 June 2009. The PACAC have since concluded that there are lessons to be learned on the inquiry process itself; PACAC, *Lessons Still to be Learned*, p. 3.

206. In comparison the Savile Inquiry into Bloody Sunday had 2,500 witness statements, took twelve years to report and cost £155 million, <http://www.bloody-Sunday-inquiry.org.uk> (last accessed 30 October 2017).
207. Chilcot, *The Iraq Inquiry*, executive summary, pp. 129–41.
208. Hammond, Hansard (Commons), DCXIII, c316, 13 July 2016.
209. Ibid., c322.
210. Private information.
211. PACAC, *Lessons Still to be Learned*.
212. Chilcot, evidence to Liaison Committee, Q37.
213. NAO, *Operation TELIC*, p. 4.

Chapter 7 Failing History or Lessons Learned?

1. Hegel, Georg Wilhelm Friedrich [1899] (1956), *The Philosophy of History*, New York: Dover, p. 6.
2. Kissinger, Henry (1994), *Diplomacy*, New York: Simon and Schuster, p. 27.
3. Liddell Hart, B. H. [1972] (2012), *Why Don't We Learn From History?*, Marston Gate: Amazon, p. 40.
4. The report is dedicated to those who lost their lives 'in the hope and expectation that lessons will be learned from their sacrifice'. Haddon-Cave, Charles (2009), *The Nimrod Review*, London: TSO, pp. 447–52.
5. Hedley, John Hollister (2005), 'Learning from Intelligence Failures', *International Journal of Intelligence and CounterIntelligence*, 18/3, p. 441.
6. Private information.
7. Crispin Blunt during Sir John Chilcot evidence to the House of Commons Liaison Committee, 2 November 2016, Q35.
8. <http://www.historyandpolicy.org> (last accessed 5 November 2017).
9. Neustadt, Richard E. and Ernest R. May (1986), *Thinking in Time: The Use of History for Decision-Makers*, London: Collier Macmillan, p. 4.
10. Private information.
11. Dickie, John (1992), *Inside the Foreign Office*, London: Chapmans, pp. 236–7.
12. Reynolds, David (2005), *In Command of History: Churchill Fighting and Writing the Second World War*, London: Penguin.

13. Record of a conversation between the Secretary of State and Eden, 30 May 1958, FO 800/728.
14. Marx, Karl [1852] (1926), *The Eighteenth Brumaire of Louis Bonaparte*, London: George Allen and Unwin, p. 23.
15. Straw, Jack (2012), *Last Man Standing: Memoirs of a Political Survivor*, London: Macmillan, p. 412.
16. N.a., 'UK Action to Combat Daesh', <https://www.gov.uk/government/topical-events/daesh> (last accessed 4 November 2017).
17. JIC, 'International Terrorism: Impact of Iraq', 13 April 2005, TII.
18. Lord Michael J. Williams, witness statement, 9 January 2011, TII.
19. Burt, Alastair (2011), 'The Power of Western Foreign and Security Policy', 1 December 2011, <http://www.gov.uk/government/speeches/the-power-of-western-foreign-and-security-policy> (last accessed 30 December 2011).
20. Cameron, Hansard (Commons), DXXV, c709, 21 March 2011.
21. House of Commons Defence Committee (2012), *Operations in Libya*, London: TSO, p. 45.
22. House of Commons Foreign Affairs Committee (2016), *Libya: Examination of Intervention and Collapse and the UK's Future Policy Options*, London: TSO.
23. Obama had reluctantly supported Cameron's Libya policy.
24. For more information see Aldrich, Richard J., Rory Cormac and Michael S. Goodman (2014), *Spying on the World*, Edinburgh: Edinburgh University Press, pp. 418–19.
25. Cameron, Hansard (Commons), DLXVI, c1440 and c1427, 29 August 2013.
26. N.a., 'Syria Crisis Response Summary: 23 October 2017', <https://www.gov.uk/government/uploads/system/uploads/attachment_data/file/653968/UK_Syria_Crisis_Response_Summary_2017_10_23.pdf> (last accessed 4 November 2017).
27. Cited in Tweedie, Neil (2012), 'We must draw on our historians', 1 August 2012, <http://www.telegraph.co.uk/history/9441669/We-must-draw-on-our-historians.html> (last accessed 1 August 2012).
28. The FCO has around forty-five research analysts who develop considerable knowledge about the history and culture of specific geographical areas. Hague, William (2011), 'The Best Diplomatic Service in the World: Strengthening the Foreign and Commonwealth Office as an Institution', 8 September 2011, <http://www.gov.uk/government/speeches/the-best-diplomatic-service-in-the-world-strengthening-the-foreign-and-commonwealth-office-as-an-institution> (last accessed 2 November 2013).

29. Ibid.
30. Author interview with Sir Alan Munro, 16 July 2014.
31. Carryl Allardice, introduction at the FCO Head of the Knowledge and Information Management Team, FCO Records Policy and Practice Forum, 17 May 2013.
32. FCO (2015), 'Annual Report and Accounts 2014–15', <http://www.gov.uk/government/uploads/system/uploads/attachment_data/file/444067/Amended_FCO_Annual_Report_2015_web__1_.pdf> (last accessed 23 July 2015), p. 20.
33. Ibid., p. 56; FCO (2014), 'Annual Report and Accounts 2013–14', <http://www.gov.uk/government/uploads/system/uploads/attachment_data/file/325896/FCO_Annual_Report_2013–14.pdf> (last accessed 23 July 2015), pp. 73, 5–6.
34. Ibid., p. 70
35. Ibid., p. 70.
36. Private information.
37. Joint and Coalition Operational Analysis (2012), 'Decade of War Volume I', <http://cgsc.contentdm.oclc.org/cdm/search/searchterm/(JCOA)> (last accessed 19 July 2015).
38. Private information.
39. Hammond, Hansard (Commons), DCXIII, c323, 13 July 2016.
40. For more on the NSC–JIC relationship see Aldrich et al., *Spying*, pp. 409–13.
41. Hammond, Hansard (Commons), DCXIII, c323, 13 July 2016.
42. See, for example, Bernard Jenkin, PACAC, oral evidence, 14 September 2016, Q45; PACAC, *Lessons Still to be Learned*, p. 17; PASC, *Who Does UK National Strategy?*, p. 18; PASC (2012), *Strategic Thinking in Government*, London: TSO, pp. 35–6; FAC, *Libya*, pp. 20–2.
43. Pilling, Sir Joseph (2009), 'The Review of the Government's Official History Programme', <http://www.gov.uk/government/uploads/system/uploads/attachment_data/file/62233/future-plans-government.pdf> (last accessed 20 July 2015), paragraph 12.
44. Ibid., paragraphs 29, 39, 42–4.
45. Hamilton, Bill (n.d.), 'Review of the Publishing Arrangements under the Government's Official History Programme', <http://www.gov.uk/government/uploads/system/uploads/attachment_data/file/62233/future-plans-government.pdf> (last accessed 20 July 2015).
46. Ibid., paragraphs 13.1, 13.2.
47. Ibid., paragraphs 13.3, 13.4.
48. Author interview with Sir Alan Munro, 16 July 2014.

49. On 17 July 2015 the government recognised the challenges of FOI and announced a new independent commission on its role. However, the Commission concluded that the process was working well and failed to examine the impact of FOI on reducing the documentation of decisions for learning from the past. Lord Burns (2016), 'Independent Commission on Freedom of Information Report', <https://www.gov.uk/government/uploads/system/uploads/attachment_data/file/504139/Independent_Freedom_of_Information_Commission_Report.pdf> (last accessed 4 November 2017).
50. See, for example, Howard, Michael (2006), 'Military History and the History of War', in *The Past as Prologue: The Importance of History to the Military Profession*, Williamson Murray and Richard Hart Sinnreich (eds), Cambridge: Cambridge University Press, p. 13.
51. Hartley, L. P. [1953] (2004), *The Go-Between*, London: Penguin, p. 5.
52. Liddell Hart, *Why Don't We Learn From History?*, p. 15.
53. Cited in Crick, Bernard (1983), 'Introduction', in *The Discourses* [1531], Niccolò Machiavelli, London: Penguin, p. 50.

Index

Page numbers followed by f indicate a figure.

Abadan Crisis 1951, 27, 44, 46
ABCA nations, 198
Abd al-Ilah, Crown Prince, 60
Abdiya, Princess, 60
Abyssinia, 28
Acland, Sir Anthony, 35–6, 140
'acquisition of knowledge', 19, 19–21, 20f
Aden protectorate, 21–2, 85, 99, 110, 120
Admiralty, 10, 115
Afghanistan, 213, 214, 215, 220
Air 2 Corps, 30
Air Historical Branch, 52, 84, 119
Air Ministry, 10
   Egyptian Air Force, 38
   Iraq, 103
   Jordan, 78
   Operation Musketeer, 42, 50
   PR, 75
   Saudi Arabia, 104
   William Luce, 115
Air Power Review, 12
Air Staff Secretariat, 41
Aitken report, 197
Akrotiti, 42
Al Anbar Province, 186
al-Assad, Bashar, 222
al-Baghdadi, Abu Bakr, 219
Al Faw peninsular, 171
Al-Ahram, 95
Aldred, Margaret, 129, 162
Alexandria, 29, 31
al-Gaylani, Rashid Ali, 61
Algiers agreements 1975 – Iraq and Iran, 158

Allied Force Headquarters, 41, 50
Allied Task Force, 50
al-Nabulsi, Sulaiman, 62
al-Qaeda, 169–70, 172, 202, 219
Al-Sabah, Emir Abdullah III Al-Salim, 92
Al-Sabah, Sheikh Muhammad, 91
Al-Sabah ruling family, 100, 130
ALSF *see* Arab League Security Force
Al-Sweady inquiry, 197
American Airlines Flight 11, 169
American Gulf Oil Group, 91
Amery, Julian, 35, 85, 88
Amman, 53, 63, 67–8, 71, 72, 78–9, 84
ammunition and weapons supply, 40, 109, 152–3
analogy, 8–9, 178
Anglo-American *see* UK–US
Anglo-Egyptian Financial Agreement, 44
Anglo-Egyptian Treaty 1936, 24–5
Anglo-French action against Egypt 1956, 29–30, 36–7
Anglo-Iranian Oil Company, 27, 91
Anglo-Jordanian alliance, 31–2
Anglo-Jordanian treaty 1948, 62
Anglo-Kuwaiti relations, 138–9
Anglo-Ottoman Convention 1913, 91
Anglo-Persian Oil Company, 91
Anschluss, 9, 28
AORG *see* Army's Operational Research Group
'appeasement', 8, 27, 165
Aqaba, 73
Arab Forces, 157
Arab League, 107, 220, 221

279

Arab League Security Force (ALSF), 92, 107, 120
Arab Legion, 25, 69
Arab nationalism, 33, 35, 57–8, 60–1, 69–70, 84–5, 138
Arab News Agency, 33
Arab Spring, 3, 220
Arab Union, 61
Arabic-speakers, 145
Arab-Israeli War, 26, 159
Arabists, 69, 100, 115
Argentina, 142
Armilla patrol, 134, 145, 180
Army, 50, 103, 106, 116, 148, 151, 192
Army Council, 41, 51, 57
Army Historical Branch, 11, 118–19, 225
Army Knowledge Exchange, 224
Army PR, 75, 108
Army's Operational Research Group (AORG), 109–10, 116, 117–18, 125
Arnhem, 32
Ashdown, Paddy, 8, 143
Aswan dam, 25
Australia, 187, 198
'axis of evil', 170, 220

Baghdad
  Ambassadors, 132
  ISIL, 219
  Jeremy Greenstock, 185
  John Christie, 111
  Kuwait, 92–4
  MNC-I, 186
  ORHA, 183
  PR, 148
  Second World War, 61
  SIGINT, 102
  SIS station, 101
  war loans, 130
Baghdad Pact 1955, 61, 68, 85–6, 90
  Liaison Committee, 85–6
  riots against, 62
Baghdad Radio, 60, 70
Baha Mousa inquiry, 197
Bahrain
  Coldstream Guards, 92
  communications, 111
  JIC, 150
  John Christie, 100

Kuwait, 124
Middle East Command, 105–6
overflying rights, 146
PR, 108
reconnaissance, 122
relations with Britain, 85
William Luce, 114
Baker, James, 140
'Baldrick lines', 134
Balkans, 180, 191, 192
barriers to learning, 57, 124
Barrons, Major General Richard, 184
Basra, 2, 90–1, 93, 100–2, 111, 183, 186–8, 192
'battle cakes', 148–9
Battle Damage Assessments (BDA), 155, 163
behaviourist psychologists, 14
Beirut, 62, 69
Bellringer, 98, 100
Ben-Gurion, David, 33, 71–2
Berlin crisis, 93
Bermuda Conference 1957, 63
Bernière, Jacques, 142
Bin Laden, Osama, 169–70
Black Watch, 183
Blair, Tony, 1–3, 9, 169, 172–8, 187, 199, 204
Blair–Bush relationship, 175, 176
Board of Inquiry, 189, 197, 198
Bomber Command, 39
Boorman, Lieutenant-General Derek, 132
'the Borrowers', 189
Bosnia, 151, 178, 191
Bosnia-Herzegovina, 189
Bowden, Colonel J. W., 100, 101
Bravo Two Zero, 152
Bremer, Paul, 185
British Army, 224–5
British Army Review, 12
British Army Review's 'Learning in Conflict' special editions, 224
British Consulate, in Basra, 101
British Defence Coordination Committee, 55
British Defence Coordination Committee (Middle East), 68–9
British Defence Intelligence Liaison Staff, 156
British East India Company, 91
British economy, 75–6, 179

Index

British Embassy
  in Amman, 62, 66, 68, 70, 85
  in Baghdad, 64, 101
  in Iraq, 60–1
  in Jordan, 65
  in Kuwait, 132
  in Riyadh, 145, 147
  in Saudi Arabia, 135–6
British Fire Group, 138–9
British Intelligence Corps liaison, 157
British Mesopotamia campaign, 61
British Muslim community, 141
'British Obligations Overseas', 56
British Office in Baghdad, 183
British Petroleum, 100
British Special Forces, 131, 134, 152
British–Kuwait defence agreement, 135
Brook, Norman, 5, 33, 44, 116, 121
Brown, George, 44
Brown, Gordon, 179, 202–3
Brown, Lieutenant General Chris, 184
Buraimi dispute, 27
Burma independence, 27
Burt, Alistair, 220
Bush, George H. W., 140, 165, 170
Bush, George W., 2, 169, 170, 172–6, 187
Butler, Lord, 164–5, 181, 201
Butler, Rohan, 11, 46, 48–9
Butler Implementation Group, 201, 208, 210–11
Butler inquiry, 166, 182, 201–2, 203, 210
Butler report, 201–2, 211, 225

Cabinet Committee, 68
Cabinet Defence Committee, 60–1, 78
Cabinet Office
  bypassed by Prime Minister, 173
  Chilcot inquiry, 203, 226
  CID, 5
  Current Intelligence Group, 181
  DIS, 150
  Foreign Affairs Committee, 199
  Harold Macmillan, 97–8, 123–4
  Historical Section, 11
  IMINT, 103
  Iraq Inquiry 2009, 2
  JIC, 55
  Jordan, 64–8, 76
  Kuwait, 115, 121, 135

Legislation Committee, 44
  lessons, 56
  Official Committee on Defence and Overseas Policy, 116
  Official Committee on the Middle East, 81
  official histories, 11
  'Review of protective security', 165
  Saddam Hussein, 170
Caccia, Harold, 36, 96, 97
Cairo, 33
Cairo International Airport, 39
Cairo Radio, 27, 70, 85
Cairo West, 39
Cameron, David, 3, 204, 220–1, 222
Campbell, Alistair, 199
Canada, 34, 37, 97, 198
CENTCOM (Central Command), 142, 155, 177
  Air Force, 140
Central Intelligence Agency (CIA), 13, 43, 58, 112, 155, 156, 176
Central Office of Information, 75, 159
Central Treaty Organisation (CENTO), 86
Centre for Historical Analysis and Conflict Research (CHACR), 224–5
Challenge Team, 202
Chamoun, Camille, 61–2
Chaplain, Colonel, 68
Chaplin, Edward, 171–2
chemical and biological weapons, 146, 153–4, 165–7, 197, 200, 222
Cheney, Dick, 176
Chiefs of Staff
  Anglo-American relations, 36, 63–8
  Charles Keightley, 38, 42–3, 51–3, 56–7
  GHQ MELF, 83
  Iraq, 179
  Jordan, 77–9, 87
  Kuwait, 116, 120–1
  lessons, 126
  Middle East Command, 105
  Operation Sodabread, 118
  Port Said, 32
  Suez Canal, 29
Chilcot, Sir John, 2, 186, 203–4, 205
Chilcot inquiry, 202–5

281

Chilcot report, 202–5, 208, 226
Christie, John, 100
'Christmas massacre', 165
Churchill, Sir Winston, 8, 218
CIA *see* Central Intelligence Agency
CID *see* Committee of the Imperial Defence
Civil Secretariat, 151
civil service, 4–5, 6
Civil Service College, 7–8
classification, 187, 198, 207
Coalition Provisional Authority (CPA), 171, 178–9, 183, 185, 197
Coghill, Colonel Sir Patrick, 69
cognitive psychologists, 13–14
Cold War, 25, 58, 129, 132, 134, 160, 163
Coldstream Guards, 92
Combined Staff College, 51–2
Commando Brigade, 40
Committee of Public Accounts, 167, 210
Committee of the Imperial Defence (CID), 5
communications, 191, 193–4
   difficulties, 39, 111, 155–6, 187
communist threat, 132
Congo, 115
Congress, 170
connectivism, 14–15
Conservative government, 65
Conservative Party, 204
Constitutional Reform and Governance Act 2010, 5
constructivism, 14–15
Convention of Constantinople 1888, 24
Cook, Robin, 174
Coombe-Tenant, Henry, 101
Cooper, Chester, 58
Cooper, Sir Frank, 41
Corbyn, Jeremy, 204
cost management, 150–1
Council of Representatives, 221–2
Counterinsurgency Warfare, 193
counterterrorism, 165
Cox, Sir Percy, 61
CPA *see* Coalition Provisional Authority
Cradock, Percy, 133, 136, 150, 168
Crisis Cell, 136
Croskery, Donald, 144

Crossman, Richard, 44
Current Intelligence Group, 181, 202
Cyprus, 27
   airbase, 31, 39, 77, 80, 99
   GCHQ, 155
   Jordan, 79
   Near East Command, 105
   overflying rights, 103
   SIGINT, 102
Czech arms deal, 28
Czechoslovakia, 137
   Russian invasion of 1968, 13

Daesh, 3, 220, 222
DCDC *see* Development Concepts and Doctrine Centre
de Gaulle, General, 74
de la Billière, General Peter, 139–40, 141, 145, 148–9, 155, 160, 193
Dean, Patrick, 32–3, 51, 55, 96, 107, 182
de-Ba'athification, 185, 219
The Decision to go to War in Iraq, 195
Defence and Overseas Policy Committee (DOP), 173
Defence Attachés, 133
Defence Committee
   JSTARS, 154
   lesson distribution, 206
   lesson identification, 167
   lesson implementation, 210
   lesson management structures, 211
   lessons, 164
   logistics, 152
   Operation Vantage, 103–4, 107–8
   PR, 190
Defence Council, 117
Defence Intelligence, 199
Defence Intelligence Agency (DIA), 156
Defence Intelligence Centre, 136
Defence Intelligence Staff (DIS), 106
   Butler report, 187
   Crisis Cell, 136
   GCHQ, 193
   IC, 10
   Iraq War 2003–9, 181
   Iraq's Republican Guard, 133
   lesson identification, 145, 154–7, 208
   lesson implementation, 150
   Operation Granby, 164

Index

Defence Lessons Identified Management System (DLIMS), 191–2, 198, 210
Defence Lessons Library, 192, 206–7, 217
Defence Medical Services reports, 198
Defence Ministry (Iraq), 60
Defence School of Languages, 193
Defence Signals Staff, 106
Defence Stores and Distribution depot, 189
Defence Strategic Guidance 2005, 192
Defence White Paper 1957, 52–3, 57, 77, 98
Defence White Paper 1962, 98, 106, 119
Defence White Paper 2003, 192
Defence Wide Lessons Board (DwLB), 197, 206, 225
Defence-wide Lessons Management (DwLM) system, 191–2
Department for International Development (DfID), 173, 183, 184
Desert Rats, 180
Development, Concepts and Doctrine Centre (DCDC), 198, 224
Development Fund for Iraq, 185
DfID *see* Department for International Development
Dhahran, 147
DIA *see* Defence Intelligence Agency
Directorate of Operational Capability (DOC), 191–2
    lessons report, 193, 197
DIS *see* Defence Intelligence Service
distribution *see* lesson distribution
Dixon, Pierson, 36–7
DLIMS *see* Defence Lessons Identified Management System
DOC *see* Directorate of Operational Capability
'the dodgy dossier', 199
Douglas-Home, Lord Alec, 44–5, 112
Dulles, Allen, 70
Dulles, John Foster, 66, 70, 71, 72, 74, 97
dust storms, 110–11
Dutton, General, 191
DwLB *see* Defence Wide Lessons Board
DwLM *see* Defence-wide Lessons Management system

Eastern and Arabian Department, 93
Eastern Europe, 134
Economic Relations Department, 29
Eden, Anthony
    analogy, 8–9
    and Eisenhower, 43
    memoirs, 45
    public and parliamentary support, 173–5
    Suez 1956, 25–8, 33–6, 47–9, 52–3, 55–8, 66–7
    Thatcher similar to, 137
    vindication, 218
    visited by French, 32
Edmonds, Brigadier General Sir James, 12
EEC *see* European Economic Community
Egypt
    Arab alliance, 139
    arms sales, 107, 152
    British troops in, 21
    Humphrey Trevelyan, 90
    JIC, 150
    Jordan, 68–9
    Nasser, 95, 138
    overflying rights, 146
    Saddam Hussein, 130
    UAR, 61
Egypt Committee, 28, 59
Egyptian Air Force, 37–8, 57
Eisenhower, President Dwight D., 28, 36, 43, 62, 63, 65–6, 72–3, 76
11th Hussars, 99, 109
Elizabeth, Queen (British), 79
Elworthy, Air Marshal Charles, 99, 105–6, 108–9, 111, 113, 117, 149
empiricist tradition, 13, 14
EOKA, 30
Episkopi, 42
equipment deficiencies, 40, 151–2, 162–3, 180–1, 188–9
Etherington, Mark, 179, 196
European Community (EC), 141–2
European Convention on Human Rights, 197
European Economic Community (EEC), 95
European Union (EU), 142, 172
    withdrawal referendum, 204
Evening Standard, 29
Exchange of Letters 1961, 92, 94
Exercise Internal Look, Qatar 2002, 180

283

Exercise Saif Sareea II, Oman 2001, 180, 189
external inquiry, 43–4, 54
extremism, 219

Fahd, King, of Saudi Arabia, 130, 138
Faisal II, King, 60
Falklands campaign
  analogy, 9
  'appeasement', 205
  command structure, 150
  compared to Gulf War, 131, 143
  FCO, 149
  Franks Inquiry, 202
  HUMINT, 145
  lesson identification, 164–5, 215
  lesson implementation, 137, 154, 162
  Operation Corporate, 133–4
  PR, 148
Fallujah, 219
Farouk, King, 25
FCO *see* Foreign and Commonwealth Office
Fergusson, Brigadier Bernard, 42
Fforter, Alexis, 69
1 Armoured Division, Kuwait 2002, 180, 189, 190
1st (BR) Armoured Division, 131
First World War, 4, 12, 91
Force Headquarters, 41
Foreign Affairs Committee, 167, 172, 196, 198–201, 206, 208–10, 216
Foreign Affairs Steering Committee, 48–9
Foreign and Commonwealth Office (FCO), 10–12, 16–17, 218
  Alistair Burt, 220
  annual reports, 183, 194, 195, 224
  Anthony Parsons, 218
  Arabian Department, 96–7, 115
  Charles Keightley, 51
  cooperation with MoD, 149
  and DfID, 183–5
  documents destroyed, 58
  Eastern Department, 82
  economics, 151
  Emergency Unit, 132, 135
  external inquiry, 44–9
  Gulf War, 138, 141–2
  Iraq Inquiry 2009, 198–9

Iraq War 2003–9, 171–6, 194–6
Jordan, 63–5, 67–8, 70–6
Kuwait, 92–6, 98–9, 101–2, 119–20
learning from history, 6, 209–15, 228
lesson identification, 53–6, 112–16
lesson implementation, 146–7
library, 217
news executive, 75
Non-Proliferation Department, 181
official histories, 158–9
Operation Fortitude, 80–2, 86–9
Operation Granby, 135–6, 165–7
Operation Musketeer, 35–7
Operation Telic, 205–6
Operation Vantage, 122–6
overflying rights, 104–8
Policy Planning Staff, 138, 139, 142
Research Department, 127
Saddam Hussein, 130–3, 144
Sèvres protocol, 29
Steering Committee, 5
Suez Canal, 26
Turkey, 188
UN, 178
UN Department, 107
Western Department, 103
William Hague, 223–4
Forward Air Controllers, 30
14th Signals Regiment, 193
4th Psyops Group, 157
40 Commando Royal Marines, 170–1
42 Commando Royal Marines, 119–20, 170–1
45 Commando Royal Marines, 99
France
  Iraq War 2003–9, 170, 195
  Jordan 1958, 74
  Kuwait, 142
  Omega, 34
  Saddam Hussein, 175
  Sèvres protocol, 26
  Suez 1956, 53
  Suez Canal Company, 24
Franks, Lord, 166
Franks Inquiry, 202, 210
Free Officers Movement, 25, 33, 60
Freedman, Sir Lawrence, 203
Freedom of Information Act 2000, 5, 227
French Airborne Forces, 41

Index

Gaddafi, Colonel Muammar, 221
Gaitskell, Hugh, 28, 66
Gallup poll, 74–5
Galtieri, General Leopoldo, 9, 164
Galula, David, 192–3
Gamil Airfield, 50
GCC *see* Gulf Cooperation Council
GCHQ *see* General Communications Headquarters
General Headquarters Middle East Land Forces (GHQ MELF), 41, 83
General Intelligence Department Jordan, 86
General National Congress (GNC), 221–2
generational learning, 16–18, 18f, 207, 212–13
George, Bruce, 162
Germany, 91, 152, 163, 178, 180
GHQ MELF *see* General Headquarters Middle East Land Forces
Gilligan, Andrew, 182
Glubb, General John Bagot, 25, 27, 62, 69
GNC *see* General National Congress
Gore-Booth, David, 139
Gore-Booth, Paul, 45, 46–7, 58–9
Government Communications Headquarters (GCHQ), 10
  DIS, 193
  Gulf War, 165
  learning from history, 13, 199
  reconnaissance, 122
  SIGINT, 121, 155, 176
  Suez 1956, 33–4
Government of National Accord, 221–2
Gowing, Margaret, 4, 7–8
Greenstock, Sir Jeremy, 172, 176, 185, 195
Gulf Cooperation Council (GCC), 158–9
Gulf War 1990–1, 22, 129–68
  'appeasement', 205
  counter-proliferation, 181
  Dick Cheney, 176
  generational learning, 206
  George H. Bush, 170, 173
  lesson identification, 215
  Operation Granby, 180
  syndrome, 154
  troops, 92

Haddon-Cave, Charles, 213
Hague, William, 8, 223–4
Hainworth, Henry, 54
Hamilton, Bill, 226–7
Hammarskjöld, Dag, 37, 73
Hammond, Philip, 204, 225–6
Hancock, William Keith, 4
Handyside, Holsey G., 112
Hare, Raymond, 104
Hart, Basil Liddell, 213, 228
Hartley, L. P., 228
Hashemite monarchy, 1
Hawley, Donald, 29
Head, Antony, 53
Headquarters British Forces Middle East (HQBFME), 134, 149–50, 156
Headquarters Middle East Land Forces, 29
Heads of Middle Eastern Mission Conference 1958, 70
Healey, Denis, 143
Heath, Edward, 144
Hegel, George Wilhelm Friedrich, 209
Heikal, Mohamed, 95
Helmand Province, Afghanistan, 21, 186
Hiller, George, 103
Hine, Air Chief Marshal Sir Patrick, 134, 140–1, 149, 156, 160
Hitler, Adolph
  learning from history, 8
  Nasser compared to, 28
  Saddam Hussein compared to, 137, 165, 173
HMS *Bulwark*, 92, 103, 109, 119
HMS *Striker*, 92, 120
HMS *Victorous*, 120
Holland, 119
Hood, Lord, 76
Horner, General, 140
Horsford, Brigadier, 108
hostages, 135, 144, 152
House of Commons
  Committee on Public Accounts, 151
  David Cameron, 220–1
  Defence Committee, 134, 135, 148, 160–3, 177, 189, 197
  Foreign Affairs Committee, 158, 194–5, 222
  Gulf War, 137, 143–4
  Harold Macmillan, 66

285

House of Commons (*cont.*)
   Iraq War 2003–9, 174
   Public Administration and
      Constitutional Affairs Committee
      (PACAC), 185, 205
   Public Administration Committee, 203
   Public Administration Select
      Committee, 184–5
   Select Committees, 211, 216
Howard, Lieutenant Colonel Bill, 30, 38
Howard, Sir Michael, 12
HQBFME *see* Headquarters British Forces
   Middle East
Hull, Sir Richard, 31, 41, 50–1
HUMINT (human intelligence)
   Charles Keightley, 42–3
   Gulf War 1990–1, 145, 154
   Iraq War 2003–9, 182, 193, 201, 207
   Kuwait, 102, 122
Humphreys, John, 188
139 Squadron, 39
Hurd, Douglas, 132, 137, 138, 140,
   143, 151
Hussein, King
   British assistance, 31, 65, 79
   Charles Johnston, 72, 75
   John Bagot Glubb, 25, 62–63
   Jordan–Kuwait–Iraq federation,
      94–5
   Nasser, 70
   Patrick Coghill, 69
   Saddam Hussein, 130
Hutton, Lord, 200

IAEA *see* International Atomic Energy
   Agency inspection
IC (intelligence community) *see* intelligence
   community (IC)
identification *see* lesson identification
IMF *see* International Monetary Fund
IMINT (image intelligence), 41–2, 102–3,
   122, 154–5, 177
imperialism, 60, 165
'imperialists', 95
implementation *see* lesson implementation
'in it together', 73
India, 136
   independence, 27
India–Pakistan war, 183

individual learning, 16–18, 18f, 123,
   211–12
information operations (Info Ops), 191
institutional learning, 16–18, 18f, 123,
   213–14
intelligence agencies, 10, 155–7
Intelligence and Security Committee, 165,
   199–200, 201, 202, 208, 210–11
Intelligence Branch, 41
intelligence community (IC), 10, 12–13,
   16–17
   Butler report, 225–6
   Cold War, 132–3
   communications, 187
   coordination difficulties, 41, 150
   Gulf War 1990–1, 144–6
   Iraq Inquiry 2009, 198–201
   Iraq War 2003–9, 172, 181–2
   Jordan 1958, 68–70
   Kuwait, 99–103, 121–2, 126–7
   language, 193
   learning from history, 57–8, 80, 84,
      88–9, 214–15, 228
   lesson identification, 207–11
   lesson implementation, 111–13
   MoD liaison, 113
   Operation Corporate, 136
   Operation Granby, 164–8
   psyops, 157
   Saddam Hussein, 130, 153–5
   Suez 1956, 32–5, 53–5
   UK–US liaison, 43, 64, 97, 176–7
Intelligence Corps training centre, 157
Intelligence Services Act 1994, 13, 165
International Atomic Energy Agency
   (IAEA) inspection, 146
International Monetary Fund (IMF), 47
interpretation *see* lesson interpretation
Iran, 27, 34–5, 103, 131–2, 159, 170,
   175, 220
Iranian Revolution 1979, 218
Iran–Iraq War 1980, 129, 134, 144,
   145, 146, 165, 166
Iraq
   1919, 1
   1920s–1930s, 172
   1941–7, 1
   1991, 1
   annexation of Kuwait, 90, 92

Index

anti-war protests, 173–4
attack, 120
Cabinet Office, 65
Chiefs of Staff, 68
economy, 129–30
JIC report, 121–2
and Jordan, 94
learning from history, 215
MoD, 210
nationalism, 68
non-aggression pact 1989 – with Saudi Arabia, 158
oil export revenue, 91, 129–30
press, 153
terrorism, 220
UK–US liaison, 73
William Luce, 114
Iraq Communications Group, 199
'Iraq: cultural appreciation booklet', 193
Iraq Fatalities Investigation, 197
Iraq Historical Allegations Team, 197
Iraq Inquiry 2009, 2, 202–5
   coordination difficulties, 184–6
   FCO, 216
   FOI, 227
   Jeremy Greenstock, 195
   learning from history, 208
   lesson identification, 173
   Mark Etherington, 196
   media, 199
   NSC, 225
   UK–US liaison, 175–9
Iraq Planning Unit, 179, 183
Iraq revolution 1958, 1
Iraq Survey Group, 201
Iraq War 2003–9, 1–3, 9, 22–3, 169–208, 212
Iraqi Air Force, 145, 163–4
Iraqi Army, 100, 145, 163–4
Iraqi Central Bank, 185
Iraqi Navy, 145
Iraqi revolution 1958, 35, 60–1, 69, 70, 85–6, 90, 99
Iraqi Security Forces, 185
Iraq's Republican Guard, 133
Islamic State in Iraq and the Levant (ISIL), 219
Islamic State in Iraq (ISI), 219

Islamic State (known as IS ISIS or Daesh), 219
Islamist fundamentalist sentiment, 159
Israel
   establishment of, 21
   and Jordan, 79
   learning from history, 3
   Omega, 34
   Operation Cordage, 31–2
   overflying rights, 71–2, 77, 87, 104
   Sèvres protocol, 26
   Syrian and Egyptian attacks on 1973, 13
Italian Air Ministry, 105
Italy, 104–5, 142

Jackson, General Mike, 186
Japan, 178
Jeddah talks 1990, 130
JFHQ *see* Joint Forces Headquarters, Riyadh
JHQ *see* Joint Headquarters
JIC *see* Joint Intelligence Committee
Johnson, David, 171, 179, 190
Johnston, Charles, 71–2, 75–6, 79–81, 87, 93
Joint Administrative Headquarters, Bahrain, 106
Joint Forces Headquarters (JFHQ), Riyadh, 140
Joint Forces Logistics Command, 224
Headquarters, 180
Joint Headquarters (JHQ), 149–50, 153, 156
Joint Intelligence Committee (JIC), 10
   9/11, 170
   assessments, 102–3, 201, 222
   Butler inquiry, 182
   Butler report, 202
   Cabinet Office, 55, 68
   Charles Elworthy, 99–100
   Chester Cooper, 58
   Cold War, 132
   coordination difficulties, 225–6
   'the dodgy dossier', 199
   Gulf War, 133
   history, 12
   Iraq War 2003–9, 172
   Kuwait, 120–1

287

Joint Intelligence Committee (cont.)
  learning from history, 80
  lesson identification, 88, 200
  lesson implementation, 51, 136–7
  Middle East (JIC(ME)), 54, 55, 58, 68–9, 84, 113, 127
  Operation Musketeer, 53–4
  Patrick Dean, 96, 107
  Percy Cradock, 150
  Suez 1956, 32–4, 38
  terrorism, 220
  UK–US liaison, 85, 156
  WMD, 146, 181
Joint Intelligence Liaison Committee, 64
Joint Intelligence Organisation, 10
'joint intention', 66
Joint Operations, 189–90
  Instructions, 78
Joint Planning Staff, 51, 77–8, 99, 106, 116
  Instructions, 78
Joint Service
  History, 84
  In-House Historian, 118
  Staff, 106
Joint Service In-House Histories, Working Party on, 52, 83–4
Joint Surveillance and Target Attack Radar Systems (JSTARS), 154
Joint Task Force Commanders, 31, 37–8
Joint Warfare Staff, 106
Jordan
  Arab alliance, 139
  British assistance, 31–2
  British mandate, 21
  Government, 108
  intervention 1977, 83
  lesson identification, 138
  Operation Musketeer, 47
  Saddam Hussein, 130
  Steering Brief, 159
  UK–US liaison, 49
Jordan 1958, 60–89
  IC, 111
  John Bagot Glubb, 27
  learning from history, 215
  lesson identification, 94, 123–7
  lesson implementation, 22, 53
  MoD, 98
  overflying rights, 104
  UN, 96, 107
Jordanian Arab Army, 68
Jordanian Army, 76, 79
Jordanian Development Board, Amman, 78
Jordan–Kuwait–Iraq federation, 95
Jordan's Royal Army, 25
JSTARS *see* Joint Surveillance and Target Attack Radar Systems

Kabul, 224
Kant, Immanuel, 14
Kay, Dr David, 200–1
Keightley, Charles
  lesson identification, 38, 53
  lesson implementation, 42–3
  Musketeer Revise, 31
  PR, 40
  report, 51, 55–7, 113
  UK–US liaison, 36
Kelly, Dr David, 200
Kennedy, John F., 93, 112
Kenya, 42, 92
Khalil, Squadron Leader Isameddine Mahmoud, 35, 54
King, Tom, 132, 148, 149, 160–1
Kinnock, Neil, 143
Kipling, Rudyard, 24
Kirkpatrick, Sir Ivone, 29, 56
Kissinger, Henry, 212
Korea, 76, 165, 166
  analogy, 137–8
Kosovo, 9, 163, 178
  analogy, 172–3
'Kosovo model', 178
Kuwait
  ammunition, 152
  Anthony Acland, 35–6
  force size, 77, 79
  invasion of, 1990, 9
  lesson implementation, 210
  Margaret Thatcher, 141
  media, 111–12
  MoD, 134
  overflying rights, 188
  relations with Britain, 85
  Saddam Hussein, 132, 168
  UK–US liaison, 65
  war loans, 129–31

Index

Kuwait 1961, 22, 51, 90–128
Kuwait New Airport, 111
Kuwaiti Army, 92, 133, 135
Kuwaiti Health Service, 109
Kuwaiti Oil Company, 111
Kuwait's Concessionary Agreement, 91–2

Lamont, Norman, 150–1
Land Warfare Centre, 197
language, 193
Lawrence, T. E., 192
leaflet scattering, 42, 157
League of Nations, 1
learning, spheres of, 18f
learning from history, 1–23, 218–26
learning process, 13–15, 18–21, 19f
Lebanon, 61–5, 68–70, 72–4, 78, 85–6, 96, 107
   civil war 1958, 35
Lee, Air Chief Marshal Sir David, 119
lesson distribution, 18–21, 19f, 163, 187, 198, 206–10, 216–18
lesson identification, 18–21, 19f, 20f, 209–10, 212–16, 228
   Chilcot report, 205–7
   communications, 187, 189
   Iraq War 2003–9, 200–1
   Kuwait, 126–7
   Margaret Thatcher, 166–8
   media management, 191–3
   Operation Granby, 163
   Richard Barrons, 184
   UK–US liaison, 177–8
   War on Terror, 195–8
lesson implementation, 18–21, 19f, 209–11, 215–18
   Butler report, 201–2
   communications, 189–91
   Defence Committee, 167
   DwLM, 197–8
   Iraq War 2003—9, 206–7
   Kuwait, 126
lesson interpretation, 19–21, 20f
lesson retention, 18–21, 19f, 209, 210, 212, 216
   Jordan 1958, 88–9
   MoD, 206–7
   Operation Musketeer, 50
   School of Land and Air Warfare, 125

'Lessons from Musketeer', 31
'Lessons from Operation Musketeer', 50–1, 57
Libya crisis 2011, 3, 194, 220, 221–2, 226
linguists, 42–3
Lloyd, Selwyn, 29, 45, 47, 63, 66, 76, 86, 97
Lloyd George, David, 8
local culture and religion respected, 139, 146–7, 193
Lockerbie, 169
Lockhart, Bruce, 69
Logan, Donald, 29
Lucas, Ivor, 29, 82, 88
Luce, Sir William, 94, 105–8, 113–16, 119, 124

Macedonia, 189
Macmillan, Harold
   analogy, 8–9, 89
   Anthony Nutting, 45–6
   Charles Keightley, 51–2
   Defence White Paper 1962, 119
   Jordan 1958, 60–7, 71–6
   Kuwait, 106–8
   learning from history, 43, 57
   lesson identification, 123–4
   Norman Brook, 116
   Operation Fortitude, 86
   Philip de Zulueta, 82, 122
   Qasim, 94
   Suez 1956, 54, 143
   Tony Blair, 173
   UK–US liaison, 96–8
Major, John, 143, 150–1, 160, 165–6
Malaya, 27
Malik, Charles Habib, 63
Malta, 39
Malta (Septex I), 30
Marines, 180
Mau Mau, 42
McNamara, Robert, 119
MECAS *see* Middle East Centre for Arab Studies
media management, 75, 87–8, 94, 108–10, 111–12, 147–9, 190
MELF *see* Middle East Land Forces, 117
Memorandum of Understanding, 185
memory, 14

289

Meyer, Christopher, 177–8, 194, 195
MI5, 10, 13, 33, 165
  history, 12
MI6, 10, 32–5, 54–5, 69, 84, 165, 181
  history, 12
  see also SIS
Middle East Centre for Arab Studies (MECAS), 35
Middle East Command, Aden, 105
Middle East Current Intelligence Group, 133, 136–7, 156
Middle East Department, 29
Middle East Land Forces (MELF), 117
Midge drones, 154
Miliband, David, 184, 217
military targets, 148
Millar, Sir Frederick Hoyer, 76
Millard, Guy, 27, 36, 47
Milosevic, Slobodan, 9
Ministry of Aviation Supply, 10
Ministry of Defence (MoD), 10–12, 13, 16–17
  bypassed by Prime Minister, 173
  Defence White Paper 1962, 106–8
  Departmental Record System, 83
  Gulf War 1990–1, 146–54, 159–64
  imperialism, 67–8
  Iraq War 2003–9, 177–81, 184–8
  Jordan 1958, 82
  Kuwait, 100–1, 105, 116–21, 125–6, 134–5
  League of Nations, 228
  learning from history, 56, 209–20, 224–5
  lesson identification, 41, 196–8
  lesson implementation, 43, 87–9
  local culture and religion respected, 139–40
  media management, 75–9
  Operation Corporate, 166–7
  Operation Musketeer, 31–2, 49–52
  Operation Telic, 205–7
  Operation Vantage, 98
  PR, 190–4
  propaganda, 39
  Staff Colleges, 217
  Suez 1956, 29
  UK–US liaison, 36–7, 64, 156
  US CENTCOM, 142
  WMD, 200

Ministry of Transport, 41
MoD see Ministry of Defence
Mosaddeq, Mohammad, 27, 34–5
Mosul, 219
Mountbatten, Lord, 59
Mubarak, Sheik, Abdullah, 91, 117, 130
Multinational Corps Iraq (MNC-I), 186
Multinational Division South East (MNDSE), 185–6
Multi-National Force-Iraq (MNF-I), 192
Munich, 49
Munich Agreement, 28
'Munich' analogy, 8–9
Munro, Alan, 132, 138, 147, 159
Musketeer Revise, 30–1, 32
Musketeer Winter Plan, 31
Mussolini, Benito, Nasser compared to, 28, 89
Mutla Ridge, 100–1

Nafisa, Queen, 60
Naguib, Muhammad, 25
Napoleon, 8
Nasser, Gamal Abdel
  analogy, 8–9
  Arab nationalism, 69–70, 84–5, 138
  external inquiry, 44
  Free Officers Movement, 60–2
  Jordan 1958, 80–1
  Kuwait, 94–5
  Operation Musketeer, 47
  planned assassination of, 35
  Suez 1956, 25–35, 53–6
  UN, 37
National Audit Office, 151, 161, 167, 189, 197, 206–7, 210
National Health Service (NHS), 198
National Security Agency memo, 176
National Security Council (NSC), 225–6, 228
National Transitional Council, 221
Nationalist Socialist Party, Jordan, 62
NATO see North Atlantic Treaty Organisation
Naval Historical Branch, 118
The Naval Review, 12
Near East Command, Cyprus, 105
negative lessons, 123–4
Nicoll, Doug, 34

Index

Nicosia, Cyprus, 71
Niger, 176
9/11, 9, 169, 170, 178, 183
Nizwa, Oman, 27
North Atlantic Treaty Organization (NATO)
 Allied Rapid Reaction Corps, 180
 ammunition, 152
 Article V, 104
 intelligence summary, 157
 lesson distribution, 198
 lesson identification, 163
 Operation Granby, 134
 reports, 195
 UK–US liaison, 140–2, 189
North Korea, 170, 220
Northern Iraq, 178
Northern Ireland, 178, 180, 184, 192
NSC *see* National Security Council
Nuremberg war crime trials, 32
Nutting, Anthony, 24, 35, 44, 45–6, 58, 66

Obama, Barack, 222
O'Donnell, Gus, 201
Office for Reconstruction and Humanitarian Assistance (ORHA), 183
official histories, 5–7, 12–13, 44–7, 210, 226–7
 Gulf War 1990–1, 159
 Iraq War 2003–9, 203–4
 Jordan 1958, 83–4
 Kuwait, 113
 Suez 1956, 58
Official History of the Second World War, 5
Official History programme, 226–7
oil, 159
Oman, 77, 150
Oman war 1957, 35, 42
Omand, Sir David, 201
Omega, 34, 35
OPEC *see* Organization of the Petroleum Exporting Countries
Operation Besemer, 189
Operation Boot, 34–5
Operation Broil, 64
Operation Cordage, 31–2

Operation Corporate, 133, 136, 149, 162, 166
Operation Desert Fox, 173
Operation Eagle Claw, 152
Operation Ellamy, 221
Operation Entirety, 197
Operation Fortitude, 63–89, 96–8, 103–4, 125–6, 178
Operation Granby, 129–68
 force size, 171
 language, 193–4
 lesson distribution, 198, 210
 lesson identification, 177–8
 and Telic, 180–2, 205, 207
 UK–US liaison, 186–90
Operation Iraqi Freedom, 170–1
Operation Jester, 69
Operation Livid, 118, 125
Operation Lodestar, 189
Operation Market Garden, 32
Operation Musketeer, 26–9
 Charles Keightley, 113
 force size, 77
 and Fortitude, 89
 HUMINT, 102–3
 and Jordan, 86
 lesson implementation, 98
 Margaret Thatcher, 166
 media management, 74
 MoD, 178
 overflying rights, 71
Operation Resinate, 180
Operation Resolute, 189
Operation Sodabread, 118
Operation Straggle, 34, 43
Operation Telic, 170–208, 219, 222–3
Operation Torch, 161
Operation Vantage, 90–128
 command structure, 149
 Defence Attachés, 133
 equipment, 135, 161
 and Granby, 129
 lesson identification, 138, 156, 165–6
 and Telic, 205, 207
 UN, 178
operational command, 189–90
operational lessons, 123–4, 191
Operational Training and Advisory Group (OPTAG), 192

291

'Options for change' defence review, 134, 167
Organization of the Petroleum Exporting Countries (OPEC), 129–30, 141–2
ORHA *see* Office for Reconstruction and Humanitarian Assistance
Oswald, Admiral Julian, 149–50
Ottoman Empire, 21, 91
overflying rights, 103–5, 146, 188
Overseas Defence (Gulf) Cabinet, subcommittee, 136
Overseas Development Secretariat, 183

PACAC *see* Public Administration and Constitutional Affairs Committee, House of Commons
Pakistan, 95, 136
Palestine, 3, 27, 35
  partition of 1947, 21
Palestine Liberation Organization (PLO), 159
Parachute Brigade, 40
Parry-Evans, David, 139, 141, 150, 157, 162
Parsons, Sir Anthony, 62, 85, 218
Parton, Group Captain Neville, 161
Paulson, Paul, 69
Pearson, Brigadier Tom, 67–8, 71, 83
Permanent Joint Headquarters (PJHQ), 164, 187, 190, 191
Persia, 119
Persian Gulf, 77, 78, 90–1, 105, 114
Persian Oil Crisis 1951, 91
Petraeus, David, 192–3
photographic interpreters (PI), 154–5
Pilling, Sir Joseph, 226
Pink, Ivor, 37
PJHQ *see* Permanent Joint Headquarters
Plowden, Lord, 5–6
Plowden report, 82
Policy Planning Staff, 166
Port Said, 26, 29, 31, 32, 37–9, 47, 54
positive lessons, 124
Potsdam Conference July 1945, 11
Powell, Charles, 144–5
Powell, Colin, 176, 178
Powell, Jonathan, 169, 175
Powell, Sir Richard, 51
Powell–Straw relationship, 176

PR *see* public relations
Prime Minister's Office, 10, 17
  CPA, 179
  FCO, 173
  HUMINT, 182
  Intelligence and Security Committee, 199
  learning from history, 56, 57, 205, 228
  UK–US liaison, 176
Profumo, John, 110, 117–18
project Alpha, 27
propaganda, 7, 34, 39, 61, 101, 138, 147–8
  anti-Western, 130
Psychological Warfare Unit, 117
psyops (psychological operations), 42, 51, 157, 194
Public Administration and Constitutional Affairs Committee (PACAC), House of Commons, 185, 205
public opinion, 74–5, 148–9, 164, 173–4
Public Records Act (1958, 1966, 2000), 5, 83
public relations (PR), 40, 51, 75, 108–10, 148, 190–1, 195
Putin, Vladimir, 175

Qasim, Brigadier Abd al-Karim, 60–1, 68, 90, 92–5, 99–102, 111, 120–2, 127
Qatar, 3, 22, 85, 150

Radford, Air Commodore, 49
radio, 101, 149, 157, 191
Radio Baghdad, 60, 70
Radio Cairo, 38
Radio Kuwait, 157
RAF (Royal Air Force)
  Amman, 71, 84
  communications, 111
  counterinsurgency training, 192
  equipment deficiencies, 116
  Gulf War 1990–1, 131
  Habbaniya, 70
  history programme, 52
  Joint Service Staff, 106
  Jordan 1958, 77
  learning from history, 213
  lesson identification, 160–1, 163
  lesson implementation, 154, 180
  media management, 147–8

Index

overflying rights, 39, 103, 146
PR, 108
UK–US liaison, 43
Ramadi, 219
Ramsden, James, 110, 125
rationalist epistemology, 13–14
Reith, Lieutenant General Sir John, 190
'Restoration Plot', 35, 54
retention *see* lesson retention
Rhineland, 28
Rhodesia, 79
Ricketts, Peter, 201
Rimington, Stella, 13
Riyadh, 142
Ross, Carne, 196
Rothnie, Alan, 113–14, 115, 119, 124
Royal Air Force *see* RAF
Royal Fleet Artillery, 171
Royal Marines Y Squadron, 193
Royal Military Academy Sandhurst, 12
Royal Military Police Red Caps, 189
Royal Navy
   counterinsurgency training, 192
   equipment deficiencies, 116
   force size, 131
   Gulf War 1990–1, 134, 137
   Iraq War 2003–9, 188
   Joint Service Staff, 106
   Kuwait, 109
   lesson implementation, 180
   Lord Mountbatten, 59
   media management, 148
   Operation Granby, 150
   UK–US liaison, 141
Royal Rhodesian Air Force, 92
Royal United Services Institute (RUSI) seminar, 191
Rumsfeld, Donald, 176
Rusk, Dean, 97, 112
Russia, 73–4, 96, 104, 172, 175

Saddam Hussein
   al-Qaeda, 202
   analogy, 9
   British–Saudi intelligence, 157
   compared to Hitler, 137
   FCO, 167–8
   Gulf War 1990–1, 129–33, 143–5, 147
   IC assessments, 153–4

Iraq Inquiry 2009, 179
Iraq War 2003–9, 170–6
lesson identification, 159
Popular Army, 163–5
UN, 141
WMD, 181–2, 200
Sandys, Duncan, 51, 53, 67, 77
SAS, 144, 152
Saud, King, 95, 104
Saudi Arabia
   Alan Munro, 132, 138
   ammunition, 152
   Donald Croskery, 144
   economics, 114
   Embassy in London, 147
   French troops, 142
   Kuwait, 95
   MoD, 134
   non-aggression pact with Iraq, 158
   Omega, 35
   Operation Granby, 135–6, 151, 157
   overflying rights, 104, 146–7
   Percy Cradock, 150
   Saddam Hussein, 130
   Saudi Group, 175
   war loans, 129
Saudi Group, 175
Scarlet, John, 182
Schlesinger, Arthur, 9
Schmidt, Dana, 112
School of Land and Air Warfare, 49–50, 57, 106, 117, 125–6
Schwarzkopf, General Norman, 140, 142, 145, 156
Scientific and Technical Intelligence Directorates, 136
2 (BR) Corps, 30
2 Corps, 53
Second World War, 7, 12, 32, 61, 63, 137, 161, 189
Secret Intelligence Service (SIS), 10, 13
   Alexis Fforter, 69
   Anthony Eden, 55
   'Christmas massacre', 165
   Information Research Department, 55
   Intelligence and Security Committee, 199
   Julian Amery, 85
   Kuwait, 100–1
   learning from history, 54

293

Secret Intelligence Service (SIS) (*cont.*)
   lesson implementation, 201
   Nasser, 35
   Operation Granby, 157
   Richard White, 58
   Saddam Hussein, 144
   Soviet Union, 28
   Suez 1956, 33
   UK–US liaison, 43, 176
   see also MI6
Security Service (SS, MI5) *see* MI5
'September dossier', 182, 198–9, 200, 208
7/7, 169
Sèvres protocol, 26, 29, 32, 32–3, 34, 59
'sexed up', 182, 200
Shinwell, Emanuel, 27, 106
Shröder, Gerhard, 175
Siemens, George, 14–15
Sierra Leone, 180, 192
SIGINT (signals intelligence), 102, 121, 155, 167–8, 176–7, 187, 193
SIS *see* Secret Intelligence Service
Six Day War 1958, 35
16 Independent Parachure Brigade, 29–30, 49, 63, 71, 83
6th Royal Tank Regiment, 30
Smith, Major General Rupert, 148, 154
Sanchez, General Rick, 186
Southern Command, 110
Soviet Union
   Crisis Cell, 136
   and Egypt, 25, 28, 34, 43, 53–4
   Jordan 1958, 80, 84
   Lebanon, 70
   Saddam Hussein, 144
   UAR, 61
Spain, 170
Stabilisation Unit, 194, 198, 206
Staff Colleges, 12
State of the Union Address 2002, 170
Stephenson, Air Vice Marshall John, 42
Stevens, Sir Roger, 93
Stewart, Michael, 46–7
Stockwell, General Hugh, 30, 38–9, 41, 42, 49–50
Strang, Lord, 48–9
Strategic Defence and Security Review 2010, 181, 201
Strategic Defence Review 2002, 192

strategic lessons, 209–20
Strategic Reserve, 77, 110
Straw, Jack, 175, 176, 177, 195, 201
Sudan, 103–5
Suez 1956, 24–59
   Douglas Hurd, 143
   Emanuel Shinwell, 106
   Harold Macmillan, 98
   learning from history, 5, 205, 210, 215
   lesson identification, 66, 69, 71, 123–7, 165, 171–3
   lesson implementation, 90, 119
   Middle East dynamics, 61
   psyops, 157
   'spectre of', 175
   'Suez syndrome', 137
   UK–US liaison, 63–4, 73
   UN, 107
Suez Base Canal Agreement 1954, 25, 26
Suez Canal, 78, 95
   closure, 79
   German–Ottoman attack on, 1914, 24
   nationalisation, 8–9, 62
Suez Canal Company, 24, 25, 28
Suez Canal Conference, 33–4
Suez Canal Users' Association, 26
Sweden, 119, 142
Swift, Carlton, 112
SWOT, 216
Sykes–Picot Agreement 1916, 21
Syria
   2013, 3
   2015, 3
   ammunition, 152
   Assad, 222
   David Gore-Booth, 139
   and Iraq, 130
   ISI, 219
   Operation Musketeer, 47
   Operation Straggle, 34, 43
   overflying rights, 39, 71–2
   Steering Brief, 159
   UAR, 61

tactical lessons, 191
Talbot, Admiral Philip, 106, 112
Taliban, 174
Tanner, Colonel, 186
Taylor, A. J. P., 4, 7

Index

Tehran, 218
Templer, Sir Gerald, 31, 32
Terrapin (codename), 33
terrorism, 35, 220
Thatcher, Margaret
   analogy, 9, 165–6, 173
   economics, 150–2
   and George H. Bush, 140, 175
   Gulf War 1990–1, 132
   lesson identification, 159
   Saddam Hussein, 133
   Saudi Arabia, 138
   'Suez syndrome', 137
   UN, 141
theatre intelligence structures, 41, 75, 103, 105, 108, 149, 186–7, 190–1
3 Commando Brigade, 30
3rd Infantry Division, 38
Thorndike, Edward, 14
Transport Command, 30, 40
Transport Task Force, 83
Treasury, 43, 179, 183
   history department, 7
Trend, Burke, 44–5
Trevelyan, Humphrey, 90, 92, 93, 101–2, 112, 120
Tripoli, 221
Tunisia, 220
Turkey, 3, 91, 103–5, 119, 188
Turki, Prince Al Faisal, 157, 175
20th Armoured Brigade, 2
24 Brigade, 92

UAE *see* United Arab Emirates
UAR *see* United Arab Republic
UK EYES A (UK citizens only) classification, 156
UK–Saudi relations, 138
UK–UN Mission, 135
UK–US liaison, 175–6
   Bermuda Conference, 63–4
   Jordan 1958, 78, 80–2
   Kuwait, 96–97
   lesson identification, 87–8, 125, 139–40, 166, 215
   Operation Telic, 185–6
   'special relationship', 43
UK–US Planning Group, 78, 96–7
Umm Qasr waterway, 188

UN (United Nations)
   analogy, 89
   Anthony Eden, 28, 36–7
   Charter Article 51, 141
   Colin Powell, 178
   David Cameron, 3
   economics, 219
   Eisenhower, 43
   Emergency Force, 37
   Emergency Special Session, 37
   FCO, 96, 107
   force, 26
   General Assembly, 37
   Gulf War 1990–1, 164
   inspectors, 174–5
   Iraq War 2003–9, 171–3
   Jordan 1958, 73–4, 123
   Kuwait, 112, 115
   lesson identification, 166, 205–6
   lesson implementation, 141, 215
   'Points for a Middle East Policy', 82
   Resolution 660, 130–1
   Resolution 1441, 174
   Resolution 1973, 221–2
   Resolutions, 138, 178
   Saddam Hussein, 144, 160
   sanctions, 138, 180
   weapons inspection, 170, 182
UN Monitoring, Verification and Inspection Commission (UNMOVIC), 170, 181
UN Secretary General, 37
UN Security Council, 37, 96, 196
UN Security Council resolution, 27
   660, 130–1
   1441, 170
   1973, 221
UN Special Commission (UNSCOM), 153, 170, 195
United Arab Emirates (UAE), 22, 130, 150
United Arab Republic (UAR), 61, 70–1, 72, 80, 85, 107
United Nations *see* UN
US 4th Infantry Division, 188
US 6th Fleet, 37–8
US Army, 184
   training colleges, 192–3
US Consul General, in Basra, 112
US Consulate, in Benghazi, 224

295

US Continental Army Command, 117
US Defence Department, 163, 169
US Embassy, 72
    in Baghdad, 112, 133
US Intelligence Community Staff, 214
US Joint and Coalition Operational
    Analysis Division, 225
US Marines, 187
US National Security Agency, 144
US Navy Task Force, 141
US NOFORN (no foreigners)
    classification, 156
US satellite systems, 154
US Senate Armed Services Committee, 200–1
US Senate Select Committee on
    Intelligence, 201
US State Department, 65, 116, 176
    Far East section, 112
USSR *see* Soviet Union

Vietnam, 148
Viggers, Sir Freddie, 179

Wafd government, 25, 33
Walker, Harold, 115
War Cabinet, 150–1
war loans, 130
War Office, 10, 50, 75, 110, 115, 117–18, 126
    Survey Directorate, 38–9
War on Terror, 170, 195
War Studies, 12
Warsaw Pact, 136
Washington Working Group, 67
Wasit province, 179
Watkinson, Harold, 119

weapons of mass destruction (WMD)
    'axis of evil', 220
    Butler inquiry, 164–5
    Colin Powell, 178
    Foreign Affairs Committee, 195, 198–9
    GCC, 158
    Intelligence and Security Committee, 200–1
    Iran–Iraq War 1980, 146
    JIC, 181–2
    Operation Desert Fox, 173
    Saddam Hussein, 153–4
    sanctions, 171
    terrorism, 170
    UK–US liaison, 156
weather conditions, 109–11, 180, 188
Western European Union (WEU), 141–2
Weston, Brigadier Michael, 49, 138
White, Michael, 175
White, Richard, 33, 54, 55, 58
White Paper 1963, 106
Wigg, George, 118
Williams, John, 199
Wilson, Harold, 6
WMD *see* weapons of mass destruction
Woodward, Llewellyn, 7
World Trade Centre, New York City, 169
Wratten, Air Vice Marshal Bill, 140
Wright, Lord, 36
Wright, Sir Michael, 60–1

Yemen, 3, 21–2, 77
Young, George, 34–5, 55
Young, Rob, 135

Ziegler, P. S., 116
Zulueta, Philip de, 82, 84, 88, 122

EU representative:
Easy Access System Europe
Mustamäe tee 50, 10621 Tallinn, Estonia
Gpsr.requests@easproject.com